MW00604927

PATCHWORK APARTHEID

Patchwork Apartheid

PRIVATE RESTRICTION, RACIAL SEGREGATION, AND URBAN INEQUALITY

Colin Gordon

Russell Sage Foundation NEW YORK

THE RUSSELL SAGE FOUNDATION

The Russell Sage Foundation, one of the oldest of America's general purpose foundations, was established in 1907 by Mrs. Margaret Olivia Sage for "the improvement of social and living conditions in the United States." The foundation seeks to fulfill this mandate by fostering the development and dissemination of knowledge about the country's political, social, and economic problems. While the foundation endeavors to assure the accuracy and objectivity of each book it publishes, the conclusions and interpretations in Russell Sage Foundation publications are those of the authors and not of the foundation, its trustees, or its staff. Publication by Russell Sage, therefore, does not imply foundation endorsement.

BOARD OF TRUSTEES
Michael Jones-Correa, Chair

Larry M. Bartels	James N. Druckman	David Leonhardt	Thomas J. Sugrue
Marianne Bertrand	Jason Furman	Hazel Rose Markus	Celeste Watkins-Hayes
Cathy J. Cohen	David Laibson	Jennifer Richeson	
Sheldon Danziger	Jennifer Lee		

ROR: https://ror.org/02yh9se80

LIBRARY OF CONGRESS CATALOGING-IN-PUBLICATION DATA

Names: Gordon, Colin, 1962- author.
Title: Patchwork apartheid : private restriction, racial segregation, and urban inequality / Colin Gordon.
Description: New York : Russell Sage Foundation, [2023] | Includes bibliographical references and index. | Summary: "Private restrictions on racial occupancy are a critical element and episode in the history of American inequality. This study draws on newly available full count (parcel-level) data on racial restriction for five Midwestern counties. The research makes four important and overlapping contributions to our understanding of the history of the American city, and to the patterns and processes of segregation and stratification that are so central to that history. First, it elevates and clarifies the role of private restriction in the history and architecture of racial segregation in the United States. Second, it documents the astonishing scale and reach of private racial restriction. Third, this record of private restriction offers a compelling documentary catalogue of both local and individual acts of discrimination or segregation, and of the racial assumptions and racial categories that animated them. Finally, the importance of private restriction to our account of racial segregation shifts our attention from public to private actors, and from the local and federal housing polices of the 1940s to the patchwork apartheid of private restriction that those policies accommodated, emulated and, over time, locked down. The trajectory of racial residential segregation in most settings simply does not support the conclusion that it was primarily or overwhelmingly a product of public policy. Public policies did not segregate America; they failed to challenge that segregation when confronted with it, and routinely deferred to the private actors who were responsible"— Provided by publisher.
Identifiers: LCCN 2023018653 (print) | LCCN 2023018654 (ebook) | ISBN 9780871545541 (paperback) | ISBN 9781610449229 (ebook)
Subjects: LCSH: Segregation—Middle West—History. | Discrimination in housing—Middle West—History. | African Americans—Housing—Middle West—History. | African Americans—Middle West—History. | Racism—Middle West—History. | United States—Race relations.
Classification: LCC E185.915 .G67 2023 (print) | LCC E185.915 (ebook) | DDC 305.800977—dc23/eng/20230424
LC record available at https://lccn.loc.gov/2023018653
LC ebook record available at https://lccn.loc.gov/2023018654

Copyright © 2023 by Russell Sage Foundation. All rights reserved. Printed in the United States of America. No part of this publication may be reproduced, stored in a retrieval system, or transmitted in any form or by any means, electronic, mechanical, photocopying, recording, or otherwise, without the prior written permission of the publisher. Reproduction by the United States Government in whole or in part is permitted for any purpose.

The paper used in this publication meets the minimum requirements of American National Standard for Information Sciences—Permanence of Paper for Printed Library Materials. ANSI Z39.48-1992.

Text design by Linda Secondari.

RUSSELL SAGE FOUNDATION
112 East 64th Street, New York, New York, 10065
10 9 8 7 6 5 4 3 2 1

CONTENTS

ILLUSTRATIONS

Figures

Maps

Tables

Datasets, additional maps, and high-resolution color versions of all maps that appear in the book are available in an online appendix at https://www.russellsage.org/publications/patchwork-apartheid.

ABOUT THE AUTHOR

COLIN GORDON is professor of history at the University of Iowa.

ACKNOWLEDGMENTS

A LOT OF people helped me write this book; my words here acknowledge those debts but leave them unpaid. The idea of mapping and documenting private restrictions in St. Louis and St. Louis County grew out of conversations with Peter Hoffman (Legal Services of Eastern Missouri) and Kalila Jackson (Metropolitan St. Louis Equal Housing and Opportunity Council). Peter and Kalila, and their organizations, provided ongoing support and encouragement. Other St. Louis collaborators and colleagues have informed my work over the years and sustained me through more recent stretches in the local property records: special thanks, on this score, to David Dwight, Dana Eskridge, the late Maggie Garb, Kennedy Moehrs Gardner, Clarissa Hayward, Walter Johnson, Phil Klinker, Molly Metzger, Andrea Murray, Kim Norwood, Jason Q. Purnell, Bryce Robinson, Jake Rosenfeld, Cori Ruff, Todd Swanstrom, Karen Tokarz, Barry Upchurch, Aaron Williams, and Erica Williams.

From the outset, this project has leaned heavily on the pioneering work on private restrictions done in Minneapolis, Seattle, and elsewhere. Kirsten Delegard and her Mapping Prejudice team out of Minneapolis (including Miles Corey, Penny Peterson, and the late Kevin Ehrman-Solberg) were a constant source of inspiration and ideas—and of course the source of the Hennepin County data (the public release of which made the comparative structure of this study possible). Jim Gregory's Segregated Seattle is a brilliant intervention in local history and a model of student- and community-engaged research. As I was finishing the research for this book, LaDale Winling pulled together a coalition of researchers engaged in "covenants" research across the country (https://www.nationalcovenantsresearchcoalition .com/). I have learned a great deal from conversations with the scholars and community activists involved in this project. I would be remiss if I did not acknowledge the profound influence of contemporary scholars of private restriction—most importantly Robert Weaver, Charles Abrams, Herman Long, Charles Johnson, and Scovel Richardson.

The research was made possible through the cooperation of county recorders and their staff in Iowa, Missouri, and elsewhere. Thanks to Sandie Smith in Black Hawk County, Kim Painter in Johnson County, Gerald Smith in St. Louis County, and Michael Butler in the City of St. Louis. In St. Louis, Sandra Irons went above and beyond in facilitating my access to paper, film, and digital records. A special shout out to Richard Buthod, whose infectious enthusiasm and detective skills were crucial to the success of the St. Louis research. In the Iowa counties, property records research was completed with the help of student research teams: Brayden Adcock, Matt Bartholomew, Kate Dennis, Tyler Dolinar, Carson Frazee, Cori Hoffman, Emily Kehoe, Cassidy Kengott, Christopher Marriott, Charlotte Stevens, Daniel Welsh, and Hannah Wegner (Black Hawk County); Gabe Bacille, Dune Carter, Colton Herrick, Daniel Langholz, Jack Lauer, and Keiran Reynolds (Johnson County). Thanks also for local support and encouragement from Kingsley Botchway and Joy Briscoe in Waterloo, and Zach Wahls in Iowa City.

While the pandemic interrupted the normal routine of scholarly discourse, I benefited from both ongoing and occasional conversations with colleagues across the country—some of whom I have known for over thirty years, some of whom I met just recently. For insights and ideas and support, thanks to Simon Balto, Richard Brooks, Kathy Brown, Brent Cebul, Laura Dresser, Ainsley Erickson, Jacob Faber, Devin Fergus, Paige Glotzer, Amy Hanauer, Amy Hillier, Andrew Kahrl, Douglas Massey, Todd Michney, John Parman, Ted Pearson, John Robinson, Joel Rogers, Carol Rose, Catherine Rymph, Larry Santucci, Patrick Sharkey, Joe Soss, Tom Sugrue, and KaLeigh White. Thanks to the Columbia City Seminar, the University of Northern Iowa, the Kinder Institute at the University of Missouri, the Philadelphia Federal Reserve, and the Russell Sage Foundation for opportunities to present this work—and for the tough and critical questions that followed.

I was fortunate to land a gig as a visiting scholar at the Russell Sage Foundation in 2022–2023 and doubly fortunate to join such a bright, committed, and collegial cohort of fellow scholars. In the truest spirt of interdisciplinary scholarship, I learned from those whose work overlapped with mine—and as much from those whose work seemed far afield. Whether at Wednesday seminar or Friday (leftovers) lunch, the conversations were unfailingly rigorous and constructive. With great appreciation and affection, thanks to Scott Allard, Liz Ananant, Sarah Carr, Jennifer Chudy, Angie Chung, Sheldon Danziger, Phil Garboden, Thomas Holt, Jen Klein, Trevon Logan, Terry Maroney, Mignon Moore, Natasha Quadlin, Adam Reich, Eva Rosen, Lara Shore-Sheppard, Jennifer Silva, Louise Story, Anna Sussman, and James (JT) Thomas. Thanks also to the Russell Sage Foundation staff for their support, including Galo Falchettore, Hyacinth Johnson, John Lee, Jennifer Rappaport, and Katie Winograd. The inestimable Suzanne Nichols shepherded the manuscript from proposal to production. The final version of the manuscript benefited greatly from the insights and suggestions of three anonymous reviewers, and from the deft editorial pen of Marcelo Agudo.

Completion of this book was made possible by research fellowships from the National Endowment for the Humanities (2021–2022) and the Russell Sage Foundation (2022–2023). The University of Iowa supported this project in myriad ways: An Arts and Humanities Initiative Grant from the Office of the Vice President for Research sustained the early stages. The College of Liberal Arts and Sciences topped off the external funding, and my colleagues in the Department of History picked up my courses and service obligations. The Digital Studio for the Public Humanities has provided ongoing in-kind support, especially in mapping (Jay Bowen) and web development (Nikki White). In St. Louis, research support was provided by Legal Services of Eastern Missouri, the Metropolitan St. Louis Equal Housing and Opportunity Council, Harvard's Commonwealth Fund (via Walter Johnson), and the St. Louis Area REALTORS.

My immediate family have sustained me in many ways, both in engagement with this research and in distraction from it. Love and thanks to Izzy, Aly, Ian, Dick, Dave, Jean, and Al; and to their partners and to generations of their offspring.

Finally, I'd like to reserve a special note of thanks and appreciation for my close friend and colleague Sarah Bruch. Sarah sets an impossible but aspirational bar as a teacher, mentor, scholar, and collaborator. For the last decade, her breadth of knowledge, commitment to engaged research, and keen and critical sociological imagination have deeply shaped my scholarship and my teaching. To the degree that any of that shows up in these pages, Sarah deserves the credit.

Earlier versions of parts of the manuscript appeared as Colin Gordon, "Dress Rehearsal for Shelley: Scovel Richardson and the Challenge to Racial Restriction in St. Louis," *Washington University Journal of Law and Policy* 67:1 (2022), 87–110; and Colin Gordon, "Dividing the City: Race-Restrictive Covenants and the Architecture of Segregation in St. Louis," *Journal of Urban History* 49:1 (2023), 160–82, and are repurposed here with permission.

CHAPTER 1

Introduction

ON FEBRUARY 11, 1893, Emma Van Wort purchased several parcels of land, fronting one hundred feet on the south side of Minerva Avenue in northwest St. Louis, from Matthew and Annie Sullivan for $3,250 (about $108,000 in 2023 dollars). The deed of sale carried with it several conditions: that seven feet at the back of the lot be reserved for an alley; that any buildings constructed on the lots be at least two stories in height and set back at least fifteen feet from the street; that none of the lots be used for "manufacturing purposes, such as soap factories, tanneries and such"; and that neither the buyer nor her heirs would ever "sell, convey or transfer any of their property to colored people." A month later, the Sullivans sold another eighty feet of frontage on Minerva Avenue, attaching the same terms and conditions.[1]

On July 30, 1952, the developers of Spoede Hills, a subdivision of twenty half-acre lots in suburban St. Louis County, filed a "Trust Agreement and Indenture," a property deed specifying mutual obligations between buyer and seller, with the St. Louis County Recorder. The indenture declared its general intent "that such subdivision shall be and remain a first class single family residential subdivision" and, toward that end, enumerated the "reservations, limitation, conditions, easements and covenants" governing the use of property in the subdivision. The first few pages outlined the duties of subdivision trustees and the terms under which property owners would be assessed for upkeep of the subdivision's utilities, easements, and private streets. In turn, the indenture laid out a long list of "general restrictions" binding lot owners and any successors for a term of thirty years, automatically renewed (absent action by the trustees) in twenty-year increments. These restrictions included detailed specifications (of the kind now commonly embedded in building and zoning codes) for building design, materials, and placement; elaborate rules for fencing and landscaping (of the kind now commonly invoked by homeowners' associations); prohibitions on business use, residential rentals, and radio aerials; and provisions for the regulation of nuisances—including the barring of "pigeons, poultry, cattle, hogs, rabbits or other animals." Restriction "J" provided that "no land or interests in this Subdivision shall be sold, resold, conveyed, leased, rented to, or in any way occupied, used or acquired by others than those wholly of the Caucasian Race, except that the foregoing does not apply to bona fide servants employed and living with families of the Caucasian Race in said Subdivision."[2]

The 1893 deed covenants on Minerva Avenue were the first racially restrictive deed covenants recorded in greater St. Louis (taking in the City of St. Louis and St. Louis County). The Spoede Hills restriction, drafted more than four years after the Supreme Court declared such agreements unenforceable in *Shelley v. Kraemer* (1948), was one of the last. In the intervening half century, property owners, neighborhood associations, real estate agents, and developers in St. Louis County and the City of St. Louis (a distinct jurisdiction with county status) would craft almost two thousand such race-restrictive agreements. These restrictions were both a dominant subset of the private land-use controls (designed to regulate a wide range of "nuisances") employed before the emergence of conventional municipal zoning, and a key mechanism of racial segregation in the era of the Great Migrations.[3] All told, these agreements set aside more than 100,000 residential parcels—over 60 percent of the combined city-county residential property base in 1950 and nearly 90 percent of county properties—for those "wholly of the Caucasian Race."[4]

The use of private racial restriction was particularly intense in "border" cities like St. Louis, but the practice was widespread. Indeed, it is hard to overestimate the importance of these restrictions, in St. Louis and beyond, as a symbol and a driver of residential segregation and as the source of durable racial disparities in housing opportunity and household wealth.

This, certainly, was the consensus of contemporary observers. "While the restrictions are private measures," one study concluded in 1943, "they can be exceedingly effective if used on a large scale." In his 1948 examination of *The Negro Ghetto,* Robert Weaver concluded that "of all the instruments that effect residential segregation, race-restrictive covenants are the most dangerous: Such covenants give legal sanction (until declared unconstitutional) and the appearance of respectability to residential segregation." For its part, the National Association for the Advancement of Colored People (NAACP) viewed residential restrictions as important in their own right— "the foremost problem confronting Negroes today" as Thurgood Marshall put it in 1945—and as the root source of segregation in education and other public goods.[5]

Scholarly assessments, in turn, identify racial restrictions not just as one mechanism in a long history of exclusion and segregation but as a foundational element of that history. Racial restrictions rendered formal and routine—even respectable and prudent—what had long been accomplished through intimidation or violence. They hardened assumptions about racial occupancy and property values that would become central tenets of professional realty and home finance. They (and their assumptions) lived on in both local land-use and economic development policies and in the tangle of public policies and private practices that constitute redlining—the use of race to rate credit risks in housing and mortgage programs.[6] In most Northern urban settings, segregation was *accomplished* by racial restrictions (and the violence and intimidation that accompanied them) and *sustained* by succeeding policies and practices.

Private restrictions on racial occupancy are a critical element in the history of American inequality. For over half a century, they decisively shaped both the development of American cities and the distribution of people within them. They were, first and foremost, a powerful form of categorical exclusion: you can't live here. In both inventing and responding to the "threat" of African American occupancy, private restriction reified racial categories and the boundaries between them. This exclusion was accomplished by legal enforcement (before 1948), by violence and intimidation, and by social and professional norms that upheld such restrictions as necessary and ethical standards. And it was justified or rationalized by frames and narratives that defined African American occupancy as a "nuisance" use of property and a threat to property values.

Such exclusion represented more than merely the hoarding of housing opportunity by white homeowners, real estate agents, and developers. Given the centrality of private property ownership to American citizenship, racial restrictions on the right to buy, sell, or occupy property effectively truncated the political, social, and economic citizenship of those they targeted for exclusion.[7] Racial restrictions shaped the distribution of housing resources and the local public goods and services that flowed from property ownership.[8] They undermined not just the economic welfare and security of African Americans, but the right—as T. H. Marshall famously put it—to "share to the full in the social heritage and to live the life of a civilized being according to the standards prevailing in the society."[9] By constraining access to such a key source and marker of full citizenship, racial restrictions amounted to an "unconscionable denial that a substantial number of our fellow citizens are full members of the rights-bearing community at all."[10]

Private restrictions entailed not just exclusion from "protected" neighborhoods but also exploitation outside them and on their borders.[11] "It is practically impossible under the present conditions which control Negro housing," as one 1931 observer put it, "to escape viscous exploitation."[12] African Americans crowded into older central city neighborhoods marked by poor housing quality and artificially high demand paid a steep "segregation tax" in the form of above market rents and—for those who overcame the barriers to homeownership—subprime lending terms.[13] At the same time, restrictions at the borders of African American neighborhoods proved fragile, and their inevitable collapses created conditions akin to blockbusting: a cascade of panicked sales and racial transition that undermined home values as African American occupancy (and ownership) increased.[14] "Slum property owners and restrictive covenant manipulators are two sides of the same coin," Weaver observed in 1948. "One reaps large returns by encouraging a limited supply of housing for minorities, the other sells a false sense of protection to white occupants in surrounding neighborhoods."[15] On both of these dimensions, private restrictions shaped attitudes, dispositions, and opportunities—encouraging and enabling whites to harbor lasting assumptions about race, neighborhoods, and property values and generating an impenetrable tangle of place-based disadvantages for African Americans.[16]

The willingness—indeed the eagerness—of public policies to emulate and institutionalize both the boundaries inscribed by private property restriction and the assumptions that animated them deepened and sustained disadvantages for African Americans. Racial restrictions not only accomplished the allocation of particular persons to particular spaces, but also shaped the real and perceived value of those spaces. The resulting segregation proved both durable and consequential: its legacy was "massive, cumulative, and mutually reinforcing inequalities in housing, education, amenities, public safety, municipal services, trust, social capital, job opportunities, and exposure to environmental hazards, crime, delinquency and stress."[17]

The original and lasting impacts of private restriction were at once intentional and ecological, structural and cultural.[18] While the Supreme Court rendered such agreements unenforceable in 1948, the residential landscape they built was sustained, emulated, and adapted by other actors. It was institutionalized, ossified, and legitimized by public policies. It was explained, justified, and internalized by persistent assumptions and narratives framing African American occupancy as a threat—or, in the preferred language of public and private appraisal, an encroachment of adverse or inharmonious land use.[19] The racial segregation that private restriction accomplished and encouraged became a lasting source of inequality, the "linchpin" as Douglas Massey and others have underscored, of the American system of racial stratification.[20]

Yet, while the importance and impact of race-restrictive property covenants are widely recognized, relatively little is known about their adoption, diffusion, or consequences in any given setting. The reason for this is simple: the practice of private restriction and its documentary record are buried in local case law and in county deed records, the latter organized and indexed by the date documents are filed with the county recorder.[21] Restrictive agreements are interspersed with property deeds, quit claims, sewer liens, and all the other routine business undertaken by the recorder's office. They are not routinely attached to chains of title (the buyer in the *Shelley* case had no idea the property was restricted), and the records themselves are vast (the deed books for St. Louis from 1900 to 1950 run over 3.2 million pages), largely handwritten, and—for the most part—unsearchable. Unless restrictions are identified in a property transaction or legal proceeding, they are virtually inaccessible and for the most part undiscoverable. As Kevin Fox Gotham observes, "there is no systematic evidence" as to the scope of such practices.[22]

This study is the first to overcome that documentary hurdle and address some of the interpretive and explanatory questions that have lingered in its shadow. It draws on newly available full count (parcel-level) data on racial restriction for five Midwestern counties, including complete data on over 800 race-restrictive agreements encompassing some 35,000 properties in the City of St. Louis, identified through a register kept by one of the city's major title firms; over 1,000 agreements encompassing more than 75,000 properties in neighboring St. Louis County, identified by cross-referencing deeds and subdivision plats with the county's internal restrictions card file; just under 100 agreements encompassing over 4,000 parcels in two Iowa counties (Black Hawk and Johnson), identified by student research teams combing the full record of deeds; and nearly 25,000 restricted parcels in Hennepin County, Minnesota, identified and documented by the Mapping Prejudice project in Minneapolis. These data (described more fully in the appendix) make it possible to craft a detailed portrait of not only the scale and reach of these restrictions but also the pace and pattern by which they spread and the driving forces behind their use. It allows us (building on scholarship on the legal history of racial restrictions,[23] and on their use in some metropolitan settings[24]) to map them in space and over time, to compare their logic and patterns in different settings, and to thoroughly examine the ways in which homeowners, homeowners' associations, developers, and real estate agents contributed to their use and to their diffusion.

This research makes four overlapping contributions to our understanding of the history of the American city and the patterns and processes of segregation and stratification central to that history. First, it elevates and clarifies the role of private restriction in the history and architecture of racial segregation in the United States. By any measure, it was private action and private restriction that segregated northern and border cities during the First Great Migration (running from World War I to the onset of the Great Depression) and inscribed the boundaries that sustained local patterns of exclusion and exploitation through and beyond the Second Great Migration (1940–1970). Racial segregation rose dramatically during the era of private restriction (the city-average index of black-white dissimilarity nearly doubled between 1890 and 1950)[25] and leveled off when the *Shelley* decision rendered such restriction unenforceable. Local patterns of restriction were assembled strategically (if not always successfully) by developers and real estate agents to exclude African Americans from new development and to contain African American occupancy where it was already established. In this sense, private property rights trumped any pretense of local planning, and private property interests—deeply invested in racial segregation—made most of the foundational decisions about the use and occupancy of land in the city and its suburbs.[26] Urban and suburban development leaned heavily on a useful mythology of universal private rights and opportunities, while systematically denying or narrowing the property rights of African Americans.[27]

The construction of racial boundaries and racialized neighborhoods, in turn, shifts our attention from segregation as an *outcome* to segregation as a *process*. As racial restriction shaped the distribution of housing opportunity, it also shaped the assumptions and social relations on which that exclusion rested. The delineation of racial neighborhoods necessarily involved the delineation of racial categories.[28] Both were fiercely contested, especially at their boundaries. The resulting segregation was simultaneously imposed and negotiated, rigid and unstable. One variety of private restriction, in this respect, labored defensively and (in the long run) unsuccessfully to shore up racial boundaries in transitional urban neighborhoods; another drew clear and long-lasting racial boundaries between cities and their suburbs.[29]

Second, this research documents the astonishing scale and reach of private racial restriction. Much of the scholarship on restriction focuses on the impact of a few key developers and developments, including J. C. Nichol's Country Club District in Kansas City, Missouri, the Olmsted Brothers' Palos Verdes Estates in Los Angeles, and the Roland Park Company's eponymous development in Baltimore.[30] But, as we see across the Midwest, racial restriction was scarcely confined to the aspirational or "picturesque enclaves" crafted by elite developers.[31] It was a ubiquitous business practice, embedded not just in the rules of tony subdivisions but in a wide variety of restrictive covenants attached to individual sales, neighborhood petitions, and subdivision rules that marked most new construction, much of it marketed to the working class, off-limits to African American occupancy.

Such restrictions were not anomalous experiments in exclusion; they were the norm—and one of the central organizing practices—in local housing markets.[32] "There are numerous sizable suburban cities in which it is boasted that no 'non-Caucasians' may live except as the employee of the white occupant," noted the NAACP's Loren Miller in the late 1940s, "and Chambers of Commerce in those cities will gladly furnish maps showing complete covenanting of all land."[33] On the eve of the *Shelley* decision in 1948, the scale of private restriction far exceeded that of either federal housing policies or local zoning ordinances, and restrictions were less prone to revision than the latter.[34] Given this scope, such a private and piecemeal practice proved an effective mechanism of exclusion and segregation. Employed systematically or extensively, even fragmented and informal mechanisms can yield stark segregation; they make "the division of the social world into ethnic groups," as Andreas Wimmer argues, "appear natural and self-evident both for the privileged and the excluded."[35]

Third, this record of private restriction—nearly 2,500 distinct restrictive agreements covering over 140,000 properties drawn from five counties and three states—offers a compelling catalog of both local and individual acts of discrimination or segregation and of the racial assumptions and racial categories that animated them.[36] It archives the "descriptive vocabulary of day-to-day existence" by which, as Barbara Fields suggests, ideologies of race and racial difference are constructed.[37] The maintenance of racial categories and the spatial and social boundaries between them depends on the willingness and ability of people to justify or rationalize their invention and their persistence. In this respect, private restriction and the economic and legal arguments on which it rested document the way in which white property interests drew on "interaction, fear, hope, and imagination to construct boundary maintaining stories."[38] The deeds in which such restrictions were inscribed (and where they can still be found) memorialize, as Maureen Brady posits, the ways in which buyers and sellers thought about property and their neighbors: restriction was "a way for owners to organize themselves around certain preferred uses in a neighborhood, but it also telegraphed the unwanted nature of emerging activities [or uses] that regular nuisance law was not so quick to prevent."[39]

The language of private restriction traces the subtle shifts in racial ideology and racial categorization across the first half of the twentieth century. The earliest racial restrictions were drafted in the throes of Jim Crow, the eugenics movement, and the "separate but equal" logic of *Plessy v. Ferguson;* the last were drafted on the eve of the modern civil rights movement—just months before the Supreme Court's 1954 *Brown* decision, the murder of Emmett Till, and the onset of the Montgomery bus boycott. Across this span, restrictions document changing conceptions of race: of what it meant to be colored, negro, or black on one hand and white or Caucasian on the other.[40] Legal challenges in district, state, and federal courts document the changing meaning of social citizenship and equal protection. The language of restriction—in the agreements themselves and in the courts—underscores the ways in which racial categories were invented and refined by the very instruments of exclusion. "The black man," as Du Bois famously observed, "is a person who must ride 'Jim Crow' in Georgia."[41]

Finally, private restriction's contribution to racial segregation shifts our attention from public to private actors and from the local and federal housing polices of the 1940s to the patchwork apartheid of private restriction that those policies accommodated, emulated and, over time, locked down. The trajectory of racial residential segregation in most settings simply does not support the conclusion that it was primarily or overwhelmingly a product of public policy. The Home Owners' Loan Corporation (HOLC, established in 1933), the Federal Housing Administration (FHA, 1934), the Public Housing Administration (1937), and the Urban Renewal Administration (1949) were all distressingly and infamously quick to embrace racial segregation and instrumental in cementing and sustaining its boundaries and its assumptions.[42] But the contours of segregation, as well as all the assumptions that animated and justified it, were already well established by private restriction. Midcentury housing policies, like so much of the New Deal, were constrained by the Congressional clout (or threat) of Jim Crow legislators, who were routinely deferential to private markets and private market actors.[43] Yet recent scholarship has devoted much more attention to the public policies that sustained segregation after the 1940s (especially the complicity of federal housing policies) than to the private restrictions that, across the first half of the century, did the initial work of establishing local racial boundaries and sorting the local population by race. This explanatory mismatch rests in part on the hope or assumption (shared by contemporary civil rights activists and current scholarship) that public agencies would not so readily dispense with equal protection.[44] And it rests in part on the availability of sources: on one hand, systematic documentation of private restriction has been (and remains) very difficult; on the other, federal housing agencies wore their racial politics on their sleeve and have been routinely condemned, as Charles Abrams put it as early as 1955, for policies that "could well have been culled from the Nuremberg Laws."[45]

My intent, in this respect, is not to discount the role of federal policies but to embed them more accurately and clearly in an account of the origins, the mechanics, and the architecture of racial segregation across the first half of the twentieth century. In 1948, Weaver saw the emergence of the

"Negro Ghetto" as a consequence of "community, neighborhood, and individual opposition to colored neighbors; race-restrictive deed covenants; agreements, practices, and codes of ethics among real estate boards and operators; FHA acceptance and perpetuation of real estate practice; local government's fear that adequate or more housing will encourage Negro migration; local political action to restrict Negroes to particular areas; [and] development of exclusive one-class neighborhoods."[46] He was right, but as important as this causal catalog are the connections between its constituent elements—and their common roots in private restriction. Local and federal policies—including land-use zoning, subsides for home ownership and suburban development, urban renewal, and public housing—emulated, adapted, and institutionalized patterns rooted in private restriction.[47] Public policies did not segregate America; they failed to challenge segregation when confronted with it and routinely deferred to the private actors who were responsible for its invention and design.

Attention to private restriction paints a history of American segregation that is fragmented, chaotic, and closely tied to local settings and circumstances. It also offers the sobering insight that racial segregation was a project shared and pursued—in any one of these settings—by thousands of white homeowners, neighborhood associations, real estate agents, developers, and civic leaders. The decision to quarantine African Americans on the blocks they already occupied, and to exclude them from concentric rings of new development at the city's edge, was ratified on the drafting tables of suburban developers, at neighborhood meetings in church basements or school cafeterias, and on the front porches of private homes. That decision was motivated by common prejudices and anxieties, and it was arrived at one house, one block, and one subdivision at a time.

The Strange Career of Private Restriction

Private restrictions on the use of private property became increasingly common in the United States across the nineteenth century. Such contractual constraints—usually agreed to by buyer and seller at the time of a property transaction—were more efficient and precise than recourse to legal remedies under nuisance law.[48] They filled the regulatory void left by the relatively late development of municipal building codes and zoning ordinances, the constitutionality of which was not settled until 1926.[49] As private agreements, such covenants reconciled the tension between regulation and private property rights. Indentures were widely used to prohibit a growing list of nuisance uses of property (such as slaughterhouses or saloons) and, in the decades before conventional zoning, to regulate both residential density and commercial use. In the first decades of the twentieth century, they were increasingly used to set racial restrictions on alienation—the unfettered right to buy or sell—or occupancy.

The practice of private *racial* restriction flourished at the intersection of three intertwined developments: the rapid urbanization (and suburbanization) of the American population during the early decades of the twentieth century; the racial dynamics of that urban growth created by the Great Migrations of African Americans north from the clutches of Jim Crow; and the tension between urban growth and urban regulation, as local property interests struggled to strike a balance between public order and private property rights. The urban share of the American population grew steadily across the nineteenth and early twentieth centuries: in 1920, half of all Americans lived in urban settings; by 1950, that share reached almost two-thirds. In 1900, there were but fifteen American cities with populations over 250,000; by 1950, there were forty-one.[50] Nowhere was this growth more apparent than in the industrial Midwest. Over the first half of the twentieth century, the population of Chicago more than doubled, that of Cleveland nearly tripled, and that of Detroit grew fivefold. This growth was bolstered by the push-pull of the Great Migrations. Between 1900 and 1950, 3.3 million African Americans left the South for employment opportunities in the North, a migration largely rural in its origins and overwhelmingly urban in its destinations.[51]

Rapid urban growth renewed an interest (initially expressed in response to the immigration wave of the 1890s) in better regulation of American cities, and the presence of African Americans among the new arrivals generated a new interest in segregation.[52] Indeed, the white reaction to the Great Migrations created a regime of racial stratification and racial exploitation in the urban North that was nearly as fierce as that of Jim Crow.[53] This reaction was evident in occupational segregation and discrimination. It was evident in local policing—marked by the pointed invention in the urban North, as Khalil Gibran Muhammad suggests, of African American criminality as the "bases for justifying prejudiced thinking, discriminatory treatment, and/or acceptance of racial violence as an instrument of public safety."[54] And—perhaps most starkly—it was evident in systemic residential segregation.

In housing, the segregationist impulse manifested itself in three ways: violence and intimidation, local zoning, and private mechanisms of racial restriction.[55] Violence in defense of racial boundaries was both petty and profound, ranging from everyday patterns of intimidation in public and private places, to routine "move-in violence" aimed at black homeowners and tenants, to the pogroms in East St. Louis (1917), Chicago (1919), Tulsa (1921) and elsewhere—all of which were animated by segregationist anxieties over urban space.[56] In the South, the implicit and explicit violence of Jim Crow was often sufficient to sustain neighborhood boundaries.[57] In the North, violence and intimidation, despite their prevalence as a form of social control and as an expression of social norms, had their limits. However successful such measures were in discouraging prospective black owners or tenants, they could not stem the flight of white residents from transitional neighborhoods. Especially in northern cities, they could neither reliably establish neighborhood boundaries nor make such boundaries respectable and sustainable.[58]

For its part, racial zoning promised to formalize neighborhood boundaries and embed segregation in a "separate but equal" logic of local planning. First passed in Baltimore in 1910, racial zoning ordinances were enacted in twenty-seven (mostly border and Southern) cities over the next decade.[59] But racial zoning rested on shaky legal ground and was struck down by the Supreme Court's *Buchanan v. Warley* decision in 1917. The decision, which rested not on equal protection but on a defense of property rights, captured the ambivalence—in American law and policy—toward local regulation of land use. Even the fiercest advocates of racial zoning often balked at the prospect of any broader "general welfare" constraint on land use.[60] Yet, at the same time, many civic leaders and large-scale developers viewed private property rights (and the use of nuisance law to reign in their neighbors)[61] as insufficient. They were strong advocates of leveraging local police power to sort out the chaos of urban development—and particularly the vulnerability of high-end residential neighborhoods to the encroachment of commerce, industry, and "inharmonious" neighbors.

Private restrictions, in effect, split the difference. As private contractual commitments, they avoided any conflict with either the "privileges and immunities" or "equal protection" clauses of the Fourteenth Amendment.[62]

Especially in new suburban developments, they promised regulatory protection at a scale sufficient to mimic conventional zoning. They proved more efficient and responsive than recourse to damage suits under nuisance law. In their enumeration and prohibition of local rules and standards—including building placement and materials, garage or fence placement, acceptable uses of property (usually by regulating or prohibiting commercial use), utility easements, and even the minimum value of houses—they could constrain a far more extensive and precise set of uses or behaviors than could either nuisance law or zoning.[63]

This mechanism of segregation, in turn, was lubricated by the courts. In prohibiting racial zoning by local jurisdictions, *Buchanan v. Warley* (1917) elevated private restriction as the best alternative. State courts consistently hewed to the view that private racial restrictions did not involve state action and so lay beyond the reach of the equal protection clause of the Fourteenth Amendment. In 1926, the Supreme Court bolstered this assessment when it declined jurisdiction in such a case from the District of Columbia—ruling in *Corrigan v. Buckley* the "alleged constitutional questions so unsubstantial as to be plainly without color of merit and frivolous."[64] It was not until after World War II that the Court reconsidered the question, holding in *Shelley* (1948) that, while the agreements themselves were private contracts, their enforcement was prohibited as state action; and then in *Barrows v. Jackson* (1953) that the same logic applied to enforcement through private damage suits.

Under the cover of private contracts, then, the practice of private restriction became a sandbox for experiments in housing policy and racial exclusion. Put another way, such covenants focused on both securing positive obligations (such as design and maintenance standards) from property owners and protecting them from negative actions by their neighbors.[65] Property owners voluntarily constrained their property rights in exchange for the promise of security or permanence. "The lot purchasers sacrifice their right to the free use of their separate lots," as Helen Monchow noted in her 1928 survey of the practice, "but they gain the right of protecting the benefit they derive from the restriction against its violation by any of their neighbors."[66] Restrictions "ran with the land" but, following the general rule against perpetuities in property law, typically expired after a generational window of twenty-five to fifty years. Various devices, including automatic renewals, were used to make such restrictions effectively permanent.[67]

As private contracts, restrictions were enforced by the parties to the agreement: a developer might set down covenants and conditions for purchasers, or residents—through the mechanism of a neighborhood improvement association (or "Civic Club") or a subdivision trusteeship—might bind each other to the agreement.[68] Local enforcement was often girded by the threat of violence and by the coordination and promotion offered by citywide real estate boards.[69] Legal enforcement was relatively rare and largely confined to disputes over neighborhood petition agreements. Technically, most restrictions were enforceable "in law or in equity," but legal remedies and penalties varied widely. The most common recourse was an injunction barring or reversing a sale, although suits for damages (loss of property value) were also an option. Some subdivision restrictions contained a reversionary clause, forfeiting title if the racial restriction was not honored,[70] but most relied on mutual obligation to racial exclusion as a widely accepted and understood social norm.

Against the backdrop of the Great Migrations, racial restrictions were a common and integral element of private restriction. The segregation accomplished by intimidation, economic exclusion, and general prohibitions against nuisances took on new urgency in the face of the World War I–era race riots, the *Buchanan* decision, and the sheer scale and rapidity of demographic change.[71] Monchow's 1928 survey of subdivision indentures found racial restrictions in half of them, most commonly limiting sale and occupancy to "Caucasians only."[72] Where restrictive agreements were assembled by petition in older neighborhoods facing "encroachment" or "invasion," their focus narrowed to the racial threat—in part because the longer list of rules and regulations (such as those regarding building design, placement, or value) were moot where the residential footprint was already well established.[73] The nature of that threat varied by city and region: "Caucasians only" was the most common construction in the racial binary of the Midwest; Asian Americans and Mexican Americans were targeted in the West and Southwest; in the East, restrictions often enumerated the races, national origins, and religions found in the last wave of immigration. "There is obviously no limit to their inclusiveness," Weaver noted bitingly in 1948, "save that of the current state of group prejudice."[74]

The practice of private racial restriction was perfected and refined by an early cadre of elite developers, including J. C. Nichols in Kansas City, the Olmsted Brothers in Los Angeles, and the Roland Park Company in

Baltimore.[75] Their impact was felt far beyond those settings. These "community builders," were important not just for their innovation of the practice but for their promotion of it—through their influence in professional associations such as the National Association of Real Estate Boards, in the fledgling academic fields of city planning and land economics, and in the administrative machinery of local zoning and federal housing policies.[76] Smaller-scale builders followed their lead, making private racial restriction—and the assumptions that girded the practice—a routine and staple business practice in new development.[77] And local real estate agents and real estate boards followed suit, cobbling together restrictions in older neighborhoods.[78] Importantly, private restriction on new construction routinely preceded local municipalization and zoning, allowing private interests to make most of the key decisions about land use and housing opportunity. Indeed, local land-use zoning before World War II often simply put a public face on the decisions made by private developers prior to either municipal incorporation or the adoption of a comprehensive zoning ordinance.[79]

The pattern, target, and urgency of racial restriction varied across settings. White realty interests in Northern and border cities with established African American populations—including Chicago, St. Louis, and Washington, D.C.—were active in both restricting new development and petitioning for the restriction of older neighborhoods—especially when the First Great Migration threatened to push those neighborhoods beyond their established racial boundaries.[80] In cities such as Milwaukee or Minneapolis, where the African American population did not grow significantly until the Second Great Migration or later, restriction was largely confined to a suburban ring, less a response to African American occupancy than a preparatory means of sorting new arrivals.[81] In the urban northeast, private racial restrictions were routine in suburban development after World War I but were less commonly employed in central cities—where (given the form and timing of urban development) segregation was more likely to be policed by real estate agents, landlords, co-op boards, and local violence.[82]

Local variations reflected local circumstances and the (often shifting) local construction of racial threat. In San Francisco, "Caucasians only" deed covenants were used to establish or reestablish boundaries between white and Asian neighborhoods after the 1906 earthquake.[83] In Shaker Heights, Ohio, a 1905 set of restrictions focused on subdivision layout and building design was retooled in 1925 to give the developer and established residents the power to veto sales to any "undesirable."[84] In rapidly expanding western settings like Los Angeles or Sacramento, private restriction parceled out new suburbs in a patchwork of race and class.[85] Across these settings, private property restrictions were often girded by, or built around, hard physical boundaries such as railroad tracks or bodies of water. And they were reinforced by, and reflected in, local planning—especially land-use zoning and school catchment zones.[86]

Our understanding of local restrictive practices relies heavily on the records of key developers, a sampling of suburban restrictions, and rough estimates of their scope or reach based on resulting patterns of segregation. In much-studied Chicago, some observers estimate that as much as 80 percent of the city was restricted, although both the numerator (the number of restricted parcels) and the denominator (the residential base) are hard to pin down. Others consider one-third to one-half of residential lots a more realistic benchmark.[87] Ongoing documentation of restrictions in Washington, D.C., estimates a coverage of about half the city.[88] In Los Angeles County, almost half of the HOLC neighborhood assessments noted the presence of racial restrictions.[89] Research sampling subdivisions outside New York City, Wilmington (Delaware), Milwaukee, and Kansas City found between half and three-quarters of new development subject to racial restriction.[90] Contemporary estimates of Minneapolis put the rate of restriction at about one-quarter of the housing stock.[91] As a general rule, the practice of private racial restriction grew more prevalent over the course of the 1920s and 1930s, especially in larger developments.[92] Even where private restriction was less extensive, its strategic use—alongside other barriers or policies, or on the racial margins of neighborhoods—was instrumental in the spatial logic and the spatial inequality of local segregation.[93]

The Settings

The restrictions studied here are drawn from five midwestern counties, strung south to north along the Avenue of the Saints running from St. Louis, Missouri, to Minneapolis–St. Paul, Minnesota (see map 1.1). The regional setting is important: the Midwest was a sandbox for segregation during the era of private restriction and today exhibits some of the starkest racial disparities in the nation. The result is a jarring contemporary juxtaposition: while Midwestern metros (such as Des Moines, Iowa;

Map 1.1 The Five Counties

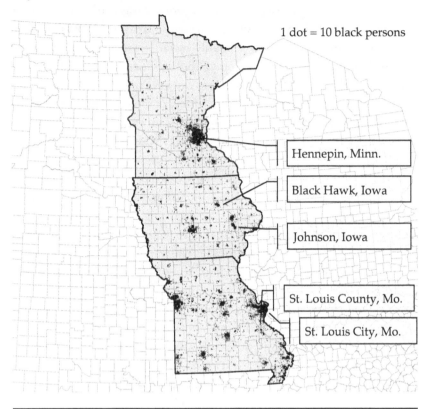

1 dot = 10 black persons

Hennepin, Minn.

Black Hawk, Iowa

Johnson, Iowa

St. Louis County, Mo.

St. Louis City, Mo.

Source: 2020 Census via Ruggles et al. 2022.

Madison, Wisconsin; and Minneapolis) typically crowd the "best places to live" lists,[94] they are also among the worst places for African Americans to live.[95] In one recent analysis ranking states on racial inequality, the five lowest states—and eight of the bottom ten—were in the Midwest.[96]

These disparities are the product of a particular regional history of race and race relations. During the Great Migrations, African Americans migrants to the Midwest settled overwhelming in the region's cities. Between 1910 and 1950, the Midwest's African American population grew more than fourfold, from 543,000 to over 2.3 million. By 1950, 90 percent of Midwestern African Americans lived in just 79 of the region's 1,056 counties, and half lived in just four: Cook County, Illinois (Chicago), Wayne County, Michigan (Detroit), the City of St. Louis, Missouri, and Cuyahoga County, Ohio (Cleveland). In these settings, the African American experience was marked by a narrow (and ultimately) fragile range of employment opportunities. Migration to the Midwest had been driven primarily by employment prospects in the region's booming industrial economy.[97] But in cities and industries across the country, that boom turned to bust as early as the 1950s. The impact was devastating—especially in the Midwest (now commonly referred to as the Rust Belt) and especially for Midwestern African Americans.[98]

Private restriction was the keystone of the Midwest's systematic architecture of residential segregation.[99] It divided the residential stock of the cities and spurred white flight into their sprawling suburbs. New residential development and municipal incorporation, relatively unconstrained by law or geography, pushed out into the cornfields—sustaining segregation not just by confining black families to some parts of the city but by reserving new housing opportunities for white families. As a result, black-white residential segregation rose dramatically. In every census year after 1890, large cities of the Midwest were more segregated than those of any other region.[100] Patterns of racial segregation extend into smaller metros throughout the region, which were—and continue to be—more segregated than similar settings in other regions.[101] African American migrants to the Midwest faced local hostility over housing and employment, the reemergence of the Ku Klux Klan, and unprecedented mob violence.[102] Over the long haul, the white response to black migration undercut the promise and the rewards of moving north.[103] As Horace Cayton and St. Clair Drake noted, African American migrants to Chicago found that "though the Midwest Metropolis was 'less prejudiced than the South,' it, too, drew the color line."[104]

The starkest and most enduring damage stemmed from the combination of occupational and residential segregation. While some manufacturing jobs were lost to regional or international competition, many simply left the central city for the suburbs.[105] Some industries, such as meatpacking, fled urban locations for rural outposts—trading a unionized workforce of whites and African Americans for a nonunion, low-wage, and largely immigrant one.[106] As a result, as William Julius Wilson and others have underscored, capital and employment were mobile but black workers were not.[107] The black working class, especially where job losses were steep and segregation persistent, became "truly disadvantaged" or "stuck in place."[108] All of this underscores the Midwest's important role in the origins and impacts of racial segregation.

The five counties studied in this project offer local variations on that regional story and regional experience (see table 1.1). In the first half of the twentieth century, the City of St. Louis (which, since its separation from St. Louis County in 1876, also has the status of a county) was a border city with a substantial and growing African American population—over 35,000 in 1900 and more than four times that by 1950.[109] Here the local institutions of segregation were particularly acute, aimed at both sustaining general boundaries (between north and south St. Louis and between St. Louis and St. Louis County) and containing the well-established African American neighborhood (originally Elleardsville, more commonly "the Ville") on the city's north side. "The border states and cities, which have represented a mixture of attitudes and compulsions," as the *Tentative Report of the Committee on Negro Housing* observed in 1931," have been most active in attempting to crystallize the ideal of complete separation in housing."[110] St. Louis flirted with racial zoning in 1916 (an ordinance voided by the Supreme Court's *Buchanan* decision a year later) and then settled into a varied pattern of private restriction. Such restriction was particularly intense across the border in St. Louis County, where developers pointedly marketed new suburban development as a white flight refuge from the city.[111]

In Iowa, the context for restriction was quite different. The African American population in Johnson County, home of the State University of Iowa, was negligible (even in 1950, less than half a percent of the total population), yet racial restrictions on individual sales and new developments were not uncommon. Iowa City had a dual housing market, abetted by the refusal of the University of Iowa to accommodate African American students in the dorms until after World War II.[112] But local restriction was animated less by the tangible threat of African American occupancy than by the diffusion of racial restriction as a professional standard and business practice. In Black Hawk County, some ninety miles north, local housing and segregation patterns echoed—albeit on a smaller scale—those of St. Louis. The county's urban core, Waterloo, was a small industrial town dominated by railroads, meatpacking, and (after 1918) the John Deere tractor works. In 1911, the Illinois Central Railroad brought in hundreds of African American workers from Mississippi to break a strike at its Waterloo maintenance yards.[113] The rapid increase in the African American population (and their

Table 1.1 African American Population and Population Shares, 1900–1950

	St. Louis City (Mo.)		St. Louis County (Mo.)		Johnson (Iowa)		Black Hawk (Iowa)		Hennepin (Minn.)	
	Population	Share (%)	Population	Share (%)	Population	Share (%)	Population	Share (%)	Population	Share (%)
1900	35,516	5.7	3,526	7.0	62	0.2	22	0.1	1,584	0.7
1905					53	0.2	15	0.0		
1910	43,960	6.4	4,253	5.2	65	0.3	29	0.1	2,646	0.8
1915					67	0.2	410	0.8		
1920	69,854	9.0	4,729	4.7	68	0.3	856	1.5	3,985	1.0
1925					157	0.5	1,030	1.8		
1930	93,580	11.4	9,645	4.6	112	0.4	1,234	1.8	4,257	0.8
1940	108,765	13.3	12,310	4.5	89	0.3	1,528	1.9	4,734	0.8
1950	154,448	18.0	17,013	4.2	201	0.4	2,702	2.7	8,769	1.3

Source: Manson et al. 2020; Executive Council of the State of Iowa 1905, 1915, 1925.

status as strikebreakers) sparked white hostility and a spate of early racial property restrictions.

Hennepin County, Minnesota, in contrast to Waterloo and St. Louis, experienced little of the First Great Migration—its African American population share did not exceed 1 percent until 1950. This did not, however, discourage local developers and real estate agents from using private restriction to define racial boundaries and racial neighborhoods. Private restriction—especially in Minneapolis's southern and western suburbs—was a staple of suburban residential development.[114] Such restrictions funneled early African American migrants into older central city neighborhoods in Minneapolis and laid the groundwork for a metropolitan patchwork of municipalization and zoning that—as in St. Louis County—would sustain the local color line for decades to come.

In some respects, these counties share a common reaction to African American migration: real estate agents and developers increasingly viewed "inharmonious" racial occupancy as a threat to property values and meeting that threat as their highest priority. In other respects, the reactions were distinctly local, resting on the timing and nature of any racial "invasion" or "encroachment," the timing and pattern of local urban and suburban residential development, and the capacity and willingness of local actors to pursue (or resist) segregation through private restriction. Where the racial threat was immediate and tangible, such as in St. Louis and Waterloo, we see particularly intense patterns of restriction by petition; where urban growth and residential development ran alongside the peak years of the Second Great Migration, as in St. Louis County and Hennepin County, we see sweeping patterns of suburban restriction.

For a number of reasons, the St. Louis case (encompassing the city and suburban St. Louis County) plays a leading role in this account; the Iowa and Minnesota counties are employed where relevant as points of comparison or contrast. Of all these jurisdictions, greater St. Louis has a longer and more extensive history of African American occupancy, private restriction, and legal challenges to private restriction—the latter culminating in the *Shelley* case in 1948. The data (as I explore more fully in the appendix) is also richer and more complete for St. Louis—yielding a full record of both the "master" agreements imposed by developers, real estate agents, and neighborhood associations and the parcels or lots included in such agreements.

Plan of the Book

Drawing on the documentation of private restriction in the five Midwestern counties described earlier, the chapters that follow trace the logic, scope, dissemination, and impact of private restriction. In chapter 2, "Caucasians Only," I outline the logic of racial restriction against a broader backdrop of racial categorization and stratification in the first half of the twentieth century. The shifting language and logic of racial restriction over time illuminate the ways in which private restriction ran alongside (and in reaction to) an era of demographic upheaval shaped by rapid urbanization, the Great Migrations of African Americans to the urban North, and the abrupt restriction of immigration. All of this was reflected in both the ferocity of private restriction and the shifting categorical terms of inclusion and exclusion. But, if the meaning of white or Caucasian in such restrictions was uncertain and contested, the logic of their targets and boundaries was clear. White developers and homeowners invented and cultivated the lasting idea that African American occupancy constituted a nuisance use of property and a threat to the stability and value of property investments. The exclusion of others, including immigrants from Southern and Eastern Europe, was rare, signaling a fleeting hierarchy within the category of Caucasian rather than any blurring of the bright boundary between black and white.[115] These frames and narratives served to buttress private restrictions as they were assembled, and they sustained and rationalized segregation for decades after.[116]

In chapter 3, "Dividing the City," I turn to the actual mechanics or process of racial restriction, describing the spatial and temporal patterns of private restriction in and across these jurisdictions. I devote particular attention to the type, timing, and terms (such as duration and governance) of restriction, as well as the spatial distribution of restrictions and the principal actors behind their local invention and diffusion. The form and efficacy of racial restriction, as I suggest, varied widely within and across metropolitan settings. Those assembled by petition in older neighborhoods facing a direct and tangible threat of racial transition differed from those, usually crafted by developers, staking out aspirational white enclaves in the suburbs. Those imposed in response to the First Great Migration differed from those imposed a generation later.

In chapter 4, "Patchwork Apartheid," I examine the relationship between private restriction and racial segregation and argue that such restrictions were the most important causal mechanism behind segregation in the urban Midwest. Where we have both documentation of private restriction and local (small unit) demographic data sufficient to construct a robust segregation index, we can trace this relationship directly. But even where this is not possible, the importance of private restriction to local segregation—and its temporal and spatial patterns—is not difficult to discern. The argument here is built out from local patterns and practices (the ways in which private restrictions were employed strategically to exclude or contain African American occupancy) to broader metropolitan patterns (the relationship between timing and scale of private restriction on one hand and the hardening of racial segregation on the other).

In chapter 5, "Dress Rehearsal for *Shelley*," I turn to the legal history of restriction, focusing on battles in local and state courts that preceded the Supreme Court's 1948 *Shelley* decision.[117] This was, to the NAACP's persistent frustration, a legal history in which the notion of equal protection was not entertained seriously by the courts until the late 1940s. Despite their ubiquity in housing markets into the 1940s, private restrictions were not extensively litigated and, before *Shelley*, challenges to the practice focused narrowly on the defects or failures of particular agreements or on the burden they posed to white property owners in contested neighborhoods. Local legal battles (drawn here largely from Missouri courts) offer a glimpse of the ways in which the practice of private racial restriction was constructed, contested, and enforced.

Chapter 6, "Long Shadow," traces the enduring impact of private restriction and the mechanisms by which this root spatial inequality was emulated, adapted, enforced, sanctioned—and sometimes challenged—by other actors and institutions. I trace the durability of private restriction—in other forms—in private appraisal and realty, in local zoning, and in federal housing policies. This brings us back to the contribution or culpability of public policy, both local and federal, in the larger trajectory of racial segregation. Without discounting the important (and unconscionable) role played by local zoning and federal housing policies, I argue that such policies served primarily to sustain, subsidize, and legitimize practices and patterns already well established by private restriction.

CHAPTER 2

Caucasians Only: Categories, Frames, and Narratives in Private Restriction

RACIAL CLASSIFICATION IS irretrievably an exercise of power, harnessing science (or pseudoscience) to the defense or legitimacy of a particular social order or social hierarchy. Across the modern era, the invention of racial difference has been an ideological handmaiden to chattel slavery, settler colonialism, empire, immigration restriction, and racial segregation. And it has been a means of justifying illiberal policies or practices in settings—like the United States—purportedly committed to liberal egalitarianism.[1] "As categorical inequality spreads," Elizabeth Anderson notes, "people explain and legitimate it by telling stories about supposed inherent differences between their groups."[2] Racial categorization is motivated by the desire to exclude or exploit; once established and acted on, its consequences only seem to justify the invented differences.

The composition, logic, and terminology of private racial restriction offers a telling glimpse into the ways in which those who drafted, agreed to, or signed on to such agreements thought about race across the first half of the twentieth century. The language of restriction, the definition of who was to be excluded or included, reflected the prevailing categories—and the sometimes bright, sometimes blurred boundaries between those categories—as to what it meant to be white or Caucasian on one hand, or what it meant to be one who was not "wholly of the Caucasian Race" on the other. As importantly, such definitions were in flux across an era marked by the persistence of Jim Crow segregation in the South, the white reaction to the Great Migrations in the urban North, and the long nativist backlash against the immigration boom that bracketed the turn of the twentieth century. Against the backdrop of a rigid black-white binary, the rest of the taxonomy—a chaos of race, ethnicity, national origin, language, and religion—was much less stable.[3] This imprecision led to legal uncertainty (as we shall see later) but also afforded those enforcing the restrictions some exclusionary discretion.

Nowhere, of course, are the motives and implications of racial classification more apparent than in the history and trajectory of residential segregation, in the systematic creation of white spaces to be protected and black spaces to be avoided and contained. The stories spun about those places—about the security and safety found on one side of the color line and the abject danger found on the other—were shaped in equal parts by the desire to justify exclusion and exploitation and by a willful blindness as to the consequences. Narratives employed by real estate agents, developers, and neighborhood improvement associations not only rationalized segregation but created a perverse feedback loop that attributed the conditions in the overcrowded and underinvested urban spaces left behind to the race of their inhabitants.[4] By the same token, white developers and homeowners routinely professed ignorance as to their own willingness or ability to hoard resources, advantages, and opportunities.[5] And they remained willfully oblivious to their own segregation, portraying and assuming all-white suburban neighborhoods as a natural consequence of individual choice and market forces.[6]

Taken together, the assumptions that those "not of the Caucasian race" were less than full (or desirable) citizens, and that their presence in a neighborhood constituted a nuisance to be avoided or eradicated, girded an increasingly central premise of private realty and public policy: that the occupancy or encroachment of "inharmonious" races destroyed property values. In their classic 1945 study of Chicago, Cayton and Drake observed that "the pattern of residential segregation results in habits of thought which characterize certain parts of the city as 'white' and others as 'Negro.'"[7] Such characterizations—about good and bad neighborhoods and the threat of racial transition to property values—cloaked segregation and discrimination with the apparent neutrality of the market, inviting white realty interests to disclaim racial animus in pursuit of good property investments and their corollaries—safe neighborhoods and good schools.[8] Manifested in private restrictions, they became a powerful mechanism of both exclusion and exploitation—barring African American access to most neighborhoods while extracting inflated rents and prices from those crowded into the residential pockets left unrestricted.[9]

"Wholly of the Caucasian Race": Exclusion and Inclusion in Racial Restriction

The private restrictions imposed in our five counties form a catalog of nearly 2,500 unique expressions of racial exclusion spanning six decades. They capture the ways in which their drafters and signatories understood racial categories and hierarchies at particular moments in time and how those understandings changed over time. Early on, property restrictions in the Midwest excluded "negroes" or "colored" people, Asians ("Mongols"), and a long and variable list of white ethnics. Over time, the logic of restriction narrowed to a simpler black-white binary. The prevailing categorization or terminology by the late 1930s, reserving neighborhoods and subdivisions for those "wholly of the Caucasian Race" reflected both a rethinking of what it meant to be white in the wake of the First Great Migration and immigration restriction and a fundamental shift from a language of exclusion (listing those to be kept out) to one of inclusion (listing those, under a singular banner, to be allowed in).

The practice of private restriction began at a time when race was a relatively elastic concept, and the category of white or Caucasian had fragmented under the pressure of recent immigration from Southern and Eastern Europe. In 1910, almost 15 percent of the U.S. population (nearly 15 million) were born abroad; of these, 87 percent (11.7 million) were born in Europe and nearly 42 percent (5.7 million) in Southern and Eastern Europe.[10] Scientific and popular schemes of racial categorization elided the distinctions between skin color, national origin, language, and religion. The *Dictionary of Races or Peoples* (1911) drafted by the infamous Dillingham Commission adopted a common five-race taxonomy: "Caucasian, Ethiopian, Mongolian, Malay, and American or, as familiarly called, the white, black, yellow, brown, and red races." But it also recognized nearly forty races "indigenous to Europe."[11] Tellingly, the dictionary's entry for Caucasian runs some eight pages and "includes all races, which, although dark in color or aberrant in other directions, are, when considered from all points of view, felt to be more like the white race than like any other of the four other races" and concludes that "although the white race would be supposed to be the one best understood, it is really the one about which there is the most fundamental and sometimes violent discussion."[12]

All of this occurred against a backdrop of white supremacy and racial capitalism; it marked a temporary shift, as Matthew Frye Jacobson suggests, "from one brand of bedrock racism to another—from unquestioned hegemony of a unified race of 'white persons' to a contest over political 'fitness' among a now fragmented, hierarchically arranged series of distinct white 'races.'"[13] Efforts to sort through the diversity of "so-called Caucasians" (as Madison Grant dubbed them in 1916) marked a political and pseudoscientific effort to shoehorn new immigrants into the established racial order.[14] For a generation after the Civil War, official distinctions (mulatto, quadroon) were made among African Americans as well, but these were eventually overwhelmed by a "one-drop" racial logic. Competing and overlapping taxonomies sorted people across and within broad racial categories but, in the United States, the core distinction between white and black remained unchallenged and undiluted.[15]

Both the early-century fascination with eugenics and the root racial order were reflected in the practice of private realty and property restriction. Homer Hoyt's 1933 disquisition on land values in Chicago rated the influence of national and racial residents in descending order: "1) English, Germans, Scotch, Irish, Scandinavians; 2) North Italians; 3) Bohemians or Czechoslovakians; 4) Poles; 5) Lithuanians; 6) Greeks; 7) Russian Jews of the lower class; 8) South Italians; 9) Negroes; 10) Mexicans"—noting as an aside that the list "was prepared chiefly by John Usher Smyth, West Side real estate broker."[16] Such lists evoked two contributing anxieties: the first a hangover from turn-of the-century concerns over urban crowding and the living standards of new immigrants, the second a blunter and more persistent expression of the conviction that nonwhite occupancy destroyed property value.[17] Similar lists were employed in racial restrictions, especially before the 1930s. In Black Hawk County, early petition restrictions (1914, 1915) held that property could not be "sold, conveyed, rented to, or occupied by any Negro, Indian, or any person of African, Chinese, Japanese, Greek, Italian, Servian, or Bulgarian race or descent."[18] In early restrictions in Hennepin County, prohibitions of "any person or persons of

Chinese, Japanese, Moorish, Turkish, Negro, Mongolian or African blood or descent" were common—sometimes listed as "Chinese, Japanese, Moorish, Turkish, Negro, Mongolian, Semitic or African blood or descent."[19]

Across the Midwest, such eugenics-inspired taxonomies were an early exception to a pattern of restriction aimed almost exclusively at African Americans. Outside of Hennepin County (where prohibitions against Asian occupancy were attached to about 6 percent of restricted properties), restrictive covenants and agreements were almost always organized around the color line. The original (1911) restriction on the *Shelley* property in the City of St. Louis was aimed at "people of the Negro or Mongolian Race," but it was one of only two restrictions in the entire city that used the latter term, and only a handful of others (all imposed in 1905) specified restrictions again Chinese occupants.[20] In St. Louis County, such departures were equally uncommon: Maple Place, developed in stages between 1909 and 1911, required that "none of said lots shall ever be rented, sold, or conveyed to negroes or to Chinese," but this was only one of two instances of the latter restriction.[21] A few developers used restrictions against "Negroes or Malays," a tack probably inspired by the liminal immigration status of Filipinos under post-1898 American occupation.[22] In settings where over 99.9 percent of the population was enumerated as white or black as late as 1940 (including all the counties in this study), restrictions targeting Asians and others were understandably uncommon. Even the sweeping catalog of exclusion employed in the early Waterloo restrictions was often narrower in practice and intent: numerous parties to the petition restrictions cited earlier added the notation "as said restrictions apply to negroes only" beside their signatures.[23]

Restrictions against Jews were also relatively rare. In Hennepin County, a few subdivision restrictions prohibited "persons of African or Semitic Race" or "Negroes or Jews." The restriction on the Tralee Addition in Golden Valley held that "no part of said premises shall ever be used or occupied by or sold, conveyed, leased, rented or given to Negroes or Mongolians or Hebrews or any person or persons of the Negro race or Mongolian race of Hebrew race or blood," and some restrictions on Walton Hills added "Semitic" to the list of restricted persons.[24] But these totaled just over a hundred parcels (less than half a percent of the total). In a setting dubbed "the capital of anti-Semitism in the United States" by Carey McWilliams in 1946,[25] the rarity of restrictions against Jews reflects an early and successful challenge to private restriction. In response to an anti-Semitic restriction, the Minneapolis Jewish community pressed the state legislature to pass a bill prohibiting religious discrimination in real estate transactions—effectively narrowing the focus of local private restrictions to the threat of African American occupancy.[26] In greater St. Louis, private restriction was overwhelmingly a response to the threat posed by the Great Migrations. In St. Louis County, only 4 of 1,042 restrictions included Jews, 2 directly and 2 by adding the qualifier "Gentile" to Caucasian.[27] In the City of St. Louis, partly due to the extensive use of the Real Estate Exchange's boilerplate agreement, not a single restriction was directed at Jews. In the Iowa counties, only two idiosyncratic parcel restrictions in Iowa City were directed at "Jews and colored people."[28]

Indeed, the most significant variation across the early history of restriction was not the range of restriction but the varying and shifting identification of African Americans as "colored," "negro" (usually uncapitalized), or "of the African race." Early restrictions often hedged their bets by employing multiple descriptors. A clause widely used in the Minneapolis suburb of Richfield, for example, held that "said land or buildings thereon shall never be rented, leased or sold, transferred or conveyed to nor shall the same be occupied exclusively by any negro or colored person or person of negro blood."[29] The only exception, commonly offered across all settings, was an allowance for African American servants. "The foregoing shall not apply," as the 1922 restriction on Sunset Terrace 1922 in St. Louis County read, "to bona-fide servants employed and living with families of the Caucasian Race." A similar accommodation was routine in Hennepin County, taking care not to restrict the occupancy of African Americans "such as may be serving as domestics for the owner or tenant of said lot, while said owner or tenant is residing thereon."[30]

Across this era, the language of restriction underwent a fundamental shift that both dramatically narrowed the range of racial terms and flipped the logic of restriction from one of exclusion to one of inclusion. As figure 2.1 plots, the inclusive term "Caucasian" (often accompanied by the modifier "wholly" to clarify its exclusion of the "mulatto" designation employed by the Census through 1920) gained popularity during the housing boom of the 1920s. By the late 1930s, it had largely displaced almost all other descriptors.

In the City of St. Louis, the language of restriction was largely set by the Real Estate Exchange's uniform restriction agreement. Through the 1920s,

Figure 2.1 Exclusive and Inclusive Terms in Racial Restrictions

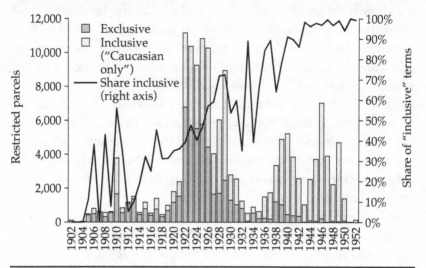

Source: Ehrman-Solberg et al. 2020; Gordon 2023b, 2023c, 2023d, 2023e.
Note: Annual parcel total is for all five counties.

this document included a prefatory reference to the goal of preserving "the character of the neighborhood consisting of the parcels last described as a desirable place of residence for persons of the Caucasian Race," and, until 1942, a restrictive clause specifying that owners could not "sell, convey, lease, [or] rent to a negro or negroes or deliver possession to or permit to be occupied by a negro or negroes (no matter how the right to occupancy or title shall be attempted to be acquired)." The restrictive clause was later changed to refer to "a person or persons not wholly of the Caucasian Race."[31] Of the seventy-one subdivision restrictions in the city, only ten used exclusive terminology (all of them "Negro"), the last of these in 1926.

Suburban subdivisions in St. Louis and Hennepin Counties show the same pattern: after the mid-1920s, their agreements or indentures were aimed almost exclusively at any "race or nationality other than the Caucasian race," "any person, other than a member of the Caucasian race," "any person or persons who are not of pure Caucasian blood or descent," or those "not wholly of the Caucasian Race."[32] In subdivisions built in stages over a number of years, developers often made the adjustment from exclusive to inclusive restrictions themselves. In St. Louis County, Moritz Place (1909) excluded "negroes" but the Mortiz Place Addition (1921) restricted occupancy or owner-ship to "the Caucasian Race." The prominent County developer Charles Vatterott excluded "negroes" from the St. Ann subdivision of Acreton in 1924, then switched to "any person other than of the Caucasian Race" when he added new houses two years later.[33] In Iowa, only the early (1914 to 1916) petition restrictions in Waterloo and a couple of parcel restrictions in Iowa City used any terms other than "Caucasian."[34]

In part, the growing prevalence of "Caucasians only" language was a product of changes in the building industry. Professional trade associations refined and disseminated model restrictive language, and local white realty boards (as in St. Louis and Chicago) developed standardized forms for neighborhood petition restrictions.[35] Subdivision development, as we have seen, increased in scale and complexity across the first decades of the twen-tieth century as community builders erected not just housing but the infra-structure to support it and the rules to govern its sale and use.[36] This meant, in turn, that the language of restriction was increasingly standardized and formulaic; large developers imposed the same general terms and conditions wherever they did business. The use of the generic "Caucasian" allowed them to skirt regionally or locally specific concerns: it was equally effective in barring African American occupancy in St. Louis, Latino occupancy in Austin, Texas, and Chinese occupancy in San Francisco. The growing prev-alence of such boilerplate language reflected both the professionalization of private realty and its commitment to racial restriction as a social norm and business practice.[37]

This shift from the exclusion of "negroes" or "colored" and other minori-ties to the blanket inclusion of "Caucasians" also reflected the intersection of a range of demographic and political factors. It was intimately bound up with the long debate over immigration restriction. Leading up to the pas-sage of the Johnson-Reed Act in 1924, which sharply curtailed new immi-gration from anywhere but Western Europe, there were sustained political pressures to distinguish among "white ethnics" and to bolster the case for restriction with an elaborate hierarchy based on race, national origin, reli-gion, and language. But after 1924, there was a general intellectual and political retreat to the long-standing "major divisions": Caucasian, Asian (Mongolian), and Black (Negroid). This was driven by the gradual assimi-lation of second-generation European immigrants and their determination to establish themselves firmly on the white side of the American color line.[38]

The ethnic enclaves emptied out by white flight, in this respect, seldom reappeared in suburban settings. "The motivation or aspiring to and becoming white," as Charles Mills underscores, "is precisely so that one can benefit from this exploitation."[39]

The urgency to "become white" and the advantages of doing so was heightened by the Great Migrations, which hardened racial discrimination and exploitation—across a number of dimensions—in northern settings.[40] The key point here, as white ethnics and housing experts alike recognized at the time, was that barriers to occupancy or mobility were permeable for some and not for others. "Except in the case of negroes and Mexicans," as Hoyt counseled in 1933, ". . . these racial and national barriers disappear when the individuals in the foreign nationality groups rise in the economic scale or conform to American standards of living."[41] National origin was not much of a barrier to residential integration, but the color line remained bright and unbreachable. Indeed, second-generation European immigrants boasted relatively high rates of homeownership, and the importance of these private investments was exaggerated in settings (such as Catholic parishes) anchored by place-based churches and parochial schools.[42]

If the racial status of Southern and Eastern European immigrants was (for a time) uncertain, their color was not—and all of the most salient and lasting dimensions of discrimination rested on the latter. Conformity to racial standards, in this respect, was determined not by the behavior or identity of those excluded but by the willingness of those above them in the racial hierarchy to accept or tolerate such standards.[43] For white ethnics, the defense of neighborhoods against African American occupancy (including participation in restrictive agreements) was an opportunity to claim or ensure inclusion under the Caucasian banner.[44] "The real history of ethnic enclave-building in this country," as Aldon Morris reminds us, "was nasty, bloody, brutish, and racist to the core."[45] For its part, the St. Louis Urban League wondered at "the Jews, Germans, and Italians in the block, all of whom seem to unite on the common plane of being white to oppose the inroads of colored tenants."[46]

While the shift to "Caucasian" served many interests and purposes, the term's precise (and legal) meaning remained uncertain. For its part, the Census defined those who were white by identifying those who were not: in 1910, enumerators were instructed that "'black' (B) includes all persons who are evidently full-blooded negroes, while the term 'mulatto' (Mu) includes all other persons having some proportion or perceptible trace of negro blood." In 1930, the instructions noted simply that any "person of mixed white and Negro blood should be returned as Negro, no matter how small the percentage."[47] This confusion or inconsistency also cropped up in the law. "Wielded by judges and juries who believed that setting racial boundaries was crucial to the maintenance of ordered society," Peggy Pascoe observes in her survey of miscegenation cases, "the criteria used to determine who fit in which category were more notable for their malleability than for their logical consistency. Genealogy, appearance, claims to identity, or that mystical quality, 'blood'—any of these would do."[48] In immigration law, a long string of prerequisite cases—juggling Congressional intent, legal precedent, and "scientific" evidence—labored over the definitional boundaries of "Caucasian." While the courts generally shored up that boundary (granting inconsistent exceptions for Armenians, Syrians, and Asian Indians), the fact that the meaning of "Caucasian" was routinely contested underscored its ambiguity.[49]

The same, of course, was true on the other side of the color line. Behind the thin scientific veneer of biology and genealogy, the designation of "colored" or "negro" proved just as slippery as that of "Caucasian." Legal definitions and bureaucratic imperatives were both bolstered and challenged by "common sense" observations and day-to-day experiences. Racial taxonomies and their distinctions did not flow from scientific criteria or methods—they conjured up the science that was useful. In and out of the courts, the question of whether one was "not wholly of the Caucasian Race" hinged on a predictable yet elastic combination (varying from place to place) of physical appearance, self-identification, family reputation, behavior, and social standing.[50]

Restrictive agreements often sought their own precision or definition. The standard agreement drafted by the Chicago Real Estate Board in 1927 held that "the term 'negro' as used herein shall include every person having one-eighth part or more of negro blood,"—a threshold it later lowered to one thirty-second—"or having any appreciable admixture of negro blood, and every person who is what is commonly known as a colored person."[51] A similar standard was used in the St. Louis County suburb of South Richmond Heights (1914), which prohibited occupancy by "any person having one thirty-second part or more negro blood." This genealogical precision was deflated by the restriction's next sentence, which held that the "Court or jury trying any case . . . may determine the proportion of negro blood in any party who may be in possession of the property by the appearance of such person."[52] Legal challenges often employed academics to testify to the social construction of racial categories and to the haziness of the term "Caucasian"—but to little avail.[53] In *Sipes v. McGhee* (1947), the Michigan case eventually resolved by the *Shelley* decision, the testimony of the plaintiff was sufficient to establish the defendants' race: "I have seen Mr. McGhee, and he appears to have colored features. They are more darker than mine. I haven't got near enough to the man to recognize his eyes. I have seen Mrs. McGhee, and she appears to be the mulatto type."[54]

In Hennepin County, some developers found the combination of "Caucasians only" restrictions and allowances for live-in servants insufficient protection and worked in prohibitions against miscegenation as well. The restriction on Franklin Steeles Minnehaha Terrace Addition in Minneapolis (1924) barred sales or rental "to any negro or person living with a person of the negro race." The restrictions on Bellevue Acres in Brooklyn (1924) and Dorman's First Addition to Minneapolis (1913) both held that lots "shall never be sold, leased, mortgaged or otherwise transferred to any person of the negro race or to any person married to or living with a person of the negro race."[55]

One reflection of this uncertainty, and a strategy for overcoming it, was the tendency of developers to pile on overlapping or synonymous categories in the hope of ensuring that the right people were excluded or included. One 1936 restriction in St. Louis County barred ownership or occupancy "by Negroes, nor by any person of the negro or dark race, including Filipinos and Hawaiians, nor by any Jews, nor by any person of the Jewish race, nor by any Chinese, nor by any person of the Chinese race, nor by any Japanese, nor by any person of the Japanese race."[56] In some cases, "Caucasian" was supplemented or displaced by "white." Some Minneapolis restrictions specified that "no dwelling shall be occupied by any person who is not of the white or Caucasian race" or that the "premises herein conveyed shall not be leased or sold to any natural person other than a white person."[57] The restriction on South Lynnhurst Park in Minneapolis (1924) barred the occupancy of "any person or persons who are not full bloods of the so-called Caucasian or white race." Some early restrictions in St. Louis County allowed only the construction of an "exclusive private residence for one white family" or "a private residence for white people," and a scattering in the 1940s prohibited the occupancy of "persons of any race other than the white race."[58] A few restrictions in Hennepin County, all of them put in place after 1945, disturbingly barred any occupant "other than of the white or Caucasian (Aryan branch) race."[59]

The fuzziness of Caucasian as a racial category could also be useful, affording on-the-fly discretion in selling or letting properties. Anti-Semitic exclusions often hid behind such language, allowing developers or homeowners' associations to pick *which* Jews they wished to exclude.[60] Some restrictions elided racial categories and nuisances by restricting those considered simply "objectionable" or "undesirable." One extensive Hennepin County restriction, for example, held that the "premises shall at no time be transferred to any colored or other objectionable person"; another prohibited any "person of Asiatic or African or of an undesirable race."[61] Similar provisions were used in St. Louis County, holding that lots "cannot be disposed of to colored or other objectionable people," or that "no lots shall be sold to negroes or other objectionable people."[62] Such language, along with the common proviso that barred any "race or nationality other than those for whom the premises are intended,"[63] gave those who were enforcing restrictions wide latitude as to the meaning of "objectionable" or "undesirable."

If the agreements themselves used varying and often vague language or terminology, there was nothing ambiguous about their motivation. The very premise of racial categorization—from the eugenics-inspired rankings found in early restrictions to the "Caucasians only" language and logic that eventually prevailed—was exclusion. In this respect, early prohibitions on "negro" or "colored" occupancy identified those to be kept out. Later restrictions identified the opportunity hoarders instead. The intent and the consequences were the same.

Offensive Trades and Objectionable Persons: African Occupancy as a Nuisance

The exclusion of African Americans through private land-use controls rested on the premise that African American occupancy constituted a nuisance use of property. At the end of the nineteenth century, private agreements prohibiting nuisances, especially industrial or commercial uses of property, were a commonplace extension of (or substitute for) nuisance law.[64] In response to the Great Migrations, racial occupancy was quickly added to and consistently featured in lists of objectionable uses. As the 1943 primer *Fundamentals of Real Estate Practice* put it: "The prospective buyer may be a bootlegger who would cause considerable annoyance to his neighbors, a madame who had a number of Call Girls on her string, a gangster, who wants a screen for his activities by living in a better neighborhood, *a colored man of means who was giving his children a college education and thought they were entitled to live among whites,*" adding that "any such deal would instigate a form of blight."[65]

Such arguments underscored how white homeowners, developers, and realtors thought about the prospect of African American neighbors; they also served strategic purposes. Under conventional nuisance law, local and state courts had proved reluctant to consider the mere presence of African Americans as a nuisance.[66] In turn, the nuisance designation was a way of leveraging support for conventional zoning; into the 1920s, state courts had consistently upheld zoning ordinances that regulated identifiable nuisances but struck down those that imposed purely aesthetic or social rules or standards.[67] In this respect, the private construction of African American occupancy as a nuisance served to both evade the narrow legal definition of the term and to leverage such assumptions into local land-use planning.

Before 1920, private property restrictions commonly included, alongside the regulation of building type and placement, a general nuisance provision covering offensive trades—often accompanied by a list prohibiting (for example) "any hotel, tavern, drinking saloon, carpenters shop, blacksmith or wheelwright shop, steam mill, tannery, slaughterhouse, skin dressing establishment, livery stable, glue, soap, candle or starch manufactory or any other building for offensive use or occupation."[68] Such lists followed the general logic of nuisance law, which focused on vice and any consequences of property use—noise, smell, smoke—that could not be confined by property lines. As the Supreme Court closed off the option of racial zoning (*Buchanan* in 1917) and offered its tacit blessing to private restriction (*Corrigan* in 1926), white realty interests increasingly added African American occupancy to lists of nuisances. "There can be no doubt, indeed, that the now quite common provision that no liquor shall be sold or used in limited area or subdivision has a marked and beneficial tendency to attract purchasers to a residential district," as one legal observer noted in 1927, "and there can be no doubt that the fear of negro invasion materially interferes with the profitable sale of almost every homesite. These restrictions, therefore, aid rather than restrict free alienation."[69]

At the same time, the assumption that African American occupancy entailed an unambiguous nuisance or objectionable use of property rested on shaky legal ground. Parties to some early restrictions, for example, often assumed African American occupancy was barred by generic references to "offensive" or "objectionable" use, to the goal of sustaining a "high class" residential area, or to the assurance that residents would be protected from any threat to "enjoyment of their property."[70] As the plaintiffs in a 1943 Michigan case (unsuccessfully) argued, "While there are no specific words in the recorded restrictions, excluding colored persons from the restricted neighborhood, still, the restriction being aimed at the maintenance of values and high residential character in the district, it must be necessarily implied that any act which intentionally destroys either or both the values and the high residential character are prohibited."[71] As in nuisance law, the courts generally rejected this equation—pressing white realty interests to specify African American occupancy as a prohibited nuisance.

In St. Louis, most early high-end residential neighborhoods (including the city's many private streets) were not racially restricted—in part because economic exclusion was considered sufficient, in part because segregation was easily sustained in other ways before the First Great Migration, and in part because residents assumed that any restriction of nuisance or objectionable use also covered the threat of African American occupancy.[72] When it was established in 1870, the private street at Vandeventer Place in central St. Louis adopted rules allowing only single-family homes valued at more than $10,000 (about $230,000 in 2023 dollars) but made no explicit provision for racial restriction.[73] As the neighborhood around Vandeventer Place changed, both nonresidential use (the original footprint is now the site of a Veterans Affairs hospital) and African American occupancy pressed residents to reaffirm and clarify their exclusionary intent. In December 1943, the residents adopted, by petition, a new clause providing that "no lot or improvement thereon in Vandeventer Place shall be used or occupied or permitted or suffered to be used or occupied by any person or persons not of the Caucasian Race (except where the same may be employed as servants or domestics on said lots)."[74]

The designation of African American occupancy as a nuisance emerges most starkly in restrictive agreements, particularly in their juxtaposition of conventional nuisances with the mere presence of any persons "not wholly of the Caucasian Race."[75] The uniform agreement used by the St. Louis Real Estate Exchange (accounting for over two-thirds of the city's restrictions) had two targets: "any slaughterhouse, junkshop, or rag-picking establishment" and any sale or conveyance to "a Negro or Negroes."[76] City subdivisions adopted similar language. The indenture for the St. Louis subdivision of Cleveland Heights provided—in a single breathless catalog of nuisances— that "there shall not be erected, kept or permitted on any lot or part of lot of said subdivision any slaughterhouse, stockyard, milk dairy, glue, candle or white lead factory, brewery or disorderly house or nuisance of any kind nor shall any lot, house, building, flat or improvement of any kind or an interest therein be sold, leased, rented, conveyed, transferred, willed, devised or in any way or manner given, granted or disposed of or occupied by any persons other than those of the Caucasian Race."[77]

St. Louis County restrictions had a similar logic and cadence. The 1928 restriction on the County's Westcamp Subdivision specified three nuisances: African American occupancy, the sale of liquor, and the erection of a hospital or sanitorium. Others typically included African American occupancy in a long list or prohibitions. The restrictions on Yorkshire Subdivision, for example, listed in order "fuel which causes the emission of soot or smoke . . . cattle, horses, swine, sheep or other domestic animals . . . breeding of any animals, birds or fowl for commercial purposes . . . noxious or offensive trades or activity . . ." and "any person or persons not wholly of the Caucasian race."[78] In Hennepin County, African American occupancy was more commonly paired with vice—ensuring that the grantee "shall not sell or lease said real estate to a colored person nor for the purpose of carrying on a liquor business or any immoral purposes."[79]

While subdivision indentures adopted an increasingly uniform set of restrictions, smaller-scale agreements often betrayed distinctly local understandings of what constituted a nuisance. One restriction in Iowa City provided that the buyer "not permit the removal of old buildings to an upon said lots nor permit a store, oil station, fraternity or sorority house, or an apartment house to be built or maintained thereon nor permit barns or outbuildings of any kind except a garage to be build [sic] thereon, nor permit any poultry to be kept thereon, nor permit any sale of properties to Jews or colored people nor permit the erection of a dwelling thereon of a design or construction costing less than Ten Thousand ($10,000) Dollars, which shall not be a bungalow."[80]

After the *Shelley* decision in early 1948, developers began to drop racial restrictions. They persisted in some subdivisions where development had begun before 1948. And they were defiantly attached to a few new subdivisions, in the hope that another means of enforcement could be found. But, across all settings, they became less and less common. Subdivision indentures leaned increasingly on—and supplemented—local zoning ordinances. And many retreated to the earlier practice of a general nuisance restriction. The St. Louis County subdivision of Cypress Gardens, for example, restricted occupancy to those "wholly of the Caucasian Race" in its original 1948 development and a 1949 addition, but the 1950 plat provided simply that "no nuisance of any kind shall be created or permitted." In St. Louis County, 226 subdivisions platted between 1890 and 1950 (just under 10 percent of the total) did not impose a racial restriction. Of these, almost half (104) were platted in 1948 or later.

Early in the twentieth century, the control of nuisances through private agreement reflected the limited "protection" offered by contemporary law and policy. With the onset of the First Great Migration, white realty interests added African American occupancy to their growing list of prohibited nuisances—an enumeration alongside saloons, glue factories, and farm animals leaving little doubt as to their sense of the nature and gravity of the threat. In the late 1940s, racial restrictions again gave way to a general nuisance clause, a tack made necessary by the *Shelley* decision and eased by the development of public land-use controls after the late 1920s. As in the early history of nuisance law and private land-use controls, the retreat to a general nuisance clause was also a retreat to private discrimination and social norms as the most reliable means of sustaining racial exclusion.

Inventing the Threat: Property Values and Racial Restriction

By justifying segregation and exclusion as a protection against nuisances, racial restrictions helped invent and entrench assumptions about racial occupancy and property values that would become a central tenet of professional realty and home finance, local land-use and economic development policies, and the tangle of public policies and private practices that constituted redlining.[81] The presumptive threat of African American occupancy to property values—what W.E.B. Du Bois dubbed "an ancient and bearded lie"—was a sort of self-fulfilling conviction, rendered real (and seemingly true) by the willingness of white homeowners and real estate agents to act on it.[82] In turn, and especially over time, it served to camouflage the racial animus behind housing choices and policies, attributing the valuation of property to neutral and inexorable market forces.[83]

Anxiety about racial occupancy and property values in the urban North predated the First Great Migration and cut across class lines. As early as 1899, Du Bois observed that "public opinion in the city [Philadelphia] is such that the presence of even a respectable colored family in a block will affect its value for renting or sale."[84] The racial zoning law at issue in *Buchanan* was justified on the grounds that "it prevents the deterioration of property owned and occupied by white people, which deterioration, it is contended, is sure to follow the occupancy of adjacent premises by persons of color."[85]

This assumption became a core premise of private realty and property valuation. It is "a matter of common observation," as *Principles of Real Estate Practice* put it in 1923, "that the purchase of property by certain racial types is very likely to diminish the value of other property."[86] Ten years later, the industry manual *Real Estate Appraisal and Valuation* emphasized that "the class of people who will be neighbors, both closely adjacent and in the general district as well, will affect the value of the house regardless of the bill of materials. A colored settlement several blocks from a white location will very often cast its influence upon the latter location."[87] For decades, both private realty and public policy sustained this "principle of conformity" and the importance of ensuring that neighborhoods maintain a "reasonable degree of homogeneity," including "families of similar race and nationality."[88] As one agent confided in the late 1960s, "No Realtor objects to dealing with Negroes, but we have that certain obligation to white people. The value of their property goes down."[89]

These convictions animated the history of private restriction. A 1947 guide to subdivision development declaimed that it would not "discuss the pros and cons or racial restrictions" but underscored the "continually demonstrated fact that infiltration of incompatible racial groups breaks down values in a residential neighborhood."[90] And, as importantly, private restriction invented and refined these convictions. Long before the notion that African American occupancy depressed or destroyed property values was dressed up in academic garb or public policy, as Margaret Garb argues, "real estate salesmen, speculators, and white property owners had defined neighborhoods along racial lines and had proclaimed that value was profoundly influenced by the race of a neighborhood's tenants and owners."[91]

Such views were routinely expressed by realty interests in Iowa, Minnesota, and Missouri. In 1916, backers of St. Louis's short-lived racial zoning ordinance argued that "property declines in value 50 percent, or more, in white neighborhoods as soon as Negroes move into them."[92] When the St. Louis Archdiocese proposed converting a church at Cook and Taylor to African American use in 1927, the local neighborhood association urged the Archbishop to reconsider: "We are not inimical to the Negro but we know that it is a fact from experience that Negroes moving into a White neighborhood greatly depreciates the value of property."[93] The St. Louis Real Estate Exchange's uniform restriction agreement was framed around "the benefits accruing and the mutual covenants and conditions herein contained and for the purpose of preserving values of our respective properties."[94] When those restrictions were contested, their defense rested largely on the promise of economic protection. "The presence of said negroes in said restricted area," as the plaintiffs argued in *Thornhill v. Herdt* (1938), "is destroying and will continue to destroy the value and desirability to the other lot owners in said area, and will continue to destroy said value, as to cause those on whose behalf this action is instituted by plaintiffs to suffer irreparable injury and irredeemable damages."[95]

In Hennepin County, concerns about property values both motivated and rationalized racial exclusion. When a few African American families moved into Minneapolis's Thirteenth Ward in 1920, over two hundred white homeowners packed a neighborhood association meeting determined to "prevent others from buying real estate, and to negotiate with those who are now residents, seeking their change of residence." The chairman of the meeting claimed not only that African American occupants were driving down property values, but that this was their goal—a gambit to turn a profit by "forcing white people to buy them out to get rid of them."[96] A quarter century later, a survey by the Governor's Interracial Commission found that over two-thirds of the state's white residents backed neighborhood segregation on the grounds that African American occupancy lowered property values.[97] In Iowa City, brokers enthusiastically pursued the assumptions and standards of the emerging real estate profession, and "protected" property values by routinely attaching racial restriction to deeds of sale.

Civil rights activists and fair housing advocates took aim at such practices, both to push back against the assumption that African American occupancy was a nuisance or threat and to argue that private restrictions distorted housing markets and eroded the very values they claimed to protect. Restrictions segmented local housing markets, creating artificial shortages of both "protected" homes and those open to African American occupancy—driving up the cost or value of both.[98] In most settings, the deteriorating quality of housing in African American neighborhoods predated African American occupancy. Private restrictions and other mechanisms of exclusion shoehorned black owners and tenants into *already* declining neighborhoods. "Instead of being responsible for the lower property values," as Herman Long and Charles Johnson argued in 1947, "the Negroes are brought into the area as a means of rescuing the property owner from the economic consequences of deterioration."[99] African Americans were ceded older, central city housing stock—often in neighborhoods unprotected by zoning or scattered through areas of mixed residential, commercial, and industrial use. "In most American cities," as Weaver underscored, "the Negro has become a handy dumping ground for obsolete property."[100]

These conditions—and the cynical explanation of African American occupancy as their proximate cause—were exaggerated by the artificial shortage of open housing during the Great Migrations and the overcrowding that resulted. Public and private interests sustained segregation (and the protection of white neighborhoods) in the face of African American migration by carving the existing housing stock into smaller and smaller units, rezoning African American neighborhoods (regardless of their housing stock) for higher density, and steering gambling, prostitution, and other vices into already stressed neighborhoods.[101]

The racial logic of property values, of course, was most directly a consequence of *white* behavior. African American occupancy "will not affect values a bit," as Du Bois observed in 1925, "unless the people in the neighborhood hate a colored skin more than they regard the value of their own property."[102] Housing values were distorted by what the FHA blithely dubbed "the market effect of buyers' and sellers' reactions." As Weaver pointed out, "It is the rapid and panic-inspired movement of the whites out, rather than the movement of a few Negroes in—that leads to the fall in property values."[103] In the end, it did not matter if the connection between the value of houses and the race of their occupants was real or invented. The result was the same. "Part of the attitude reflected in lower land values is due entirely to racial prejudice, which may have no reasonable basis," as Hoyt conceded in 1933. "Nevertheless, if the entrance of a colored family into a white neighborhood causes a general exodus of the white people, such dislikes are reflected in property values."[104] It was not African American occupancy that lowered housing values; it was white sellers, acting on an assumption of their own invention, that made that assumption seem real.[105]

In a pitch to city planners, land economists, and realty interests, Weaver and others argued that private restrictions actually *prevented* market forces from determining an orderly succession in property use, occupancy, or value. The inevitable transition, instead, looked more like blockbusting. "People, like water if dammed into too little space, create pressure and, when the pressure passes a certain point, finally break out of their bounds," as Weaver put it, adding that "once a break is made, it is impossible to hold back the tide."[106] In this view, racial restrictions served no one's material interests.

Such arguments found little purchase. The destructive tide that Weaver described was only a threat in areas (as on the north side of St. Louis or the south side of Chicago) where defensive neighborhood petitions were employed to stem or delay racial transition or in areas (as in the inner suburbs of north St. Louis County) where early restrictions on small-lot subdivisions were abandoned by white flight. On much of the suburban footprint of St. Louis, Hennepin, and Black Hawk Counties, racial restrictions proved an effective mechanism of exclusion and a guarantor of stable or rising property values.[107] In turn, it was the architects of neighborhood and suburban restriction who were able to wave the invisible hand and press the claim that homeowners and tenants were simply responding to market forces and market incentives. "The restrictive covenant and other measures of exclusion are considered as protective devices operating at the level of economic interest," as Long and Johnson observed, "rather than instruments of attack and aggression against racial, religious or national minorities at the social level of segregation and discrimination," adding that it did not seem to matter "whether this distinction in function is true or whether it is a comfortable rationalization for obvious undemocratic practices."[108]

The defense of property values, polished in the era of private restriction and persisting to the present day, pulled a veil of market forces over the grim reality of segregation. "The problem of loans for Negroes, on both first and second mortgages," as one banker put it in the early 1930s, "is bound up with the economics of the situation."[109] This shield of economic justification imagined a pristine original position in which buyers and sellers met each other somewhere on the supply curve and residential patterns (including segregation) were but the aggregate consequences of individual choices.[110] This assumption, as Charles Mills suggests, marked a particular instance of willful white ignorance—in which white single-family homeownership was the imagined norm, any other arrangement a threat to that norm, and any defense of the norm a rational economic response free of animus or bias.[111]

Taken together, these assumptions about race and property hardened into a narrative frame for racial threat and racial privilege and a foundational rationale for racial restriction. The racial hierarchy born of the immigration debate proved short-lived and superficial. At least in the Midwest, racial property restriction focused increasingly and nearly exclusively on African American occupancy. That color line, in turn, was buttressed by the fierce (and invented) conviction that African American neighbors were nuisances—akin to tanneries or glue factories—that destroyed the value of any property they approached.

CHAPTER 3

Dividing the City: Patterns of Private Restriction

AGAINST THE BACKDROP of racial categorization and property valuation, private racial restriction was motivated by the dramatic demographic shifts of the early twentieth century, shaped by the social and professional aspirations of developers and real estate agents, and necessitated by the failure of other strategies of segregation or exclusion. Accordingly, private restriction exhibited common elements and patterns across settings (especially as it was embedded in the business model and professional ethics of private realty), as well as distinct local trajectories and practices. In the Midwest, private restriction was overwhelmingly a response to the Great Migrations and focused almost exclusively on the threat—real or imagined—posed by African American occupancy. In new construction, especially on the suburban fringe, racial restriction was a routine business practice, decisively shaping the character and accessibility of the housing booms that preceded and followed the Great Depression. In older neighborhoods, private restriction responded to local variations on the racial threat and was assembled, often frantically and sloppily, to create or buttress neighborhood boundaries and to block the "encroachment" of African American neighbors.

Behind the two principal modes or strategies of exclusion—subdivision and petition—the form and pattern of private restriction varied according to local demographic patterns (and threats), local trajectories of urbanization and suburbanization, and the agents or actors responsible for the invention and diffusion of local restrictive practices. The type (or legal form), scale, and timing or pace of private racial restriction, along with the local geography and the terms of individual covenants or agreements, shaped the impact of racial restrictions and reflected the motives of developers across these settings.

Varieties of Racial Restriction

Racial restrictions in the Midwest took several forms (see table 3.1). The most common of these—across jurisdictions—was the subdivision restriction, which accounted for almost all restricted parcels in Johnson, Hennepin,[1] and St. Louis Counties; over half of those in Black Hawk County; and just over a third of those in the City of St. Louis. Subdivision development, especially in the formative years of urban and suburban growth, was fragmented and speculative.[2] Landowners recorded the most rudimentary division of land, selling off large parcels (often subject to further subdivision) to developers—most of them local and operating at a small scale. As late as 1938, 95 percent of housing starts nationwide were undertaken by builders or developers who erected fewer than one hundred houses a year.[3] As we have seen, early plats were often accompanied by general (but not racial) restrictions against nuisance uses of property. Of the 839 restrictions recorded in St. Louis before 1900, 92 percent imposed conditions other than racial occupancy. After 1900, restrictions against "colored" or "Negro" occupancy became increasingly common. In St. Louis County, about two-thirds (34 of 78) of restricted subdivisions platted before 1920 included a racial restriction; between 1920 and the *Shelley* decision in 1948, over 90 percent (872 of 955) of subdivision restrictions included a racial clause.[4]

Across the first half of the twentieth century, subdivision development grew in scale and complexity. A new generation of community builders began to develop residential subdivisions—and attach restrictions to them—on a much larger scale.[5] These developments involved not just the subdivision of land but the provision of basic infrastructure (streets, sewers, water, gas), the cost of which was rolled into home prices and responsibility for which was often ceded to public authorities when development was complete.[6] These developers were selling not just lots but aspirational neighborhoods promising permanence and exclusivity. The conception and marketing of such subdivisions leaned heavily on both the provision of

Table 3.1 Racial Restrictions by Type (Cumulative Totals through 1952)

Restricted parcels	City of St. Louis		St. Louis County		Johnson		Black Hawk		Hennepin		Totals	
	Number	Share (%)	Number	Share (%)	Number	Share (%)	Number	Share (%)	Number	Share (%)	Number	Share (%)
By subdivision	13,158	36.8	76,271	99.9	553	95.8	2,103	58.3	24,119	100.0	116,204	82.8
By petition	20,500	57.4	70	0.1	0	0.0	1,480	41.0	0	0.0	22,050	15.7
By parcel	1,888	5.3	—		24	4.2	23	0.6	—		1,935	1.4
By private street	163	0.5	0	0.0	0	0.0	0	0.0	0	0.0	163	0.1
TOTAL	35,709		76,341		577		3,606		24,119		140,352	

Source: Ehrman-Solberg et al. 2020; Gordon 2023b, 2023c, 2023d, 2023e.

public goods (especially modern sanitary infrastructure) and the promise that private investments would be protected—calming the fears and anxieties of prospective homeowners in an era when land-use zoning and building codes were in their infancy.[7] Such patterns were especially evident in the Midwest, where concentric rings of automobile-based development expanded into the cornfields during the years of the Great Migrations.[8]

Restrictive agreements were a central feature of the new suburban landscape. While the conventional land-use and building codes had the advantage of public authority, they could not "ordinarily cover many of the protective phases desirable to the prospective homeowner," as one observer noted in 1931, adding that "many otherwise good subdivisions are spoiled by careless or eccentric or greedy acts on the part of homeowner."[9] Subdivision restrictions included rules for subdivision governance (election and terms of trustees, assessments for common costs); prohibited nuisances (industrial or commercial use, vice, animals); building size, design (including design review), and materials; lot setbacks; minimum cost requirements; and design or placement of fences, plantings, and outbuildings.[10] "Restrictive covenants in deeds specifying the exact use of the property, the side, rear, and front yards, the cost of the house, the architecture, and even the race inhabitants, are extremely useful in design," as the American Society of Civil Engineers underscored in its 1939 *Manual on Land Subdivision*. "They should be outlined at the time the design is made. The judicious use of restrictive covenants will do much to establish and protect property values. Such covenants are valuable in all residential developments; subdivisions for the poor, as well as for those of more ample means, benefit from such controls."[11]

Before 1925, most restrictions were perfunctory, often simply listing building standards, a minimum housing value, prohibited nuisances, and racial restrictions in the margin of the original plat or in the document for each property transfer. As restrictive agreements became increasingly elaborate (often combining private zoning with long catalogs of restricted uses or activities), they were filed separately as "dedications," "indentures," or "declarations of restrictions," and individual property transfers would refer to them—either by book and page number or commonly just as "restrictions of record."[12] Often, these documents came to resemble full-blown private zone plans.[13] The indentures for Eldorado Park and Eldorado Lakeview (1929) in St. Louis County ran thirty-four handwritten 11-by-18-inch pages and featured five pages enumerating the duties of the trustees, a complete zoning scheme listing seven use districts and height and area regulations for each, a list of sixty-four prohibited activities in the "light industrial" district—and the provision that "no lot or other part of said subdivision shall be sold, conveyed, rented, or leased, in whole or in part, to any persons of African or Asiatic descent."[14] These agreements were often drafted by developers, but occasionally developers established basic rules of governance and left the details of restriction to the subdivision's first board of trustees. In most cases, trustees settled on restrictive language within a year or two, but later (and retroactive) restrictions were not uncommon. The racial restriction on Stark Place in St. Louis County was added in 1922, a year after construction and first sales, "for the benefit of all those persons who have already purchased and those who may hereafter purchase" a home in the neighborhood.[15]

Subdivision-based racial restrictions had many advantages. Unlike parcel or petition restrictions, they could accomplish restriction at scale. This meant both that large swaths of development could be restricted at once and that the "integrity" of the restriction was enhanced.[16] In St. Louis, seventy-two subdivision restrictions recorded between 1890 and 1950 account for only 9.4 percent of all restrictive agreements but—due to their scale—42.6 percent of all restricted parcels. The average size of race-restricted subdivisions across Black Hawk County, Johnson County, the City of St. Louis, and St. Louis County was seventy-six parcels or lots, with some development (such as St. Louis Hills in south St. Louis) counting more than a thousand homes.[17] In property law, agreements established by a single original grantor (the developer) and based on a general scheme of restriction (often laid out in a preamble) were understood as "negative reciprocal easements." Under the Sanborn rule, these were understood to be binding on all grantees—even if the restriction in question was not present in every chain of title.[18] In turn, professional networks and contacts made it easy to disseminate restrictive strategies and practices.[19] In suburban Hennepin and St. Louis Counties, developers clearly borrowed each other's restrictive terms and language or copied from national leaders like J.C. Nichols or the Olmsted Brothers.[20] As it was standardized as a business practice, racial restriction increasingly adopted boilerplate "Caucasians only" language, and increasingly cropped up in settings such as Johnson County, where the racial threat was nonexistent.[21]

At the end of the era of private restriction, and especially during the housing boom that followed World War II, subdivision-based agreements flourished with the blessing and active encouragement of federal housing policies.[22] For the FHA, large-scale and restricted suburban development checked all the boxes. It added housing units at a pace that both met the agency's housing goals (in an era when central city units were being razed in the name of urban renewal) and underwrote postwar growth. Backing large suburban developments (often with "conditional commitments" to large builders) ensured that housing subsidies flowed to areas of low "risk."[23] The result was not just an uneven subsidy for private development and home-ownership but, as David Freund underscores, "a decisive shift in the means of achieving residential segregation and—inextricably linked to this—in the rationale advanced to justify it."[24] For all of these reasons—their scale, their contractual structure, their broader articulation of neighborhood norms and expectations, and their congruity with local and federal policies—subdivision restrictions were rarely contested and easily enforced.

In settings where residential construction largely predated the use of racial restrictions, and in older neighborhoods facing the threat of racial transition, restrictive agreements were assembled by petition. Unlike the expansive subdivision restrictions, petition restrictions were often exclusively racial. In St. Louis, the uniform restriction agreement employed by the St. Louis Real Estate Exchange sought to "preserve the character of said neighborhood as a desirable place of residence for persons of the Cauca-sian Race," holding that homeowners could not "erect, maintain, operate or permit to be erected, maintained or operated any slaughterhouse, junk shop or rag-picking establishment" or "sell, convey, lease or rent to a negro or negroes."[25] Petition restrictions were a defensive response to a tangible threat, an often-futile tactic to create or sustain the boundaries between black and white neighborhoods; they were less an expression of aspirational exclusivity than a last-ditch effort to block both the expansion of black occupancy and the defection of white neighbors.[26] Accordingly, petition restrictions were rarely employed in areas of new development or in settings where there was no threat of black occupancy. They were systematically used in the blocks surrounding the Ville in north St. Louis, a patchwork of restriction that eventually included over 500 distinct agreements and over 20,000 parcels. (In all, petitions accounted for over two-thirds of the city's restrictions and almost 60 percent of restricted parcels.) In Waterloo, petition restrictions accounted for over 40 percent of restricted parcels—much of the damage done by a single petition in 1914 that included over 600 parcels. But they were rare elsewhere: only one of the thousand-odd agreements in St. Louis County was a petition (an older subdivision that adopted a racial restriction in 1940);[27] and no petition restrictions were recorded in Hennepin or Johnson Counties.

The areas covered by such petitions variously included contiguous city blocks, houses facing each other across a given street, and broader and often ill-defined neighborhoods. The standard agreement in St. Louis assumed a city block as the natural unit, describing a generic geography "bounded on the ___ by ___ Street; on the ___ by the center line of a public alley running ___ and ___ through City Block ___; on the west by ___ Street; and on the south by the center line of a public alley running ___ and ___ through City Block ___."[28] In St. Louis (and in Missouri more generally), these compact agreements (the median size was forty parcels) were understood as neighborhood schemes of restriction and premised on complete subscription of affected property owners. In other settings, petition restrictions were much larger in scale and understood as "community" schemes in which a threshold of signatures (75 percent of owners in Chicago, for example) was sufficient to accomplish restriction.[29]

Petition restrictions were often the work of local neighborhood "protective" or "improvement" associations, but in both St. Louis and Waterloo the local white realty board was the driving force—both in assembling the petitions and in organizing the local associations that enforced them. The St. Louis Real Estate Exchange worked closely with organizations like the Marcus Avenue Improvement Association (the impetus behind the *Shelley* restriction) but also worked to restrict blocks where no local organization existed.[30] The exchange drafted and recorded more than 90 percent of the city's petition restrictions. It offered not just the fill-in-the-blanks boilerplate agreement but also support in collecting notarized signatures, filing documents with the city, defending restrictions in court, and renewing them when the original term (usually fifteen or twenty years) ran out. The exchange was a third party to all the agreements it drafted, allowing it to take actions against violators even when white homeowners were reluctant to do so.[31]

On both practical and legal grounds, petitions were a shakier form of restriction than those drawn up for new subdivisions. The task of collecting signatures and maintaining signature thresholds forced petitioners to choose between small-scale agreements or spotty ones. At best "this process would be a patch-work enterprise," as one observer noted in 1928, "responding only to neighborhood initiative and leaving inevitable gaps here and there through which undesirable inroads could be made."[32] Because petitions were not drafted or imposed as a condition of sale, they were often "wild deeds" unattached to the chain of title for the properties they covered.[33] They were often sloppily assembled and easily challenged; indeed, their validity as contracts dominated the legal history of private restriction until the late 1940s. Employed defensively in neighborhoods facing racial transition, petition restrictions were at best stopgap measures—prone to erosion, defection, and eventual failure.

Private restrictions could also be attached to individual lots or parcels as a covenant to the deeds of sale. Such covenants were included in both transfers of individual parcels and sales of small groups of parcels to small-scale developers. These lot-by-lot restrictions accounted for a small share (1.4 percent) of restricted parcels across all five counties, and many were later absorbed by or included in larger-scale subdivision or neighborhood restrictions. While dwarfed by the subdivision- and petition agreements, restrictions on individual sales call attention to the importance of private realty in the practice and dissemination of race restriction. The creation of the National Association of Real Estate Boards (originally the National Association of Real Estate Exchanges) was a largely Midwestern project: thirteen of the twenty founding exchanges were from the Midwest, and its early leadership included August Frederick of the St. Louis Exchange (1908), Minneapolis developer Samuel Thorpe (1911), and St. Louis developer Cyrus Crane Fillmore (1943). Charles Chadbourn of the Minneapolis Real Estate Board drafted the organization's first code of ethics in 1916.[34] While the early codes were largely concerned with curbing unethical business practices (an effort sullied in 1915 when Frederick was indicted for fraud)[35] a major revision in 1924 introduced the "ethic" of racial restriction: "A Realtor should never be instrumental in introducing into a neighborhood a character of property or occupancy, members of any race or nationality, or any individuals whose presence will clearly be detrimental to property values in that neighborhood."[36] This article stood until 1950, when it was quietly truncated to remove the "race or nationality" phrase.[37]

In the era of private restriction, the line of influence from the National Association of Real Estate Boards (NAREB) on down was clear. National policies informed state-level licensing (and the threat of sanction) and the policies of local realty boards (which often took the lead on crafting and disseminating restrictive practices).[38] Local boards and emerging professional standards, in turn, encouraged individual brokers to sustain segregation at the point of sale. This was broadly accomplished by steering, the practice of showing prospective African American buyers homes only in areas of established African American occupancy.[39] But it was also accomplished through explicit professional standards and expectations. "As the first step in an attempt to drive negroes from the white residential sections," as the *Waterloo Courier* reported in 1916, "the realty board last night passed a resolution restricting members of the board from selling to any negro property in the white district."[40] In turn, real estate agents also took it upon themselves to attached race-restrictive covenants to individual sales where subdivision or petition restrictions did not offer protection. This was evident in Johnson County, where nearly two-thirds of restrictions were the work of a few Iowa City real estate agents, one of whom attached "Caucasians only" provisions to the terms of twenty-two sales between 1927 and 1947.[41]

Racial exclusion was assumed by white residents; contractual restrictions merely formalized that expectation. Early in the twentieth century in particular, segregation was largely a product of social norms, other forms of exclusion (such as direct discrimination by realtors or landlords), and violence. When the sprawling Forest Park Addition in north St. Louis was platted in 1888, its indenture provided that occupancy and land use were "subject to such rights, privileges, and restrictions as may be expressed in the deeds from the Forest Park Improvement Association to its purchasers."[42] In the following decades, a few parcels were restricted at sale. As the city's African American population grew in the early years of the Great Migrations, white residents of Chouteau Place (a neighborhood of some 1,300 properties in the Forest Park Addition) claimed that African American occupancy was prohibited—even though no such explicit restriction had been filed— and pressed to "renew" the restriction.[43]

Assumptions of exclusivity and racial restriction were punctured by the threat posed by the First Great Migration. In St. Louis and St. Louis County, the most exclusive neighborhoods were organized as private streets in the later nineteenth and early twentieth centuries. These streets (which were not public rights-of-way) were gated, basic services were provided through local assessments, and building design and placement were carefully regulated.[44] Here, racial restrictions were largely implicit, generated by the exclusivity of the property and not by formal restrictive language. Only two of the city's numerous private streets, West Cabanne Place (1905) and

Thornby Place (1908) included racial restrictions in their founding documents.[45] For the rest, high property values and tony building standards offered uneven protection. In St. Louis and elsewhere, class-based exclusions failed when neighborhood transitions eroded property values or when African American professionals dared to cross the implicit color line.[46] Tellingly, a few private streets added restrictions by petition or reaffirmed their racial restrictions in response to the Great Migrations. Vandeventer Place, platted in 1870, added a racial restriction by petition in 1943.[47] The original (1908) restriction on Thornby Place had a twenty-five-year term, but residents redrafted it in 1920 with more precise race-restrictive language—and extended it with another twenty-five-year term.[48]

Private racial restrictions formalized, by private contract, often implicit assumptions about race and place. The form of those restriction was crucial to their immediate and long-term impact. Racial restrictions on individual parcels, or those pursued through economic exclusion alone, proved fragile—and were eclipsed by larger-scale agreements that either restricted entire subdivisions at their development or cordoned off city blocks and neighborhoods for "Caucasians only." Subdivision restrictions were preemptory efforts to sustain racial exclusion on the suburban fringe. Petition restrictions were almost always defensive responses to the threat of "negro encroachment" in the central city.[49] Accordingly, and across our settings, each had a distinct logic, trajectory, and impact.

The Timing of Restriction

The timing and trajectory of private restriction rested on both national and local factors and the ways in which national developments were filtered through local settings. The first private racial restrictions were recorded in 1893 in St. Louis, 1902 in St. Louis County, 1910 in Hennepin County, 1914 in Black Hawk County, and 1921 in Johnson County. Early restrictions were mostly small scale. In St. Louis, for example, sixty-two of all sixty-eight restrictions recorded before 1910 were attached to individual parcels. As the pace of restriction picked up, local trajectories reflected a wide variety of factors—including local experience of the Great Migrations, the specter of racial disorder raised by the World War I–era race riots, the Supreme Court's 1917 *Buchanan* decision prohibiting racial zoning, and local patterns of private realty and private development.[50]

Private restriction was well established before the demographic, social, and legal upheaval of the World War I era. In St. Louis, subdivision-based racial restrictions in the city were first drafted in 1906 (Waustrath Place) and before 1917 included twelve subdivisions totaling over 2,000 parcels—including three large developments in South St. Louis: Morningside Park (518 parcels), Nottingham (389), and Hadley Park (213).[51] The only restrictions by petition before 1917 were on the 4400 (1910) and 4600 (1911) blocks of Labadie Avenue (the latter including the parcel challenged in the *Shelley* case three decades later) and in two neighboring blocks in 1912.[52] In St. Louis County, seventy-three subdivisions encompassing nearly 8,500 parcels were developed before 1917. In Hennepin County, about forty subdivisions encompassing at least 4,000 parcels were developed before 1917.[53] In Black Hawk County, two sweeping petition restrictions drawn up in 1914 and 1915 totaled almost 700 parcels.

While the events of 1917 to 1919 certainly motivated private restriction, their immediate impact was muted. Perhaps most importantly, private restriction was overwhelmingly attached to new construction. Across our five counties, 83 percent of all restrictions were imposed on subdivision lots at development. As a result, the pace of private restriction was tied closely to local housing starts. Nationally, and for the two settings for which we have local data (St. Louis and Minneapolis), housing starts dipped during the war and did not recover until the early 1920s: national permitted housing starts averaged 282,000 a year in the first four years after the war (1918–1921), and 854,000 a year in the next four years (1922–1925).[54] As figures 3.1–3.4 make clear, the pace of restriction closely followed the pace of housing starts in the City of St. Louis and in St. Louis, Hennepin, and Black Hawk Counties.

Petition restrictions could be drafted at any time, but here too there was no discernible response to either the *Buchanan* decision or the war-era riots. After a flurry of petition restrictions in St. Louis between 1910 and 1913, the next recorded petition was not until 1922—after which the practice took off, restricting almost 1,000 parcels a year over the next decade. From 1913 to 1917, local white realty interests had focused their efforts on the city's racial zoning ordinance, which passed by referendum in 1916. After 1917, the practice of petition restriction hinged on the local pace of the Great Migrations and on the development of a strategic response—shaped and informed by national real estate interests—by the St. Louis Real Estate Exchange.[55] In Black Hawk County, the other setting with significant petition-based

Figure 3.1 Racial Restrictions by Year and Type, City of St. Louis, 1890–1950

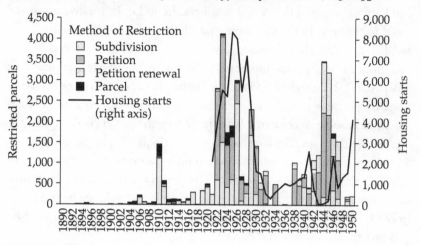

Source: Gordon 2023b; U.S. Department of Commerce 1966, table B-5.
Note: A small share of restrictions imposed through private streets is included in subdivision totals.

Figure 3.2 Racial Restrictions by Year and Type, St. Louis County, 1890–1952

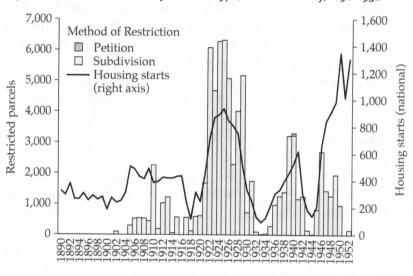

Source: Gordon 2023e; Snowden 2006, table Dc510-530.

Figure 3.3 Racial Restrictions by Year and Type, Hennepin County, 1890–1950

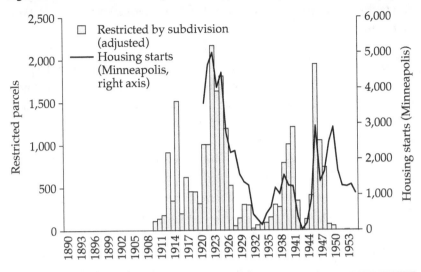

Source: Ehrman-Solberg et al. 2020; U.S. Department of Commerce 1966, table B-5.
Note: Date of restriction (from deeds) adjusted to date of original development. All Hennepin restrictions presumed to be subdivision-based.

Figure 3.4 Racial Restrictions by Year and Type, Black Hawk County, 1890–1950

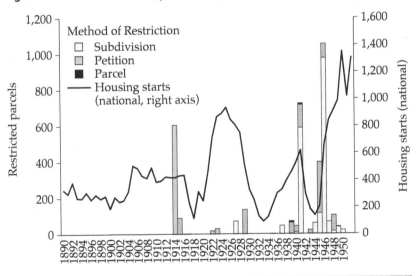

Source: Gordon 2023c; Snowden 2006, table Dc510-530.

restriction, the local racial threat was the only consideration—yielding the two petitions that reacted to the arrival of African American migrants, both before 1917.

The filing of new restrictions slowed dramatically at the end of the 1920s. For subdivision restrictions, this lull reflected the onset of the Great Depression and the collapse of the construction business. Nationally, annual new home starts fell from over 500,000 to under 100,000 between 1929 and 1933.[56] In both St. Louis and Minneapolis, new permits at the trough of the Depression (1934–1935) were a tiny fraction—less than 4 percent—of what they had been in the peak year of the 1920s housing boom. In St. Louis, the only significant new (and restricted) development between 1930 and 1939 was St. Louis Hills No. 2 (252 units), completed in 1930. In Hennepin County, the decade before the stock market crash saw over 1,000 parcels restricted each year on average; in the decade after the crash, the average shrank to just 168 parcels a year. In St. Louis County, the rate of restriction contracted by more than three-quarters, from over 4,200 parcels a year in the decade before 1929 to just 975 parcels a year over the following decade. In Black Hawk County, only 47 parcels were restricted between 1929 and 1939.

The pace of restriction by petition also slowed. St. Louis petition restrictions added just over 3,400 parcels in the 1930s, less than half the number (8,510) added by petition during the 1920s. This too reflected the turmoil in housing markets and housing finance, as foreclosures spiked and 16 percent of the city's homeowners sought relief from New Deal housing programs.[57] The pace of African American migration also slowed during the Depression decade, lessening the immediate threat of racial encroachment or neighborhood transition.[58] But it also reflected the scope of restriction that had already been accomplished during the 1920s. The Real Estate Exchange and its allies recorded 207 neighborhood petition restrictions between 1921 and 1930, almost all of them on the borders of the Ville, with the exchange's standard term of twenty years. The 86 petition restrictions added in the 1930s mostly filled in the gaps in this ragged circle of restriction.

As the economy recovered in the late 1930s, the pace of restriction picked up again. Hennepin County subdivisions restricted another 8,000 parcels after 1938, with most of the activity between 1938 and 1941 and after 1946. In St. Louis, 1,939 parcels were restricted between 1938 and 1950 in new subdivisions—although land available for new development in the city was dwindling. Restriction accompanying suburban development in St. Louis

County—where almost 20,000 parcels were restricted by subdivision over the same span—was now a more important driver of local segregation. In Black Hawk County (like Hennepin County, a Second Great Migration destination), subdivision developers recorded almost all their race restrictions after 1937.

During the Second Great Migration, mobilization for World War II brought with it white and black population growth in northern cities and fierce racial competition over economic opportunities, public goods, and residential space. The limited housing supply generated demand for public housing (to be built on a segregated basis) and a renewed interest in private restriction. In Black Hawk County, 14 established subdivisions encompassing 691 parcels adopted restriction by petition between 1939 and 1950. In St. Louis, another 4,699 parcels were restricted by petition after 1938. And, as importantly, 4,357 previously restricted parcels in St. Louis had those restrictions extended by 118 hastily assembled renewal petitions as the expiration (usually twenty years) of those filed in the early 1920s approached. Indeed, the war years, as Weaver noted in 1948, marked "veritable fetish for maintaining and strengthening racial covenants developed in many northern cities."[59]

All this occurred as legal challenges, including the *Shelley* case out of St. Louis, wound their way through the courts. When the Supreme Court ruled in May 1948 that enforcement of such agreements was unconstitutional, new restriction slowed. But it did not come to a complete halt. Local white realty interests hoped to find other means of enforcing restriction, including civil suits for damages (which targeted white sellers instead of black buyers)—an option that, although not widely employed, was not halted by the federal courts until 1953.[60] To the degree that private restrictions served as aspirational or social norms, white realty interests hoped they might still serve a purpose even without the threat of enforcement. And many developers, especially those in the middle of multistage developments, continued to copy and paste race restrictions from one subdivision or subdivision stage to the next. In St. Louis, another 363 parcels were restricted in the months after the *Shelley* decision, including the last two phases of the sprawling St. Louis Hills development in south St. Louis.[61] Post–May 1948 restriction was much more pronounced in suburban settings, amounting to 10 subdivisions totaling 581 parcels in Hennepin County,[62] 5 small subdivision totaling 47 parcels in Black Hawk County, and 93 subdivisions totaling almost 4,000 parcels in St. Louis County.

These pockets of hopeful or inertial defiance aside, the practice tailed off quickly (although *Shelley* offered no mechanism for redacting or revising any of the race restrictions recorded in the previous half century). Most St. Louis County developments adopted new language after 1948—either replacing explicit racial restrictions with building criteria and a generic nuisance clause ("No noxious or offensive trade shall be carried on upon any lot, nor shall anything be done thereon that which may be or become an annoyance or nuisance to the neighborhood")[63] or deferring most "conditions and restrictions" to local zoning and building codes. This transition is especially evident in staged developments, most of which quietly dropped race restrictions in 1949 or 1950.[64]

Across this history, and even as the practice faded after 1948, it was rare for subdivision trustees, homeowners' associations, or neighborhood associations to rescind restrictions once they were filed. Of the 781 distinct race-restrictive agreements recorded in St. Louis (not including renewals or duplicates), only 5 were formally withdrawn: 4 of these were in fiercely contested blocks just south and north of the Ville, while the other was a single parcel restriction that was pulled in 1940 on the grounds that "no other property adjacent to or near the above-described property was similarly restricted."[65] In St. Louis County, no record of race restrictions being rescinded before 1948 exists—only that of a scattered and piecemeal process of removal if and when indentures were revised in later years does. In Black Hawk County, the small Lily Dale Acres subdivision (10 lots) was restricted by 2 separate agreements in April 1949; less than a year later, the racial restriction was struck on the grounds that "it appears that said covenant and restriction is unreasonable and is in restraint of free alienation."[66]

The Geography of Restriction

The importance of the type and timing of racial restriction is evident in the spatial patterns of restriction that emerged in each setting. Individual restrictive agreements (invoked at sale, assembled by petition, or imposed by developers) created distinct patchworks of exclusion, which reflected local urban and suburban growth, local demography, and local geography. Chapter 4 details the ways in which private restriction pursued or sustained local segregation in both new subdivisions on the urban fringe and central city neighborhoods threatened by racial transition. My goal here is to simply describe the pace and spatial pattern of restriction, over time, in each setting.

In greater St. Louis, private restriction was driven by two related logics.[67] The first was aimed at "hemming in" the borders of the Ville, the well-established African American neighborhood north of Easton Avenue between Sarah and Taylor. The Ville was the center of African American life in St. Louis, home to Sumner High School (the first high school west of the Mississippi to admit black students), Lincoln University School of Law, Homer G. Phillips Hospital, and a thriving black business and professional community.[68] The short-lived 1916 zoning ordinance circumscribed the Ville; the restrictive agreements that followed were an effort to stem its expansion as the city's African American population grew. The second strategy, especially in the neighborhoods surrounding Forest Park, in the lightly developed south-west corner of the city, and across St. Louis County, was to close off new construction to African American occupancy. The spatial distribution of restriction closely tracked both patterns of occupancy and the type of restriction being employed. The city's private streets, the first marker of residential exclusion, were (excepting Shaw Place, near the Missouri Botanical Gardens on the south side) all located in the neighborhoods immediately north and west of Forest Park. Early parcel-based restrictions were scattered across the city, most of them eventually accompanied or eclipsed by larger-scale restrictions by petition or subdivision.

As early as 1910, restricted subdivisions were established along the city-county line in north St. Louis, in south St. Louis (south of the Burlington-Northern rail corridor that runs east to west from downtown), and (in this pre-automobile era) along the rail lines that extended northwest and south-west into the county. By 1920 (map 3.1[69]), the footprint of restricted subdivisions had grown markedly in the county, and the first efforts to quarantine the Ville developed on its northern border, with petition restrictions recorded on the 4400 and 4600 blocks of the Labadie in 1910 and 1911. The latter, which would eventually become the centerpiece of the *Shelley* case, held that "said property is hereby restricted to the use and occupancy, for the term of Fifty (50) years from this date. . . . That hereafter no part of said property or any portion thereof shall be, for said term of 50 years, occupied by any persons not of the Caucasian Race; it being intended only to restrict the use

Map 3.1 Racial Restrictions on Property in St. Louis, 1920

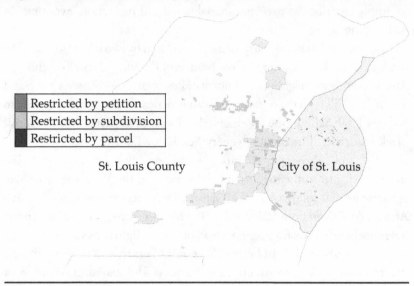

Source: Gordon 2023b, 2023e; Nolan 2018.
Note: Map shows county municipalities incorporated as of date of map. Private street restrictions are mapped with subdivisions.

of said property for said period of time against the occupancy by owners or tenants of any portion of said property for resident or other purposes by people of the negro or Mongolian race."[70]

The 1920s saw both the dramatic expansion of subdivision-based restrictions in the county (and in the corners of the city where new development was possible) and the furious persistence of the St. Louis Real Estate Exchange's effort to encircle the Ville with neighborhood agreements blocking its expansion (map 3.2). While subdivision restrictions in south St. Louis and St. Louis County created aspirational pockets of exclusion, the spread of petition-based covenants on the north side was much more frantic and defensive.[71] In 1922 and 1923 alone, the exchange sponsored over 100 restrictive agreements encompassing almost 4,700 parcels surrounding the Ville in all directions. Over the next two decades (maps 3.3 and 3.4), developers in the county continued to routinely attach racial restrictions to new construction, effectively barring African American occupancy from more than 80 percent of the county's 1950 housing stock. And real estate agents in the city continued to fill holes in the ring of restriction around the Ville.

Map 3.2 Racial Restrictions on Property in St. Louis, 1930

Source: Gordon 2023b, 2023e; Nolan 2018.
Note: Map shows county municipalities incorporated as of date of map. Private street restrictions are mapped with subdivisions.

Map 3.3 Racial Restrictions on Property in St. Louis, 1940

Source: Gordon 2023b, 2023e; Nolan 2018.
Note: Map shows county municipalities incorporated as of date of map. Private street restrictions are mapped with subdivisions.

Map 3.4 Racial Restrictions on Property in St. Louis, 1950

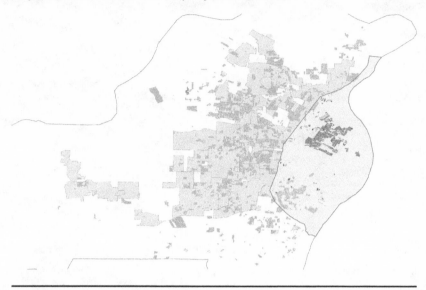

Source: Gordon 2023b, 2023e; Nolan 2018.
Note: Map shows county municipalities incorporated as of date of map. Private street restrictions are mapped with subdivisions.

In Hennepin County, the spatial pattern of restriction was much simpler—composed almost entirely of subdivision-based restrictions at the edges of the City of Minneapolis and in its immediate southern and western suburbs. As of 1920 (map 3.5), restriction was limited, consisting of a scattering of developments in south Minneapolis and in the first-ring suburbs of Edina, St. Louis Park, Golden Valley, and Robbinsdale. By 1930 (map 3.6), restriction had thickened and spread south to Richfield (the boundaries of which had extended north into present-day Minneapolis before 1927) and further west to Eden Prairie, Minnetonka, and the more remote western suburbs. Over the next two decades (maps 3.7 and 3.8), this basic pattern of suburban restriction—especially pronounced in the suburbs to the southwest—created a ragged circle of exclusion promising protection from the adverse impact of African American occupancy and a reassuring distance from any "hit or miss city neighborhood."[72]

In Black Hawk County, the pattern of restriction echoed elements of both St. Louis and Minneapolis. In 1920 (map 3.9), the singular impact of the railroad strike (and its strikebreakers) is evident in the sprawling

Map 3.5 Racial Restrictions on Property in Hennepin County, 1920

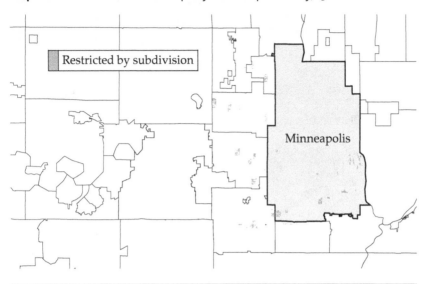

Source: Ehrman-Solberg et al. 2020.
Note: Minneapolis and county municipalities reflect their 2023 boundaries. All Hennepin County restrictions are mapped as subdivision restrictions (see appendix).

Map 3.6 Racial Restrictions on Property in Hennepin County, 1930

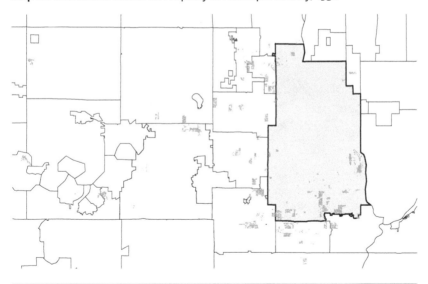

Source: Ehrman-Solberg et al. 2020.
Note: Minneapolis and county municipalities are mapped at their 2023 boundaries. All Hennepin County restrictions are mapped as subdivision restrictions (see appendix).

Map 3.7 Racial Restrictions on Property in Hennepin County, 1940

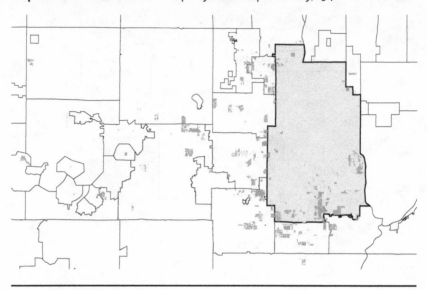

Source: Ehrman-Solberg et al. 2020.
Note: Minneapolis and county municipalities are mapped at their 2023 boundaries. All Hennepin County restrictions are mapped as subdivision restrictions (see appendix).

Map 3.8 Racial Restrictions on Property in Hennepin County, 1950

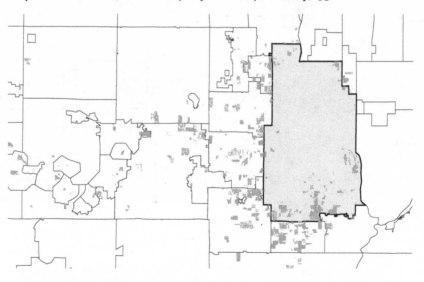

Source: Ehrman-Solberg et al. 2020.
Note: Minneapolis and county municipalities are mapped at their 2023 boundaries. All Hennepin County restrictions are mapped as subdivision restrictions (see appendix).

Map 3.9 Racial Restrictions on Property in Black Hawk County, 1920

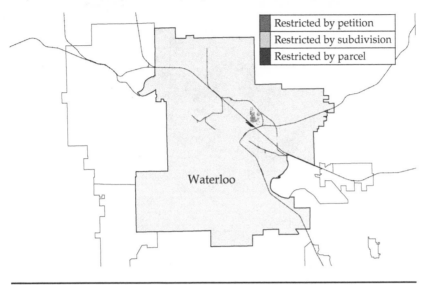

Restricted by petition
Restricted by subdivision
Restricted by parcel

Waterloo

Source: Gordon 2023c.
Note: Waterloo and other Black Hawk County municipalities are mapped to their 2023 boundaries. Major rail lines are shown for reference.

1914 petition restriction northeast of the railyards and the 1915 subdivision restriction north of that. But aside from that blunt intervention, Waterloo was, like Minneapolis, a Second Great Migration city where African American population growth began during World War II. Aside from the addition of a large subdivision restriction in the city's southwest corner (1937–1939), the footprint of restriction had changed little by 1940 (map 3.10). The bulk of restrictive activity in Waterloo (and in neighboring Cedar Falls, Evansdale, and Elk Run Heights) occurred in the decade after 1940 (map 3.11).

In Johnson County, which saw neither significant suburbanization nor African American settlement before 1950, the geography of restriction was not particularly pronounced or strategic (map 3.12). Aside from a string of individual sales restricted by real estate agents, private restrictions were confined to two large subdivisions, University Heights (1928) and Cottage Reserve (1934), and a scattering of smaller ones—their locations largely driven by the timing of construction and the whim of their developers.

Map 3.10 Racial Restrictions on Property in Black Hawk County, 1940

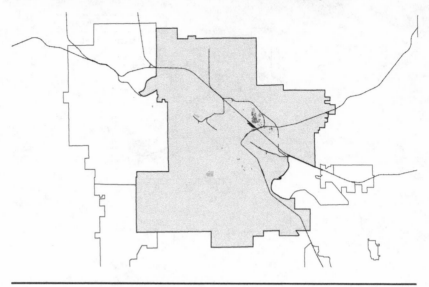

Source: Gordon 2023c.
Note: Waterloo and other Black Hawk County municipalities are mapped to their 2023 boundaries. Major rail lines are shown for reference.

Map 3.11 Racial Restrictions on Property in Black Hawk County, 1950

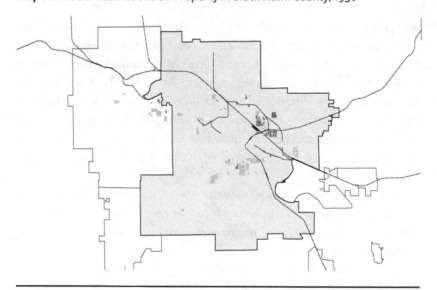

Source: Gordon 2023c.
Note: Waterloo and other Black Hawk County municipalities are mapped to their 2023 boundaries. Major rail lines are shown for reference.

Map 3.12 Racial Restrictions on Property in Johnson County, 1950

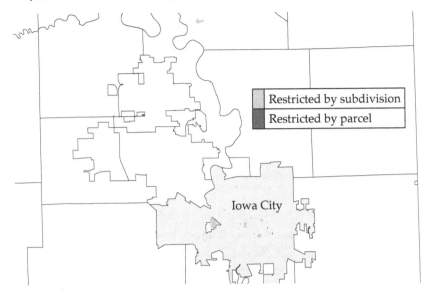

Source: Gordon 2023d.
Note: Iowa City and other Johnson County municipalities are mapped to their 2023 boundaries.

The Terms of Restriction

Finally, the terms of restriction varied widely across settings. This reflected differences over time and type of restriction, as well as distinct legal requirements or recording conventions in different state and local settings. As we have seen, many of these substantive differences—especially as they pertained to the scale or scope of private restrictions—were driven by the form of the restriction itself; that is, subdivision-based restrictions were generally larger and more expansive than petition-based restrictions. Across all forms of restriction, three questions that would influence individual conditions stood out: How long would they last? How could they be modified? And how would they be enforced?

Most private restrictions were drafted to "run with the land," a common reference in property law that attached such restrictions to the property regardless of changes in ownership. At the same time, most restrictions were attentive to another common convention in property law: the "rule against

Table 3.2 Restriction Terms and Expiration

	Share with Terms (%)	Term of Restriction		
		Average	Median	Longest
City of St. Louis	82.5	18.8	15	96
St. Louis County	38.7	29.1	25	99
Hennepin	—	—	—	—
Black Hawk	77.2	24.6	25	58
Johnson	18.3	21.5	22	30

Source: Calculated from Gordon 2023b, 2023c, 2023d, 2023e; Ehrman-Solberg et al. 2020.

Note: First column shows the share of restrictive agreements that contained expiration terms. Restriction terms are not available for Hennepin County.

perpetuities" that confined restraints or conditions on property to a generational window of 15 to 30 years, although local practice and compliance varied widely (table 3.2).[73] Where petition-based racial restrictions were common, either individual restrictions or the uniform agreement employed in St. Louis set a clear term of 15 to 25 years. In St. Louis City and Black Hawk County, over three-quarters of restrictions specified a term or expiration date. In Johnson County, where nearly two-third of restrictions were imposed by real estate agents on single sales, only 7 of 34 restrictions set time limits. In Black Hawk County, 55 of 75 restrictive agreements set time limits, with a median term of 25 years (and little variation). The average (18.8) and median (15) terms in St. Louis reflected short (less than 10-year) terms for many early restrictions, the heavy influence of the exchange's uniform agreement, and its strategy in the 1940s to encourage participation by shortening the term of both new agreements and renewals.

In Minnesota, a uniform "sunset" of 30 years was imposed on all restrictions, although parties could elect shorter terms.[74] In other settings, defined terms were less common in subdivision restriction, especially those drafted before the 1930s. Fewer than 40 percent of the subdivision restrictions in St. Louis County set time limits. Those that did tended to run longer: of the 402 developments with expiration terms, 161 were for 30 years or more, and the median was 25 years. The longest listed term was 99 years, while others flouted expiration entirely. The indenture for Westmoor Park (1922) averred that occupants were "forever subject" to restrictions. The one on Belvair Place (1946) held "that no vacant property nor building or buildings are to be sold, rented, leased to anyone not of the Caucasian race forever and ever."[75]

The process for modifying, extending, or renewing those terms also varied. The standard St. Louis petition agreement allowed restrictions to be terminated by a supermajority (75 percent) of owners, and the city's subdivision restrictions often invoked similar terms—allowing a designated majority of owners to modify, remove, or add restrictions at any time.[76] Some subdivisions delegated this authority to elected trustees. Agreements commonly contained distinct rules or triggers for extension of the original terms; these often skirted the rule against perpetuities by specifying automatic renewals (five, fifteen, or twenty-five years) in the absence of action by owners or trustees.[77] Regarding both extensions and other modifications, restrictive agreements and subdivision indentures often specified a narrow window at the end of the original term (or extension) in which restrictions were open for modification. All such provisions were aimed at underwriting protection by making it difficult for even a majority of owners to substantively change the original agreement. One St. Louis County indenture singled out its racial restriction in this respect, holding that "the above restrictions shall remain in force from and after this date until amended, modified, or abolished by a majority of the lot owners," while insuring that "paragraph 8 [the racial restriction] of this agreement shall never be amended, modified or abolished."[78]

Enforcement of private restrictions was complicated. They were not extensively challenged or litigated, and such litigation was mostly confined to the drafting deficiencies in petition agreements. As Richard Brooks and Carol Rose have underscored, restrictions were largely enforced as social norms or expectations, often expressed as move-in violence or intimidation.[79] In turn, intermediaries—especially real estate agents and realty boards—did much of the work of enforcement under the auspices of professional ethics and licensing.[80] The hold and validity of such agreements was buttressed by both the law and recording conventions: the Sanborn rule assumed the universality of subdivision restrictions, and public recording lent weight to restrictions even if they were absent from the chain of title.[81] For these reasons, subdivision-based restrictions were rarely contested, and petition restrictions showed up on court dockets either when they failed or when third parties (such as real estate boards) felt compelled to defend them.

However enforcement worked in practice, the contractual language of private restrictions commonly cited or assumed recourse to the courts. Restrictions typically stated that "such right may be enforced by the owner of any said lots by appropriate proceedings at law" or that "it shall be lawful for any other person or persons owning any real property situated in said development or subdivision to prosecute any proceedings in law or in equity against the person or persons violating, or attempting to violate, any such covenant and either to prevent him or them from so doing or to recover damages or other dues for such violations."[82] This option or threat was more acute in St. Louis, where the Real Estate Exchange (as a third party alongside the buyer and seller) could—and often did—bring legal action against those violating agreements.[83]

A small subset of subdivision-based restrictions (about fifty in St. Louis County and about five in St. Louis) raised the stakes by adding a reversionary clause—an option usually invoked solely for the racial restriction.[84] Reversion forfeited title, returning the lot to the original developer with little or no compensation if the racial restriction was violated. The indenture on Yorkshire Hills, for example, specified that no lot "shall be sold, leased, rented, conveyed, transferred, willed, devised, or in any other way or manner given, granted, or disposed of to, or occupied by any person or person not wholly of the Caucasian race." The indenture then added the kicker that "any violation of this restriction shall instantly, per se, operate as a forfeiture of the title to said lot or portion of lot and improvements thereon, and said title shall, because of such forfeiture, and for the consideration later mentioned therein, immediately pass to and vest in the undersigned, her heirs, representatives and assigns and she or they shall have the right to enter upon and take possession of such lot or portion of lot and improvements thereon." The restriction on St. Louis Hills No. 4 similarly held that "in the event of a breach of this restriction, by any reason of sale, grant devise, lease or rental of any lot or improvements thereon, to any person not of the Caucasian Race, the title of said lot shall immediately revert to the corporation and the Corporation may thereupon re-enter and take possession of the lot, with all the improvements thereon."[85] Such draconian enforcement mechanisms were rarely invoked, but their presence—alongside long terms, automatic renewals, and complicated modification procedures—underscored the urgency and importance of racial restrictions for white realty interests.

In the end, the impact of these restrictions rested less on the scope or enforcement of individual agreements than on their larger spatial patterns and logics. As the timing and geography of exclusion in each setting suggests, private agreements restricting racial occupancy by race were at once a frantic reaction to the Great Migrations (especially in neighborhoods threatened by racial transition) and a routine condition of new residential development (especially in the suburban ring). The resulting patchwork of private contracts reflected the combined efforts and anxieties of white homeowners, real estate agents and realty boards, and developers. The details of these agreements, in this respect, were less important than the ways in which they fit together—sometimes strategically, sometimes haphazardly—to accomplish and sustain racial segregation.

CHAPTER 4

Patchwork Apartheid: Private Restrictions and Racial Segregation

PATTERNS OF BLACK-WHITE racial segregation, particularly in the urban North, are well-documented. The dimensions of that segregation—dissimilarity, isolation, concentration, clustering—suggest different strategies of exclusion and a wide array of outcomes or consequences, both distributional and relational.[1] Racial segregation has proved a remarkably durable and consequential form of inequality, lasting long after the practices and policies at its roots have been successfully fought in the courts and decisively shaping local inequality, local opportunity, and the meaning of local citizenship to the present day.[2]

But our understanding of the trajectory, persistence, and consequences of racial segregation is not accompanied by a particularly satisfying account of the mechanisms or practices or policies that created it in the first instance. Massey and Nancy Denton's synthetic account leans heavily on the influence of social norms and intimidation, especially the hardening of white racism or hostility in response to the First Great Migration.[3] Local violence, in this respect, both enforced racial segregation and animated its extension: private citizens and public authorities policed and reinforced neighborhood boundaries in response to the World War I–era race riots in Chicago, east St. Louis, and elsewhere.[4] The black response to white hostility only fortified ghetto walls, as necessary reliance on parallel local business and services yielded—as Cayton and Drake noted of Chicago—"a pattern of relations which reduces to a minimum any neighborly contacts, school contacts, or chance meetings in stores, taverns, and movie houses between Negroes and whites of approximately the same socio-economic status."[5]

Acknowledged but understated in this account is the role of private restrictions—the only formal mechanism of racial segregation available to local developers, realtors, and homeowners between 1917 (when the Supreme Court prohibited racial zoning) and the era of redlining that began in the late 1930s. Private restriction was the most prevalent and formal expression of white hostility to black occupancy and, at both the suburban fringe and the contested borders of existing black neighborhoods, layered explicitly racial criteria atop other tactics of economic and social exclusion. The close spatial and temporal correlation of private restriction and emerging segregation underscores the ways in which private restriction did the work of creating (and enforcing) broad areas of outright exclusion, as well as the boundaries between racialized neighborhoods. Private restriction was both a driver of broad patterns of racial segregation in the formative decades of American urbanization and an on-the-ground mechanism by which African Americans were excluded from some neighborhoods and "hemmed in" to others.

Such mechanisms are important to our understanding of segregation not just as a distributional outcome but as a process.[6] Spatial and racial inequalities rely on the creation and justification of boundaries, which, in turn, are experienced, recognized, and respected or challenged by those on either side of them.[7] Close attention to the pattern and logic of private restriction, along with recent innovations in the use of original census enumeration districts to uncover fine-grained distributions of local populations, offers an opportunity to see how segregation played out over time.[8] Private racial restrictions, mapped to the parcel level, provide a precise block-by-block record of the (often strategic) location and timing of restriction. The scale of the enumeration district data, in turn, highlights the subtler physical dimensions of local segregation—including streets and other demarcations between white and black neighborhoods, outlying pockets of black or white occupancy, and potential zones of racial transition or conflict.

Mechanisms of Local Segregation

Segregation is conventionally measured using units of census geography, but these are not an effective guide to either the real-life boundaries that delineate patterns of racial occupancy or the lived experience of racial segregation in cities and their neighborhoods. Census geography itself is a statistical invention; census tracts and blocks are unstable and invisible to those who live in them and align imperfectly with the physical and political forces that create meaningful borders or distinctions between urban neighborhoods.[9] Such boundaries might be hard or soft, real or fictive, stable or shifting. They might evolve organically alongside urban development or (as in the case of a new urban highway or land clearance) mark a brutal interruption.[10] Segregation, in sum, was generated by defining the terms of exclusion or inclusion, managing land use, exploiting (or constructing) physical barriers between neighborhoods, reaching collective agreement as to neighborhood boundaries, and institutionalizing those boundaries with public policies.[11] Such patterns are reflected in common parlance about neighborhoods ("skid row," "the gold coast") and their borders ("the other side of the tracks," "across 110th Street"), but these descriptors do not tell us how or when such lines were drawn.

The creation and maintenance of racial segregation rely on policies and practices that sort the population into neighborhoods, set neighborhood boundaries, and justify both of these actions. In many settings, racial segregation was (and is) also accomplished by exploiting preexisting physical barriers, such as rivers or rail beds. Cities bisected by railroads, as Elizabeth Ananat has shown, became markedly more segregated during the Great Migrations than those that were not.[12] Such barriers facilitated the sorting of new arrivals, not just by providing clear and enforceable divisions but by "yielding agreement among residents, real estate agents, and other institutional actors about where one neighborhood ends and another begins."[13] They succored segregation by disconnecting neighborhoods, interrupting the street grid with limited points of access (such as bridges and rail crossings) and, in the bargain, circumscribing commercial and social networks as well.[14] Residential segregation was distributional, a categorical exclusion from given neighborhoods. And it was relational, a pattern of occupancy that created and exploited social categories and shaped or constrained social and civic interactions.[15]

Where natural or historical features proved insufficient as physical barriers, planners, developers, real estate agents, and homeowners did not hesitate to create their own. The footprint of urban highways and urban renewal projects has often been used to create or harden neighborhood boundaries.[16] The provision (or neglect) of basic infrastructure (such as sanitary and storm sewers, potable water, paved streets and sidewalks, and streetlights) has been a common marker—and creator—of "good" and "bad" neighborhoods.[17] Design and planning choices, including gating, landscaping, building orientation, and street scale or orientation (such as dead ends or cul-de-sacs), serve as real and symbolic borders.[18] "Natural or artificially established barriers will prove effective in protecting a neighborhood and the locations within it from adverse influences," as the FHA noted in its 1938 underwriting manual, describing such influences as "infiltration of business and industrial uses, lower class occupancy, and inharmonious racial groups," and noting that "hills and ravines and other peculiarities of topography often make encroachment of inharmonious uses so difficult that protection is afforded" or that a "high speed traffic artery or a wide street parkway may prevent the expansion of inharmonious uses to a location on the opposite side of the street."[19] Such elements of local planning and development were (and are) often accompanied by blunt local innovations such as barricades on streets or concrete walls between neighborhoods,[20] by exclusionary amenities such as country clubs, or by an architecture of security and surveillance sufficient to ensure that even ostensibly public spaces, as Mike Davis put it, "bristle with malice" in their "architectural policing of social boundaries."[21]

Segregation can also be accomplished, maintained, or accommodated by political and policy choices. Land-use zoning can create buffers between neighborhoods or, by managing density, facilitate the clustering (or flight) of populations. Many cities, for example, rezoned black neighborhoods from single family to multifamily use in order to stem their expansion during the Great Migrations and after.[22] School district boundaries and school catchment zones, alongside school closings and new construction, replicate or reinforce patterns of residential segregation and often define neighborhood boundaries—indeed, neighborhood monikers commonly echo that of local elementary schools.[23]

Neighborhoods and neighborhood boundaries are also sustained by a wide array of symbols, assumptions, and practices. Even when arterial streets or other features did not entail hard physical boundaries, they could still serve as "deadlines," as borders based on mutual agreement or implied threats.[24] The architecture of "grassroots redlining" (everyday patterns of discrimination, intimidation, and move-in violence) entrenches patterns of segregation and carefully manufactured anxieties about housing values.[25] Segregation sticks, as Kyle Crowder and Maria Krysan suggest, by "driving systems of economic stratification, shaping neighborhood perceptions, cir-cumscribing social networks and systems of neighborhood knowledge by race and ethnicity, and creating patterns of mobility and immobility that differ sharply across racial and ethnic groups."[26]

Racial property restrictions were instrumental to the initial establishment of racial boundaries and neighborhoods. Local restrictions, as the Chicago Real Estate Board boasted in the 1940s, took the form of a "fine network of contracts that like a marvelous delicately woven chain of armor is being raised from the northern gates of Hyde Park at 35th Street and Drexel Boulevard to Woodlawn, Park Manor, South Shore, Windsor Park, and all the far-flung white communities of the South side."[27] Such restrictions could be "delicately woven" (as in Chicago or St. Louis) in a concerted campaign to confine an existing African American neighborhood. They could take the form (as in St. Louis County and the Minneapolis suburbs) of a common commitment to exclusion in new development—often in settings where "their only appar-ent function," as Johnson and Long noted in 1947, "is that of giving psycho-logical support to other economic and social factors which make possible the maintenance of neighborhoods of exclusive residency."[28] Or they might, as in Waterloo, lean more heavily on a single blunt intervention (the large petition restriction assembled in 1914) to set the boundaries of racial occupancy. In each case, private restriction established the initial patterns and boundaries of African American occupancy and sorted new arrivals into segregated neigh-borhoods during the waves of the Great Migrations.[29]

Important, in this respect, was not just the practice of private restric-tion but its strategic implementation—whether it was one element of a broader strategy of exclusion in new suburban development or a desperate and defensive tactic employed at the boundary between black and white occupancy.[30] "No less significant than the absolute amount restricted prop-erty, or its proportion to the entire residential property community," as one observer noted in 1945, "may be the location of the restricted property with relation established areas of Negro settlement. Restrictions covering a relatively small amount of property may effectively constrict the area of settlement, if the restricted property substantially surrounds the Negro-populated area or stands as a barrier to expansion in the only direction toward which expansion is feasible."[31] In their 1947 comparison of restric-tive practices in St. Louis and Chicago, Johnson and Long argued that the placement of restrictions, usually to block or channel the expansion of black neighborhoods, was more important than their scope.[32]

Private restriction, in turn, served as an important intermediary in the calculus of private housing decisions. Such restrictions were more than just an exclusionary barrier: they were also an implicit or explicit consideration in the "social sorting" of housing choice and opportunity undertaken by prospective tenants or owners—acting on prevailing but imperfect local knowledge—in any segregated setting.[33] They could, even in the absence of legal enforcement, serve as powerful social norms or expectations.[34] And even when they failed they shaped local attitudes and expectations—albeit in different ways and with different consequences.[35]

Often, of course, these mechanisms worked in concert.[36] Private restrictions exploited physical barriers as well as local policies such as zoning. A local restrictive agreement might use an arterial street as a hard boundary, reinforced by the decision to zone its frontage for commercial use. In their design and orientation, the residential neighborhoods on either side turn away from the thoroughfare—and each other. The school district, not wanting small children to navigate crosswalks, draws the boundary between attendance zones down the center of the street. Even when original restrictions expire (or are rendered unenforceable by the courts), all the ancillary policy choices—and the assumptions behind them—remain. Racial inequality, organized in space, was not just a distributional consequence; it was "a real social structure," as Sarah Bruch, Aaron Rosenthal, and Joe Soss underscore, "a complex of boundaries and positions in which rules, norms, practices, and ideologies regulate relations between dominant and subordinate actors."[37]

We see this play out, across the era of private restriction and across our jurisdictions, at three scales. First, at the metropolitan level, private restriction was instrumental in creating and enforcing a general pattern of macrosegregation marked by suburban exclusion and central city concentration or clustering.[38] In St. Louis, Minneapolis, and Waterloo, restriction was particularly intense at the suburban fringe—especially in the new developments that fed the housing booms of the mid-1920s and late 1940s. In greater St. Louis, for example, the pace and pattern of restriction erected a clear racial divide between the City of St. Louis and suburban St. Louis County. The density of subdivision-based restriction in the county (encompassing over 87 percent of the its owner-occupied units by 1950) confined African American occupancy to a few small enclaves. While the African American population share in the county fell steadily from 9.5 percent in 1890 to just 4.2 percent in 1950, it more than tripled in the city over the same span, from 5.9 percent to 18 percent. As of 1950, 15.4 percent of housing units in the city, but just 3.8 percent of housing units in the county, were occupied by nonwhite families.[39] This scale of segregation was largely accomplished through subdivision-based restrictions and sustained by municipal incorporation and zoning.

Second, private restriction shaped patterns of segregation within central cities. Alongside hard physical boundaries, private restriction, reinforced by local land use and planning, helped to create the north-south, east-west, or "other side of the tracks" divides so common to American cities. In St. Louis, the city's geography and development, including Forest Park, an east-west rail corridor, and the central business district, sustained the gap between the predominantly (and increasingly) black north side and the predominantly white neighborhoods to the south. The latter, not developed until the 1920s, was, like the county, also blanketed with subdivision-based restrictions. Waterloo also developed a north-south divide, the original African American population contained by the Cedar River and the rail lines that followed its course. In Minneapolis, central pockets of African American occupancy reflected the suburban ring of exclusion, the natural boundary provided by the Mississippi River, and the postwar construction of Interstate 35W.[40] This scale of segregation was driven by a combination of petition- and subdivision-based restrictions and sustained by local planning and physical boundaries.

Finally, private restriction was employed strategically (if not always successfully) to set racial and neighborhood boundaries at finer scales. Any given private restriction or agreement, in this respect, served to isolate pockets of African American occupancy, stem their expansion, and work alongside other restrictions (along with physical boundaries and other practices and policies) to accomplish segregation, street by street or block by block. In St. Louis, the city's established African American neighborhood (the Ville) became the necessary focus of African American migration and, in the bargain, garnered the attention of local segregationists determined to use private restriction to stem its expansion. In Waterloo, physical boundaries blocking African American settlement to the south were buttressed by sweeping private restrictions to the north. In Minneapolis, private restriction largely preceded African American migration, creating a template for segregation that effectively sorted migrants on arrival.

My examination of private restriction and racial segregation works outward from the smallest of these scales, beginning with the use of petition restrictions to set neighborhood boundaries in St. Louis and Waterloo. I then turn to the strategy of suburban exclusion, using the development of restricted enclaves in Hennepin and St. Louis Counties to trace the ways in which developers worked at a larger scale to block African American occupancy and facilitate white flight. I close with a measure of the consequences of the close causal relationship between private racial restrictions and the racial segregation of American cities before 1950.

Setting the Edge: Racial Boundaries in Waterloo and St. Louis

Private restrictions were used to establish, enforce, and reinforce neighborhood boundaries—and to shape public policies toward the same ends. Of particular interest, in this respect, are petition restrictions, which were drawn up almost exclusively at the edges of African American neighborhoods and offer a unique window into segregation as a strategic process. Unlike subdivision restrictions (which accompanied new construction and waxed and waned with local housing markets), petition restrictions could be drafted and assembled at any time, in response to perceived threats or changing conditions. Although often bearing the imprint of local neighborhood or improvement associations, these restrictions were largely conceived and disseminated by local realty interests. Of the more than 513 race-restrictive agreements that encircled the Ville by 1945, 466 (over 90 percent) were drafted by the St. Louis Real Estate Exchange. Such interests gave careful thought not just to the practice and principle of restriction but to the ways in which neighborhood restrictions fit together to sustain segregation.

Waterloo

The timing and pattern of private restriction in Waterloo offers a blunt example of the ways in which local segregation was accomplished and sustained. The conditions and circumstances underscore the harsh logic of the Great Migrations, during which the industrializing North welcomed the influx of African Americans as workers but resented and resisted their presence as residents or neighbors. The scale of restriction and that of African American occupancy in Waterloo are such that it is possible to map both in close detail to trace the logic of restriction and its impacts block by block and house by house.

In 1910, the African American population of Black Hawk County was negligible. In Waterloo's four wards, there was but one African American head of household and a scattering of African American servants.[41] Over the next decade, this changed dramatically. The Illinois Central Railroad responded to a 1911 shop strike by recruiting African American workers to keep its maintenance yards in Waterloo running. Some workers were already employed by Illinois Central in Mississippi; some were brought in to staff the commissary and other services for those crossing the picket line.[42] The 1915 Iowa Census counted 410 African Americans in Black Hawk County. The 1920 federal Census counted 856 African Americans in the county, 837 of them in Waterloo.

For new arrivals, housing options were limited. Many of the workers who were recruited by the Illinois Central were initially put up in boxcars on the rail yards that ran north of the river.[43] As the strike came to a close in early 1912, the company began to phase out this temporary solution, and workers settled into housing adjacent to the tracks (often as boarders), in an area bounded by Sumner Street to the north, Mobile Street to the east, and the Illinois Central tracks to the south and west.[44] This neighborhood—known locally as "the Triangle" or "Smokey Row"—was almost immediately identified as a threat.[45] As in other settings, the police began to steer businesses considered immoral or unsavory into the growing African American neighborhood. Local newspapers trafficked heavily in overwrought accounts of the danger posed by the neighborhood and its inhabitants.[46] In late 1918, the *Waterloo Courier* lent its editorial support to a local "crusade to remove all idle colored men and women from the city."[47]

White property interests also responded swiftly, drawing on both local anxieties and professional interest in private restriction to contain the threat. The Illinois Central railbed, and the commercial district between the railbed and the river, set a hard physical boundary to the south and west of Smokey Row. To the north (map 4.1), property owners assembled, by petition, a sweeping restriction that stretched some forty-two

Map 4.1 Restriction and Residence in Waterloo's Triangle, 1920

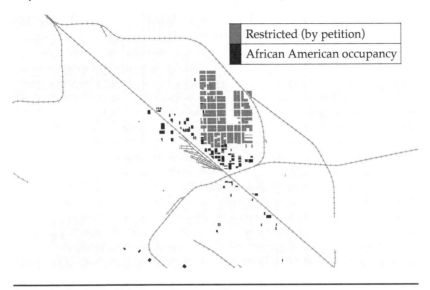

Restricted (by petition)

African American occupancy

Source: Gordon 2023c; U.S. Census Bureau 1920.
Note: Major rail lines are shown for reference.

blocks—between North Barclay and Linden Streets, from the edge of African American settlement north to Newell. The restriction, filed with the Black Hawk County Recorder in April of 1914, bore 154 signatures and covered just over 600 residential parcels. A year later, in August 1915, owners in the next subdivision north of Newell adopted identical restrictive language covering all lots.[48] In 1916, an effort by the Waterloo Board of Realtors to formally prohibit home sales to African Americans in white districts failed, but the board expected local brokers to respect the ban and enforce the boundaries of the Triangle.[49] In August 1922, owners in a small subdivision on the other side of the tracks and northeast of downtown adopted a racial restriction, blocking the expansion of the Triangle to the southwest.[50]

As was common in petition restrictions (as we shall see in St. Louis as well), the agreement was ragged and uneven, especially where it bordered the African American blocks. Owners in areas already undergoing racial transition were often reluctant to sign the petition, while others added their names even on blocks where African American occupancy was already established. It was, for those assembling the restrictions and for those being

Map 4.2 Restriction and Residence in Waterloo's Triangle, 1930

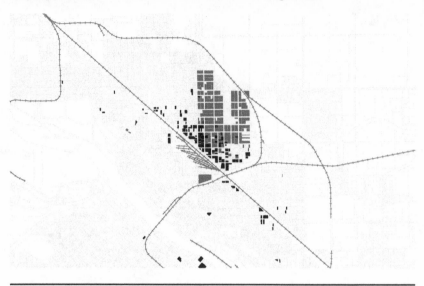

Source: Gordon 2023c; U.S. Census Bureau 1930.
Note: Major rail lines are shown for reference.

asked to sign, both a blunt gesture of exclusion and a strategic calculation. Those collecting signatures sought to contain or minimize African American occupancy while also ensuring that enough owners signed to make the agreement viable. Those who signed the restriction weighed the protection it promised against the likelihood of its success—and with it the risk of surrendering their right to sell to any willing buyer.

Waterloo's African American population increased by a third between 1920 and 1930 and by a fifth during the 1930s—totaling about 1,500 on the eve of World War II. Although African Americans made up less than 3 percent of the city's population in 1940, the African American neighborhoods strung along the north edge of the Illinois Central tracks were deeply segregated and highly visible. New arrivals, by and large, settled in the footprint of established African American occupancy or pushed that footprint out into adjacent blocks (maps 4.2 and 4.3) in ways that did not challenge the spatial logic of restriction. Segregation was hardened by adaptation to private restriction and discrimination. African Americans in Waterloo, as in other settings, built and relied on parallel or local institutions in the face

Map 4.3 Restriction and Residence in Waterloo's Triangle, 1940

Source: Gordon 2023c; U.S. Census Bureau 1940.
Note: Major rail lines are shown for reference.

of white hostility.[51] This meant, among other things, acknowledgment—if not acceptance—of the neighborhood boundaries established by private restriction. Such necessary adaptations cemented the distributional as well as the relational patterns of local segregation. Waterloo's African Americans largely lived in the neighborhoods ceded to them; residential segregation, in turn, rippled through local commerce, leisure, schools, labor markets, and social networks.

These patterns persisted through the 1940s, with one significant difference. Aside from the single burst of African American labor recruitment and migration between 1910 and 1920, Waterloo was a Second Great Migration city. Of Black Hawk County's African American population in 1980 (just over 8,500), more than 80 percent arrived (or were born) after 1940. The pattern of private restriction in the 1940s echoed that of other Second Great Migration cities like Milwaukee or Minneapolis: it relied not on petitions in older neighborhoods facing African American incursion, but on sweeping subdivision restrictions on new construction at the city's edge (map 4.4). Such restrictions (as we trace later) operated on a different

Map 4.4 Restriction and Residence in Waterloo's Triangle, 1950

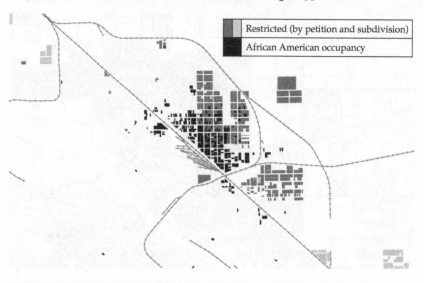

Source: Gordon 2023c; U.S. Census Bureau 1950.
Note: Major rail lines are shown for reference.

logic—shaped less by the immediate threat of African American occupancy than by the "protective" aspirations and anxieties of suburban developers, real estate agents, and homeowners.

St. Louis

The Delmar Divide runs like a scar across the City of St. Louis, outlining a long-standing demarcation between predominantly black north St Louis and predominantly white south St. Louis. The neighborhoods on either side of Delmar Boulevard, virtually identical in their platting and initial development, underscore the history and consequences of racial segregation. North of Delmar, poverty and crime are prevalent, much of the housing stock has been demolished or stands vacant, and private and public infrastructure are thin. South of the divide, by contrast, neighborhoods are marked by new development, robust public investments, and gentrification. "In St. Louis, the break between races—and privilege—is particularly drastic," as Chico Harlan noted recently, "so defined that those on both sides speak often about a precise boundary."[52]

Map 4.5 Race Restrictions in North St. Louis, 1920

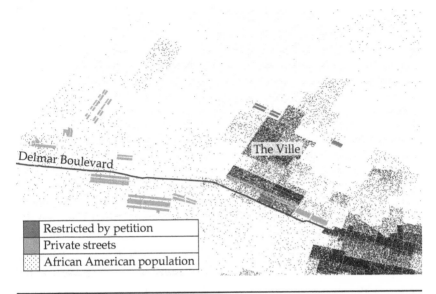

Source: Gordon 2023b; Shertzer, Walsh, and Logan 2016.
Note: The 1920 African American population is mapped by enumeration district; 1 dot = 1 person.

In the decades between World War I and World War II, the Delmar Divide was crafted as a racial boundary in response to the substantial African American population before 1920, the dramatic increase in that population generated by the Great Migrations, and the shifting boundaries of African American occupancy and racial transition.[53] On the eve of the Second Great Migration, in 1910, St. Louis's African American population of 43,960 (6.4 percent of the total population) was concentrated in the Ville (map 4.5); on a five-block stretch on Cook, Finney, and West Belle Place just south of the Ville; and in the Mill Creek Valley, a swath of working-class multifamily housing south of Olive, between the Ville and the downtown.

Each of these neighborhoods would play a role in the development of the Delmar Divide. The early establishment of the Ville made it the focus of efforts to contain African American occupancy. The Mill Creek Valley was largely contained on the east by Union Station and on the south by the rail lines running west from the station. The 1918 city plan designated much of this area "industrial," leaving it essentially unprotected and slated for eventual redevelopment.[54] The Ville, by contrast, was surrounded by white residential neighborhoods, including the gated private streets north and east of Forest Park—although the black enclave at Cook, Finney, and West Belle Place complicated efforts to set the edge between black and white occupancy. As the City's African American population grew after 1910, local planners, real estate agents, white homeowners, and city planners used every tool at their disposal—including street planning, land-use zoning, and racial restrictions—to seal the Ville's borders. This was an exercise in overt racial hostility and anxiety, but it also required a series of strategic calculations, negotiations, and retreats. The Delmar Divide reflected the successes, and the failures, of this effort.

The first push to contain the expansion of the Ville came in 1911 and 1912, with the filing of three neighborhood restrictions along Labadie Avenue, one block north of St. Louis Avenue (see map 4.5). These included the restriction—establishing that "no part of said property or any portion thereof shall be, for said term of 50 years, occupied by any persons not of the Caucasian Race"—that would be the centerpiece of the *Shelley* case three decades later. But these private restrictions were early outliers. At the time, real estate agents and white homeowners were largely focused on the prospect of a racial zoning ordinance that would formalize neighborhood boundaries. In 1916, real estate agents succeeded in getting the racial zoning ordinance on the ballot, where it won passage easily.[55]

The logic of the 1916 ordinance, which prohibited black or white occupancy on any block with a population composed of 75 percent or more of the other race, was to freeze the borders of established black neighborhoods (map 4.6). The ordinance drew clean lines around the Ville and the Mill Creek Valley. But it was also forced to acknowledge small breaches in those lines, designating a few blocks north of Mill Creek, as well as those blocks of Finney, Cook, and West Belle Place, for black occupancy.[56] These pockets where black occupancy was already well established but where the boundaries of segregation were still contested would play a key role in the development of the Delmar Divide.

Within a year of the passage of St. Louis's racial zoning ordinance, the Supreme Court struck down racial zoning as an invasion of "the civil right to acquire, enjoy, and use property." As a result, efforts to contain African American occupancy turned to conventional land-use planning. In 1918, St. Louis passed its first comprehensive zoning ordinance, which, because so much of the city was already developed, was more descriptive than

Map 4.6 St. Louis Racial Zoning Ordinance, 1916

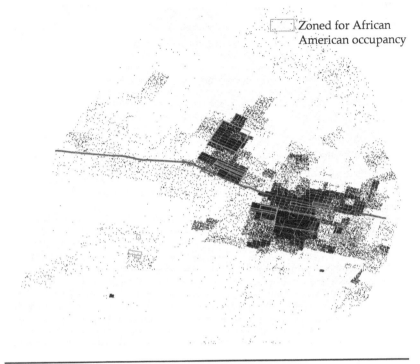

Zoned for African
American occupancy

Source: Gordon 2008; Shertzer, Walsh, and Logan 2016.
Note: African American population (gray dots) is mapped by enumeration district; 1 dot =
1 person.

prescriptive. It reserved its most exclusive "first residential" district largely
for the city's private streets and lumped all other neighborhoods (including
the Ville) into a single "second residential" zone in which the range of use
("all forms of dwelling, tenement, hotels, lodging or boarding houses") was
determined by existing development.[57] In drafting the ordinance, planners
made clear that its primary purpose was the protection of "first residential"
neighbors from the incursion of industrial or commercial land use and the
nuisance of African American occupancy. "The dead districts of our city
are witness to the folly of an absence of regulation," as one observer wrote
in 1919. "It is the ignoring of this right that has largely contributed to the
colonization of certain peoples . . . whose advent into a community has
depreciated property to such an extent that it has been almost community
robbery of an individual."[58]

The 1918 zone plan had little immediate impact. The legal status of municipal zoning, as well as its threat to private property rights, was not settled until the Supreme Court's *Euclid v. Ambler* decision in 1926.[59] Three years earlier, the St. Louis ordinance had been struck down by the Missouri Supreme Court,[60] which held that the ordinance was as an overreach of the local police power, its regulations bearing "no relation to the public health, safety, comfort or welfare" and imposing "an unreasonable and oppressive interference with the use of private property."[61] This view aligned closely with that of local realty and development interests, who, despite their enthusiasm for racial restrictions, were leery of more general land-use regulation and fought the imposition of a zone plan at every turn. Local realty interests did not concede to municipal zoning until the passage of a new zoning ordinance in 1925,[62] buttressed by the 1926 *Euclid* decision and a parallel 1927 decision by the Missouri courts (both of which confirmed the right of municipalities to zone land use for general welfare). Not long after, developers began to exploit municipal zoning to harden racial boundaries.[63]

Once the legality of zoning was settled, local regulation of land-use helped to set the edge between black and white occupancy in three ways. First, the discretion afforded by the "second residential" designation allowed planners to push neighborhoods toward exclusion or transition. Most of the residential footprint of the Ville was reclassified as "multiple dwelling" in 1925, in the hopes that it would better absorb the growing African American population. "A decade ago," as the Urban League complained in the late 1930s, "the Zoning Commission left not a single block or neighborhood zoned as residential in the area from Delmar to Labadie and from Grand to Taylor and Cora. . . . This wide Negro section was zoned as multiple dwelling, commercial, and industrial districts."[64] Allowing higher density development in established African American neighborhoods effectively contained those neighborhoods even as their population grew.[65]

Second, zoning could create nonconforming uses and facilitate the eradication of "blighted" residential pockets. Just as zoning regulations were designed to "protect" some residential areas, they were designed to expose others to redevelopment.[66] In 1925 (as in 1918), the entire Mill Creek Valley was zoned "industrial" or "unrestricted," a designation that pushed it toward eventual redevelopment. In 1938, the City Plan Commission designated much of the northern area east of Kingshighway and north of Easton as "blighted" and recommended commercial and industrial redevelopment.

This was a common tactic, the impact of which would be magnified by federal urban renewal after World War II. Private restrictions and discrimination steered African Americans into low-value, mixed-use neighborhoods; local planners then cited the results to argue for redevelopment. "Will you kindly give us a definition of what is blighted," as the St. Louis Urban League responded rhetorically (and bitterly), "if the majority of property in the area you mentioned is owned by Negro residents?"[67]

Third, industrial and commercial zones created buffers between neighborhoods. South of the Ville, the arterial streets Easton and Finney (north of Delmar) and Olive (one block south of Delmar) were zoned for commercial frontage in both the 1918 and 1925 plans.[68] Commercial arterials, in much the same manner as railbeds or rivers, limited access to and between neighborhoods and widened the physical gap between residents on either side. In turn, other local demarcations (such as school catchment zones) were often drawn along such barriers, reinforcing them and their impact on residential patterns.

Zoning sustained segregation not just in its premises and design but in its administration. The establishment of a zone plan also created a machinery for adjudicating disputes, considering amendments, and granting exemptions. In St. Louis, administrative discretion sustained segregation by consistently upzoning property in African American neighborhoods, spot zoning to create buffers between black and white neighborhoods, and ensuring that public zoning respected and echoed the spatial logic of private restriction.[69] In turn, private restrictions adapted on the fly to new circumstances and threats. In 1917, a developer erected an apartment building on Delmar Boulevard, within the footprint of Washington Terrace (a private street) and in direct violation of its prohibition on multifamily housing. Rather than challenge the transgression, the trustees of Washington Terrace granted a waiver—conceding the frontage on Delmar to reinforce restrictions to the south.[70]

Such zoning and land-use decisions reflected efforts to set the southern border of African American occupancy, as well as the confusion or uncertainty as to where that border should be. As city planners noted in 1918, most of the city's wide (over sixty feet) streets—including Easton, Evans, Page, Cook, Finney, West Belle, and Delmar—ran parallel to each other south of the Ville.[71] Any one of these, through street planning and zoning, could have been developed as a hard arterial boundary between the Ville and the neighborhoods to the south. White homeowners were torn between defending the neighborhoods immediately south of the Ville from African American occupancy and abandoning them before it was too late. Organizations of white homeowners (various local "improvement associations") and the St. Louis Real Estate Exchange were reluctant to give up on any block. At the same time, black real estate agents were looking to expand the market for African American sales at the margins of the Ville, and local civil rights activists (especially the Urban League) were battling both private restrictions and the under zoning or downzoning of black neighborhoods.[72]

Over the next decade, all of this played out in the local politics of racial restriction. In 1920, the St. Louis Real Estate Exchange adopted a rule to expel any member who sold to an African American in the area bounded by Grand, Kingshighway, Forest Park Boulevard, and the Hodiamont Tracks (a half block north of Delmar), claiming that an "incursion of negroes would 'shoot real estate values all to pieces.'"[73] In 1923, the exchange formalized this rule but flipped its logic, establishing three "unrestricted" zones—roughly corresponding to the footprints of the Ville, the Mill Creek Valley, and the central business district—in which sales to African Americans were allowed.[74]

In turn, the exchange began a concerted campaign to assemble petition restrictions at the edges of the Ville. In St. Louis, as we have seen, this form of restriction was particularly widespread, intense, and coordinated among local realty interests. Between 1910 and 1947, the exchange drafted and filed almost 500 such agreements (and another 130 renewals), marking some 15,000 residential parcels in north St. Louis off-limits to African American occupancy.[75]

Like some perverse board game, the proliferation of such petitions was an exercise in marking or capturing territory. It was also an effort to establish a hard boundary between black and white neighborhoods. As of 1920, the only petition restrictions around the Ville were the 1911 and 1912 agreements on Labadie (see map 4.5). Not long after, the exchange began to extend and buttress those boundaries. In 1922, it sponsored and filed agreements in all of the areas surrounding the Ville. On the south, between the Ville and Delmar, this included new restrictions on Page, Evans, and Newberry Terrace (map 4.7). In 1923, the Exchange added two new restrictions on Evans and, hedging its bets, restrictions five blocks south on either side of Delmar between Taylor and Vandeventer (map 4.8). In 1924, the exchange assembled a series of restrictions south of Evans between Vandeventer and

Map 4.7 Racial Restrictions in North St. Louis, 1922

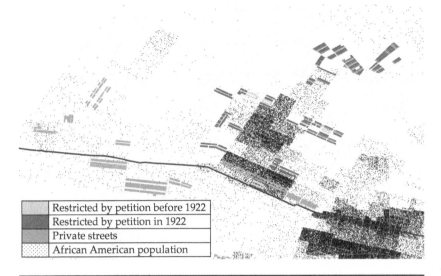

Restricted by petition before 1922
Restricted by petition in 1922
Private streets
African American population

Source: Gordon 2023b; Shertzer, Walsh, and Logan 2016.
Note: The 1920 African American population is mapped by enumeration district; 1 dot = 1 person.

Map 4.8 Racial Restrictions in North St. Louis, 1923

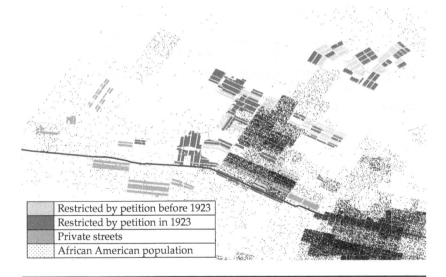

Restricted by petition before 1923
Restricted by petition in 1923
Private streets
African American population

Source: Gordon 2023b; Shertzer, Walsh, and Logan 2016.
Note: The 1920 African American population is mapped by enumeration district; 1 dot = 1 person.

Map 4.9 Racial Restrictions in North St. Louis, 1924

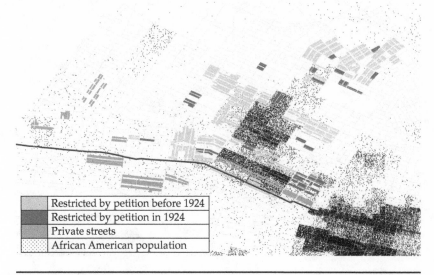

Source: Gordon 2023b; Shertzer, Walsh, and Logan 2016.
Note: The 1920 African American population is mapped by enumeration district; 1 dot = 1 person.

Grand and filled in the last block of Evans (between Newstead and Pendleton) immediately south of the Ville (map 4.9). Over the next few years, the exchange concentrated on restricting blocks north and west of the Ville.

This flurry of restriction created a strategic and practical dilemma on the Ville's southern boundary. A band of restriction along Evans and Page, centered on St. Anne's Church and its immediate parish, hemmed in the Ville immediately to the south.[76] But, between Page and the band of restrictions on Enright and Delmar, there were well-established African American neighborhoods on Finney, Cook, and West Belle Place.[77] In some respects, by cordoning off this already established area, the exchange was engaged in its broader goal of containing the growth of the Ville, a task that suggested a retreat to clear and defensible borders between white and black occupancy. But, at the same time, it was reluctant to give up on any block or to set the precedent of abandoning any restrictive agreement—and so often dug in its heels even where racial transition was well underway.

While the exchange assembled and defended local restrictions, property owners turned to city planners for support. In 1927, in the wake of a

tornado that cut a swath of damage along Finney Avenue north of Vandeventer, property owners along Delmar lobbied to be included in a municipal street-widening project that was pointedly configured to harden racial
boundaries. But, as with the broader pattern of property restriction, there
was uncertainty as to where that line should be drawn. When property
owners balked at a special assessment to pay for the Delmar widening, the
project stalled and attention shifted a few blocks north to Page. The city
tore up a grass median, residential properties fronting Page increasingly
turned to commercial use, and white property owners began to sell.[78]

In the face of white defection and a string of legal challenges to the
contractual validity of many petition restrictions, the exchange's efforts to
sustain restrictions north of Delmar began to fray. In June 1927, white
property owners on Finney between Grand and Vandeventer filed a petition in the circuit court to void a restrictive agreement that they had signed
four years earlier—on the grounds that "the whole neighborhood is now
a colored section and plaintiffs' property is completely surrounded by colored inhabitants." The court agreed, finding that the original restrictive
agreement was flawed and that—in any case—it had failed in its intent.
Later the same year, the circuit court declined to enforce a restriction on
Bayard Avenue between Page and Delmar on the grounds that the owners
of the property in question were not signatories to the original petition. In
1930 and 1931, the Missouri Supreme Court upheld both rulings.[79]

While the exchange continued the legal fight, one block and one restrictive agreement at a time, it was also busy erecting the next line of defense.
The pace of restriction slowed in the late 1920s, but the exchange continue
to plug holes; two new petitions in 1929 (map 4.10) completed the restriction of properties fronting Delmar, from Taylor on the west to Spring on the
east. Because Delmar was, like Page, increasingly commercial, the exchange
also turned its attention to the next residential block south. Between 1932
and 1934 (map 4.11), it assembled ten adjacent restrictions along Washington Boulevard, from Euclid to Spring. Taken together, these restrictions
sketched in Delmar Avenue as an arterial no-man's-land between black and
white St. Louis.

The exchange's efforts were a sort of battlefield strategy.[80] It engaged
on each of the fronts it had established at the borders of the Ville while
also fortifying a safe retreat south of Delmar. This echoed the pattern elsewhere, where segregationists often fell back to hard, recognizable, or chosen

Map 4.10 Racial Restrictions in North St. Louis, 1930

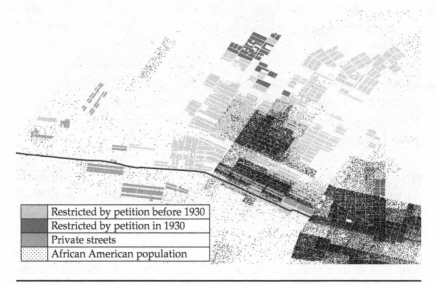

Restricted by petition before 1930
Restricted by petition in 1930
Private streets
African American population

Source: Gordon 2023b; Shertzer, Walsh, and Logan 2016.
Note: The 1930 African American population is mapped by enumeration district; 1 dot = 1 person.

Map 4.11 Racial Restrictions in North St. Louis, 1934

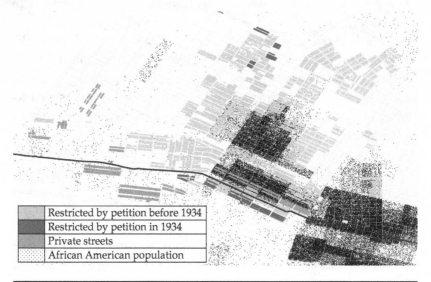

Restricted by petition before 1934
Restricted by petition in 1934
Private streets
African American population

Source: Gordon 2023b; Shertzer, Walsh, and Logan 2016.
Note: The 1930 African American population is mapped by enumeration district; 1 dot = 1 person.

boundaries.[81] Restrictions closest to established areas of African American occupancy were the most fragile. "Once a break is made" as Weaver noted, it is impossible to hold back the tide . . . [and] a new barrier is established somewhere beyond the location of the old one."[82] The retreat to Delmar, however, did not mean that the exchange was fully conceding the blocks between Delmar and The Ville. If only to bolster the validity of agreements elsewhere, it continued to defend restrictions long after they had failed. At the same time, it quietly engaged in negotiations with the Urban League, which urged the real estate agents to strategically concede some blocks even if it meant defending others.[83]

By the late 1930s, the fabric of restriction in the blocks between Easton and Delmar was unraveling. Many agreements, as the 1927 legal challenge on Finney underscored, had simply failed in their stated purpose. "The district south of Page and north of Evans," as the *Post-Dispatch* observed in 1939, "has been occupied by Negroes for many years."[84] When the HOLC rated the area a year later, it observed "some better homes along Finney Ave. and adjacent blocks" but warned that "the colored occupants are slowly pressing the white people for more space and it is logical to conclude that deeper infiltration is only a matter of time."[85] Here, as elsewhere, the emerging architecture of redlining signaled the willingness of white homeowners and mortgage lenders to give up on the neighborhood, even as the officers of the exchange were digging in.

On such blocks, the Real Estate Exchange faced opposition from white homeowners and prospective black property owners alike. As a result, its efforts were flawed and incomplete. In July 1937, the Page Avenue Home Protective Association met to consider the "means of combatting further encroachment," but admitted that gaps in the exchange's "iron ring" of restriction made that a difficult task.[86] As black families began to move onto the 4300 block of Page, the local improvement association discovered that the agreement in question had been a swindle: the notary public who had drawn up the restriction "took money from the property owners to pay the filing costs, then departed with both the money and the deeds."[87] Finally, the restrictions assembled by the exchange in the early 1920s, most of which had twenty-year terms, were starting to expire, and many property owners were reluctant to sign on to renewals that would constrain their right to sell.[88]

This uncertainty was reflected in the courts. In most cases—as in a 1939 confrontation over African American occupancy in the 4200 and 4300 blocks

of Evans—local courts upheld restrictions.[89] In turn, state appellate courts
hewed to the logic of state (*Koehler v. Rowland* in 1918) and federal (*Corrigan v.
Buckley* in 1926) precedents that viewed restrictive agreements as enforceable and binding private contracts, not as public policies subject to the
equal protection clause.[90] But the courts were also increasingly attentive to
the flaws in the original agreements and their failure to stem racial transition. In 1937, the circuit court voided a restriction on Vine Grove (just
north of the Ville) on the grounds that it had failed in its purpose. In 1939,
the Missouri Supreme Court agreed, arguing not just that the agreement
had failed but that the original petition (signed by only eleven of forty-six
property owners) should never have been considered a credible instrument
for neighborhood restriction. "While it is true that covenants or agreements
creating racial restrictions of the kind in question are generally sustained
by the courts," as the court argued, ". . . this can only be so where they are
entered into in such a manner and with such completeness as to give them
force and effect."[91]

As African American migration to St. Louis swelled in the 1940s, African
American real estate agents, the Urban League, and others argued for lift-
ing restrictions at the borders of the Ville as the only viable response to the
city's emerging housing crisis, an argument often upheld by local courts.
"Housing is desperately short-handed in St. Louis as it is in most other large
cities," as the Urban League underscored, "but the lack of housing facilities
for Negroes in St. Louis is critical for peculiar reasons. Approximately 97%
of the Negro population in St. Louis lives at the geographical heart of the
city, surrounded on the east by commerce and business, and on the south,
west, and north by neighborhood covenant agreements. There are no out-
lets to the open county for any kind of expansion. There is a complete circle
of restriction."[92]

But it was a fragile circle. Racial restrictions cobbled together at the
margins of African American occupancy "have not prevented and cannot
prevent the expansion of the living space for mounting Negro populations,"
as Weaver noted in 1948. "They delay this movement, make this final break-
through almost a rout, and create vested interest on the part of present
occupants to keep Negroes out."[93] In early 1942, the Enright Avenue Property Association moved to enforce a restriction, originally signed in 1923
and renewed in 1938, on the 4500 block of Enright. In September 1943,
a circuit court judge refused to issue an injunction enforcing the agreement,

noting that while 95 percent of owners had signed the original petition in 1923, barely half had agreed to the renewal. The decision echoed earlier cases in which racial transition had already "defeat[ed] the very purpose of the neighborhood scheme," but it also cast the problem more broadly. "They must live somewhere," the judge argued. "East of the area involved, property is occupied solely by Negroes and there is a sprinkling of Negroes to the west and northwest. Conditions have changed in the 20 years since the restrictive agreement was signed."[94]

These circumstances—the failure or expiration of restrictions, the ambivalence of white homeowners in transitional blocks, the growth of the African American population, and eroding support from the courts—compelled the Real Estate Exchange to trade confrontation for negotiation. In the end, as the exchange reasoned, settling on a clear and defensible boundary between black and white occupancy was more important than the precise location of such a boundary. While the challenge to racial restrictions on equal protection grounds was gaining momentum, both the Urban League and African American real estate agents proved willing to bargain with the exchange block by block. Since the 1920s, James Bush, one of the real estate agents at the center of the original *Shelley* transaction in 1945, had been working to undermine restrictions along Delmar and elsewhere.[95] He persuaded the exchange to give up on agreements on the 4200 and 4300 blocks of Page in 1937, pointing out that the area was "a virtual island in the Negro district and that owners of property in the area had decided to place the houses at the use of Negroes."[96]

Strategically, in this respect, African American real estate agents were willing to meet the exchange halfway. As long as the only legal recourse was to demonstrate that a restrictive agreement was fundamentally flawed (in its original form or in its impact), Bush and others pressed the exchange to concede those blocks it had clearly lost in exchange for a grudging acknowledgement of a bright line *somewhere* between black and white occupancy. By this approach, the blocks between Delmar and the Ville would be allowed to tip completely to African American occupancy and the ragged circle of restriction around the Ville would be recast as hard northern and southern boundaries. In 1944, Bush championed "extending Negroes in territory adjoining where they are," adding his assessment that this was "the best thing for the negro, the best thing for the city, and the best thing for real estate values."[97]

Such negotiations at the edges of the Ville challenged the boundaries of segregation but not its larger logic. Bush described his role in brokering sales along Delmar as "part of a program to expand the Negro community as far west as Kingshighway," but also, he conceded, "to keep the northern and southern borders respectively at St. Louis Avenue and Delmar Boulevard."[98] By the mid-1940s, the NAACP had begun to question this strategy and the accompanying assumption that racial restrictions could only be dismantled where they had failed. "Expanding existing Negro areas," as Weaver reminded his colleagues in 1945, "simply creates new islands and ghettos."[99]

Over the ensuing decades, St. Louis was transformed by the Second Great Migration and white flight from north St. Louis. Between 1940 and 1960, the African American population of St. Louis doubled to just under 215,000, while the white population fell by over 170,000. White flight was concentrated in the area north of Delmar, after the *Shelley* decision rendered all of the exchange's restrictive agreements unenforceable in 1948.[100] In the process, the presumed northern border of the Ville had evaporated. But the southern edge set at Delmar, where restrictive agreements had been fortified by street planning and land-use zoning, held fast. As a result, African American occupancy and homeownership pushed north after 1950, and the ragged circle of restriction around the Ville was replaced by a stark north-south divide.[101]

The Delmar Divide, in turn, became—and remains—the central reference point for local housing and economic development policies. Private and public architects of urban renewal in St. Louis cynically used residential and social "blight" north of Delmar as a pretext for redevelopment—and then spent the money (local and federal funds) elsewhere.[102] With the end of the federal urban renewal program in the early 1970s, struggling north-side neighborhoods were left to the whim of local policy that was premised less on the renewal of north-side neighborhoods than on their displacement—a combination of benign neglect and steep subsidies for private redevelopment schemes.[103] By the same token, scattered public and private investments along Delmar itself marked an effort less to erase the black-white divide then to push it north[104]—effectively rolling back the "retreat" of private restrictions in the 1920s and 1930s.

Today the Delmar Divide persists as a relic of private restriction, sustained and reinforced by local planning and policy. Since the 1970s, pedestrian and vehicular access from Delmar to the neighborhoods to the south (in the city and the county) has been blocked or constrained by a combination of barriers and "traffic-calming" adjustments to the street plan. Many of the streets running south from Delmar toward the city's Central West End or (across the county line) toward the Washington University campus were (and remain) barricaded by iron gates or large concrete planters—known locally as "Schoemehl pots" after the mayor who innovated their use in the early 1980s.[105] Chokers (narrowing a street to a single lane or sidewalk), diagonal diverters (blocking through-traffic at four-way intersections), and one-way streets make it virtually impossible to turn south off Delmar into the residential blocks stretching south to Forest Park. Commercial and institutional development on both sides of Delmar (including a block-long metro bus garage built in 1983) effectively widened the boundary between white occupancy to the south and black occupancy to the north.[106]

"A Desirable Place of Residence": Suburban Exclusion in Hennepin and St. Louis Counties

The strategic quarantine of neighborhoods like the Triangle in Waterloo or the Ville in north St. Louis was executed block by block to contain the residential impact of the Great Migrations. The result, unsurprisingly, was the concentration and isolation of African Americans in neighborhoods already characterized by aging housing stock and mixed-use zoning—further burdened by crowding, downzoning, and predatory housing costs. Those boundaries proved both impactful and fragile, undermining housing opportunity regardless of whether they held or failed.[107]

The boundary between city and suburb, by contrast, was starker and longer lasting—and accounted for most of the increase in black-white residential segregation between 1940 and 1970.[108] It set apart new development on the urban fringe as a white refuge from African American occupancy. Because such restrictions accompanied new construction, they often leveraged local topography and planning (such as street layouts, zoning, and parks) to reinforce the borders of restricted developments.[109] Suburban segregation, in this respect, depended not just on private strategies of exclusion but on a jurisdictional scaffolding (especially municipalities and school districts) that reinforced and sustained it.[110] Tellingly, when private restrictions were held unenforceable in 1948, white residents fled north St. Louis (where the fabric of private restriction was unraveling) for the suburbs (where such exclusions still held).[111] Indeed, suburban exclusion did not begin to fray until the 1970s, and then only because central city decline and "slum clearance" compelled black flight, turning inner suburbs platted during the first generation of white flight into "secondhand suburbs" marked by racial transition.[112]

The American suburb was conceived, developed, and marketed as a world apart from the density and disorder of city life. Suburban developers offered a range of "picket fence" amenities but, even more importantly, they offered them at a scale that promised security, stability, and protection. Just as important as the house you were buying, in this view, was the assurance that "harmonious" neighbors were making the same choices for the same reasons.[113] Minneapolis suburban developers promised "a community where you can be proud to live, proud of your home, your grounds, *and your neighbor's home as well.*"[114] Across Hennepin County, developers marketed the promise of racial homogeneity alongside idyllic lake frontage carved out of the unfarmable wetlands.[115] Advertisements for the new housing spreading west from St. Louis cited the virtues of "elegant Suburban homes, protected by restrictions guaranteeing absolute security against any objectionable feature," and assured prospective buyers that "the class of houses to be built has been fixed and the restrictions protect the future."[116] Such promises were routine in the "fashionable residential" developments immediately west of Forest Park, but they were also the stock in trade for modest working-class developments on the city's northwest border. Vinita Terrace (the 1910 indenture of which held that no sale "be made to a negro")[117] was "restricted to protect," as its developers attested; it "offers every refinement that the richest enjoy in more highly restricted districts, without costly ostentation and prohibitive building expense."[118]

There was little doubt—in both the pattern and the aspirations of suburban development—that these were intended as white spaces. The goal of racial homogenization was evident in the early and explicit conviction that African Americans were bad neighbors, as well as in the persistent and thinly camouflaged anxiety about property values, crime, or good schools that expressed the same belief.[119] These anxieties were embedded in the increasingly exhaustive catalog of the standards, prohibitions, and conditions that developers imposed on buyers and that buyers imposed on each other in the practice of private suburban restriction. Such restrictions captured the aspirations and anxieties of white realty interests at development and at first sale, and they formalized and legitimized those aspirations and anxieties. Racial exclusion, in this respect, motivated suburban development in the first instance, then became one of its persistent and defining features: suburbanization described the emerging development pattern; white flight identified its motivation and its consequences.

We see this play out in metropolitan patterns of restriction—in the concentric rings of exclusion moving west through St. Louis County (see maps 3.1–3.4), in the dense fabric of exclusion south and west of Minneapolis in Hennepin County (maps 3.5–3.8), and in the scatter of restricted subdivisions far removed from Waterloo's near north side in Black Hawk County (map 3.11). While these larger spatial patterns and logics were important, they were largely unplanned. They emerged from a patchwork of local efforts (more than one thousand distinct restrictions in St. Louis County and more than five hundred in suburban Hennepin County) with common motivations and goals, only loosely coordinated by professional networks of developers and other realty interests. A closer local focus reveals the pace and pattern of local restriction, as well as the ways in which local efforts were stitched together into the larger pattern.

Consider the footprint of Ferguson, one of the first incorporated municipalities in St. Louis County. An inner north-county suburb, Ferguson was an early destination for working-class white flight from north St. Louis. Like most of its peers, Ferguson comprised a crazy quilt of private subdivisions—87 in all, of which 41 were race restricted. Of those, 24 subdivisions were platted before 1923, none of which was restricted; of the 63 platted after 1923, two-thirds were race restricted. Restriction was cobbled together by 31 different developers, only 2 of which completed multiple Ferguson subdivisions.[120] Restricted developments varied by size: the largest was over 500 parcels, the median 85. Building lots were relatively modest by later suburban standards. While a few post-1945 subdivisions boasted half-acre building sites, the median lot size was just 7,500 square feet. By the end of 1925 (map 4.12), Ferguson's recent development included 13 race-restricted subdivisions; by 1950 (map 4.13), that number had swollen to 41—accounting for about three-quarters of the housing stock built over that span.

As in many similar suburban settings, the scale of private race restriction in Ferguson—as well as the share of housing stock it covered—was sufficient to create and sustain an assumption that exclusion could be

Map 4.12 Ferguson Restrictions, 1925

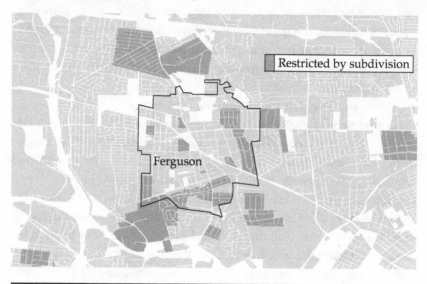

Source: Gordon 2023e; Nolan 2018.

Map 4.13 Ferguson Restrictions, 1950

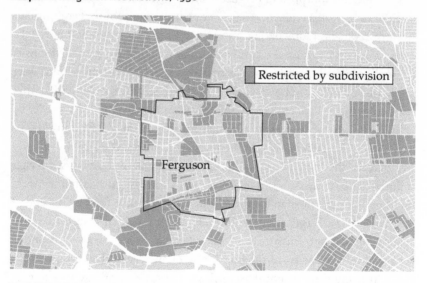

Source: Gordon 2023e; Nolan 2018.

generalized beyond the boundaries of particular developments. When the HOLC rated Ferguson neighborhoods in 1940, its appraisers concluded some area descriptions with the blunt assessment that "town restrictions prohibit the residence of negroes inside its limits" and that a "major portion of area located in Ferguson, Mo. . . . is restricted to prohibit residence of negroes in its limits."[121] These claims were inaccurate—no such law was on the books—but spoke powerfully to the cumulative effect of private restriction: that entire jurisdictions were simply off-limits to African Americans, a perspective shared by those included and excluded alike.[122]

Consider St. Ann, a small suburban municipality in north St. Louis County. Unlike Ferguson, St. Ann was largely the work of a single developer: Charles Vatterott, a major force in St. Louis County development and realty. His portfolio included some forty subdivisions, and, by one estimate, his builders accounted for a third of all permits issued in the county in the 1930s.[123] A devout Catholic, Vatterott was acutely aware of the uncertainty and anxiety among white parishioners in the city, especially north of Delmar. White Catholics in St. Louis, as elsewhere, were deeply rooted in urban parishes and—for that reason—uniquely threatened by demographic change and racial transition.[124] Vatterott's solution was to offer working-class Catholics a foothold in St. Louis County, which required not only housing but the creation—in cooperation with church officials—of new parishes and parish assets in the suburbs spreading west from St. Louis.[125]

The first such effort was Mary Ridge, a 1940 development of about 150 homes in what is now the southeast corner of St. Ann. Mary Ridge was marketed to Catholic families—Vatterott even offered a discounted down payment to prospective purchasers with four or more children.[126] In turn, the subdivision plans made allowance for a parochial school.[127] Mary Ridge was race restricted, its founding indenture prohibiting occupancy by "any other than those of the Caucasian Race."[128] Vatterott, a racial liberal by St. Louis standards, was torn between a social and religious interest in racial equality and the business imperative of segregation. "In a question that is so bitterly debated on both sides," as one colleague advised him regarding private race restrictions, "no individual person could be bound, either in justice or even in charity to undertake a move that would bring havoc to his Mary Ridge, and still larger St. Ann's Village, and expose his houses to bombings."[129] Indeed, Vatterott was inconsistent on the question.

Map 4.14 St. Ann Restrictions, 1950

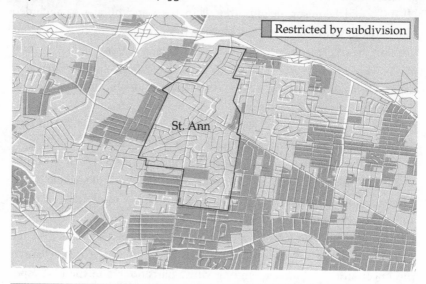

Source: Gordon 2023e; Nolan 2018.

Eleven of his St. Ann developments were race restricted, but others were not (map 4.14). Sometimes the unrestricted developments simply dropped the race clause; sometimes they substituted a general nuisance clause. The determining factor seems to have been timing: Vatterott developed thirty-three subdivisions in the county between 1922 and 1950. Of the twenty platted before 1945, only one (Buder Park in St. Ann) was not race restricted. Of the thirteen platted after 1945, only three (all in Florissant) were race restricted. Vatterott consistently restricted his early large-lot developments to the west (all annexed into St. Ann after 1950), while the small-lot subdivisions in central St. Ann (most built between 1945 and 1950) were largely unrestricted.

Or consider Richfield, an early suburban municipality (incorporated in 1908) directly south of Minneapolis. The original footprint of Richfield (see map 4.15) extended north and east into present-day Minneapolis; the city annexed the area north of 62nd Street in 1927 as part of redevelopment to accommodate the new airport. The development of Richfield included some 270 residential subdivisions through 1952 (just under a third of which were in the area annexed by Minneapolis).[130] Here the pattern of restriction

Map 4.15 Richfield Restrictions by Year Built

Source: Ehrman-Solberg et al. 2020; John R. Borchert Map Library, n.d.; Hennepin County Library, n.d.
Note: The dotted line is the Richfield boundary prior to the 1927 annexation.

was dominated by a series of large-footprint subdivisions: 30 platted before 1925, 33 from 1925 to 1945, and 11 after the war.[131] Indeed, Richfield's 1908 boundaries encompass nearly a third of all restricted parcels in Hennepin County. While these developments accomplished restriction at scale (the median size of restricted subdivisions was 88 lots), the process itself was fragmented. Racial restriction in Richfield was the work of 39 different developers, only 11 of which were responsible for multiple subdivisions. The only developer to complete more than 5 projects, the Estates Improvement Company, did most of its work (10 developments totaling some 2,000 lots) before 1930.[132] The intensity of restriction, and the scattered gaps in the pattern, were almost entirely driven by the date of construction. Most of Richfield's residential development (except for its southeastern corner) was completed between 1920 and 1950—the peak years of private restriction—during (and in response to) the Second Great Migration. Except for the Irwin Shores subdivision directly south of Wood Lake (1938–1940), almost all of Richfield's unrestricted pockets were developed after 1950.

These examples are telling. While private restriction was common, in none of these settings—for a variety of reasons—was it systematic or complete. Yet it clearly served its purpose. In Richfield, the timing of local development was such that almost all of the residential base was restricted at development. In the older inner suburb of Ferguson, the timing of development and private restriction created an uneven checkerboard of exclusion—but it also fostered the popular and professional conviction that African American occupancy was prohibited everywhere in town. In St. Ann, race restrictions were common in early developments on the outskirts, but inconsistently imposed on the footprint of the municipality itself, incorporated in 1948. The broader logic of suburban exclusion, in this respect, depended on how these local patterns fit together—either through intentional coordination or through sheer repetition. And it depended on the degree to which developers, and those they included or excluded, understood such practices and patterns—at various scales—to constitute a general scheme of restriction.

In part, the effectiveness and durability of suburban restrictions rested on the fact that they were embedded in the logic and motives of new development. Alongside the racial restrictions themselves, the design and layout of such developments further accomplished and sustained segregation or exclusion.[133] As one observer noted in 1931:

> Each subdivision should be designed to fit the local conditions of housing, topography and other features. *One reason for lack of stability and permanence of home districts has been the lack of definite boundaries* or the inability to terminate a particular type of district because of the standardized type of rectangular street pattern which invites endless spread of urban expansion. It is important that *advantage be taken of existing natural boundaries* such as suitable park land, stream valleys, ridges, bluffs, and the like, in order to more nearly insure a controlled growth of the neighborhood unit. In the absence of such natural boundaries, artificial boundaries may be created.[134]

Indeed, HOLC area descriptions routinely referred to the "protection" offered by arterial streets, creeks, and railbeds.

Subdivision development also accomplished racial exclusion at scale, allowing developers or trustees to impose conditions and restrictions against tracts of hundreds—sometimes thousands—of homes with one recorded document or plat. Private agreements, in turn, could restrict occupancy

Table 4.1 Race and Racial Restrictions, Central City and Suburbs, 1950

1950	Greater St. Louis			Greater Minneapolis		
	Total	City of St. Louis	St. Louis County	Total	City of Minneapolis	Minneapolis Suburbs
White population	1,091,684	702,348	389,336	667,810	513,250	154,560
Black population	171,461	154,448	17,013	8,769	6,807	1,962
Black population share	15.71%	18.03%	4.19%	1.30%	1.33%	1.27%
Occupied housing units	372,627	258,136	114,491	201,456	159,345	42,111
Owner-occupied units	176,236	89,811	86,425	119,665	83,737	35,928
Restricted units	106,677	30,553	76,124	24,119	8,231	15,888
Jurisdictional share of restricted units		28.64%	71.36%		34.13%	65.87%
Restricted units as share of owner-occupied units	60.5%	34.02%	88.08%	20.16%	9.83%	44.22%

Source: U.S. Census Bureau 1952, 1953; Ehrman-Solberg et al. 2020; Gordon 2023b, 2023e.

and alienation in ways that (after the *Buchanan* decision) could not be accomplished in public land-use controls. "Deed restrictions are apt to prove more effective than a zoning ordinance in providing protection from adverse influences," as the FHA reasoned in 1938, adding that "where the same deed restrictions apply over a broad area and where the restrictions relate to types of structures, use to which improvements may be put, and occupancy, better protection is afforded."[135]

The attraction of suburban restriction—carefully planned and bounded, far removed from immediate threats of racial transition, and completed at a scale sufficient to ensure meaningful protection—is evident in greater Minneapolis and greater St. Louis (table 4.1). In each setting, the practice of private restriction became increasingly prevalent outside the central city, often in unincorporated areas. Suburban restrictions accounted for about two-thirds (66 percent in greater Minnesota, 71 percent in greater St. Louis) of all restrictions, creating an effective barrier to black occupancy outside the central cities. In St. Louis, the frantic effort to quarantine the Ville by petition was accompanied by the systematic restriction of new suburban construction—which served as both a distinct strategy of exclusion and a failsafe boundary should the effort to contain the Ville fall short. In Minneapolis itself, new residential construction between 1920 and 1950 was haphazardly restricted, while bordering developments in Richfield, Edina, and Robbinsdale were much more rigorously and uniformly restricted.

Making the First Ghetto: Patterns of Restriction and Segregation before 1950

The strategic use of private restrictions to contain African American occupancy in central cities, and to prohibit it outright in the suburbs, underscores its singular importance in creating and sustaining racial residential segregation. Private restriction, in this respect, both accomplished segregation on the ground and defended it as a prudent foundation of urban planning and private investment; it simultaneously set the boundaries between white and black neighborhoods and justified those boundaries as bulwarks of security or protection. This is evident in the emerging architecture of urban and suburban segregation, as well as in the close relationship between private restriction and aggregate measures of segregation.

The measure of residential segregation (defined by Massey and Denton as "the degree to which two or more groups live separately from one another")[136] poses significant challenges with respect to both the form and character of the segregation being measured and the appropriate scale of the segregated area and its constituent statistical units. Segregation is captured in different ways by different indices, all of which measure the difference between the demographic distribution in a given whole (a city or a metropolitan area) and the demographic distribution in a part of that whole (a ward, a census tract, or a neighborhood).[137] Such indices can capture distributional outcomes, such as whether a given population resides evenly across a given jurisdiction or is concentrated in particular areas. And they can capture relational dynamics, such as the isolation or exposure of the members of one group to the members of another.[138] Indices of segregation are notoriously sensitive to the size and organization of the spatial units on which they are based: if the smaller unit (the part) is too large, it is unlikely to capture much of the underlying patterns of segregation because that segregation is likely to occur within each of the parts in much the same way as it occurs in the whole. If the smaller unit is too small, it will overstate the degree of segregation. The spatial units themselves (census tracts

or enumeration districts, political wards) may be artifacts of the very phe-
nomenon they seek to measure.[139]

With these caveats in mind, every statistical survey of black-white residential segregation concurs on this basic account: At the end of the nineteenth
century, African Americans in the urban North were no more residentially
segregated from native-born whites than were recent immigrants.[140] Black-
white segregation in the urban North grew dramatically between 1890 and
1940 and then leveled off; in most settings the index of dissimilarity peaked
in 1940 or 1950 while the index of isolation continued to climb.[141] Under
their working definition of a "ghetto" (a black-white dissimilarity index
greater than 0.6 and an isolation index greater than 0.3), David Cutler,
Edward Glaeser, and Jacob Vigdor identified a single case (Norfolk, Virginia)
in 1890, and fifty-five by 1940—a list that included all the northern industrial cities on the receiving end of the Great Migrations.[142] For the ten largest
northern cities as of 1880, fully 97 percent of the twentieth-century increase
in black-white dissimilarity and 63 percent of the increase in black-white
isolation occurred between 1900 and 1930.[143] By 1930, as Massey and Denton
underscore, "the perimeters of black settlement were well-established in
most cities and the level of black-white residential dissimilarity had reached a
stable and very high level." By World War II, "the foundations of the modern
ghetto had been laid in virtually every American city."[144] This assessment is
sustained by qualitative and quantitative research on the emergence of segregation in particular settings.[145]

Recent work leveraging full-count census data has qualified and complicated this story. Alternative measures of segregation, built up from the
household level, find that a pattern of black-white segregation emerged
earlier, beyond the northern urban settings on which so much segregation
research is focused.[146] The use of enumeration districts (instead of political
wards) as the unit of analysis has shed new light on levels of segregation
early in the century—suggesting the appearance of "embryonic ghettos" as
early as the 1890s and underscoring the importance of early white flight in
Great Migration cities.[147] Yet, while these accounts reconsider the timing
and initial levels of racial segregation, they too underscore the importance
of private restriction. Smaller census units yield higher initial levels of segregation but confirm the same arc of rapid segregation after 1910, peaking
before 1950. White flight, in turn, was fundamentally shaped by the intermediary of private restriction—both in contested neighborhoods where

Figure 4.1 Black-White Dissimilarity Index for Five Counties, 1880–2000

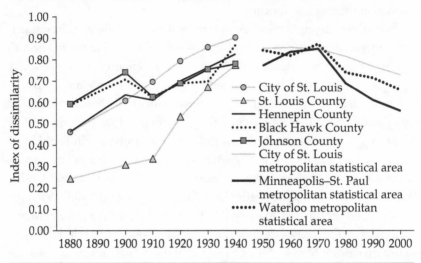

Source: Manson et al. 2022; Cutler, Glaeser, and Vigdor 1999 (tracts).
Note: Dissimilarity is measured by county (enumeration district) through 1940, and by metropolitan statistical area (census tract) thereafter. Data for missing years are interpolated.

such restrictions attempted to hold the line and in suburban enclaves offering "protected" options when that line gave way.[148]

The dramatic growth in racial segregation, nationally and locally, runs alongside the trajectory of private restriction—from the early years of the First Great Migration through the end of the Second. To illustrate this, I employ two measures. The dissimilarity index measures segregation between groups as the share of one group that would have to move within a city to accomplish equal distribution (under conditions of complete segregation, the index would approach 1.0; under conditions of racially even distribution, it would approach 0). The isolation index measures the percentage of the same-group population that lives in the area (ward, tract, or enumeration district) where the average member of that group lives. As both measures suggest, the scale of the area affects the level of segregation. But regardless of the measure used, the trends are unmistakable.

Across all five settings (figure 4.1) the dissimilarity index rises steadily across the era of private restriction and peaks between 1940 and 1950. A dissimilarity index greater than 0.6 is generally considered a marker of segregation, and a score of 0.8 or above a marker of extreme segregation. The index

Figure 4.2 Black-White Dissimilarity Index and Restrictions in St. Louis, 1880–2000

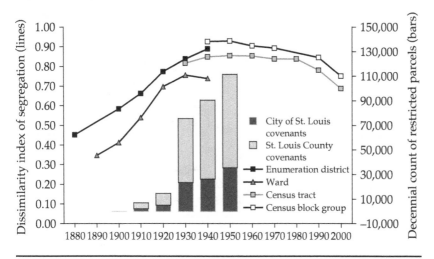

Source: Manson et al. 2022; Decennial Census (blocks and tracts); Cutler, Glaeser, and Vigdor 1999 (wards); Gordon 2023b, 2023e.

for 1940 ranges from 0.79 (Johnson County) to 0.91 (City of St. Louis). Because these measures are sensitive to the size of the underlying population (a small population can never be distributed evenly),[149] the early values are higher in those settings (Johnson, Black Hawk, and Hennepin Counties) where the African American population constitutes a very small share of the total.

In the two large metropolitan settings (Hennepin County and greater St. Louis), the relationship between private restriction and rising segregation is particularly clear. Figure 4.2 charts the index of dissimilarity for the City of St. Louis, using three census-based measures (enumeration districts, census tracts, and census block groups) and the cruder ward-level data. The clustered bars (calibrated on the right axis) show the count of race-restricted parcels (at ten-year intervals) for the City of St. Louis and St. Louis County. Figure 4.3 does the same for Minneapolis (narrowing the segregation data to just the enumeration district through 1940 and tracts thereafter). Figure 4.4 extends the analysis to the isolation index for the City of St. Louis. In every case, the parallel timing and trajectories underscore Weaver's blunt 1948 assessment that such restrictions were the "principal instrument for effecting residential segregation in northern and border states."[150]

Figure 4.3 Black-White Dissimilarity Index and Restrictions in Minneapolis, 1880–2000

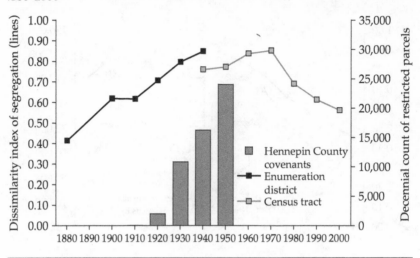

Source: Manson et al. 2022; Ehrman-Solberg et al. 2020.

Figure 4.4 Black-White Isolation Index and Restrictions in St. Louis, 1880–2000

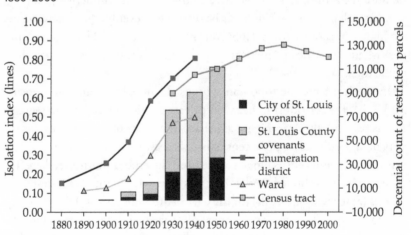

Source: Gordon 2023b; Manson et al. 2022; Decennial Census (blocks and tracts); Cutler, Glaeser, and Vigdor 1999 (wards).

Conclusion

Private restriction was not a simple mechanism of exclusion, sketching in one set of neighborhoods for white occupancy and another for African Americans. Petition restrictions cobbled together in transitional neighborhoods and subdivision restrictions on the suburban fringe accomplished and sustained racial segregation, but they did so in distinct ways. Subdivision restrictions, imposed by the original developer and accepted—as a condition of purchase—by the first buyers, were pointedly designed to hoard both housing opportunities and the public goods (such as schools and infrastructure) that flowed from private development. Petition restrictions, by contrast, were not an escape from the prospect of African American occupancy but a defensive response to its immediate threat. In suburban settings, developers strove for scale—both in the design and execution of their own subdivisions and in the hope that adjacent developments would follow suit. In transitional urban neighborhoods, realty interests just hoped to hold the line.

In a sense, subdivision restrictions contributed to segregation by succeeding, and petition restrictions contributed to segregation by failing. Restricted subdivisions, for the most part, sustained the promise of exclusion and protection; they posed a "lasting impediment to Negro occupancy"[151] well beyond the point at which their racial restrictions were deemed unenforceable.[152] Petition restrictions were practically and legally more vulnerable and far more susceptible to African American incursion or white defection—especially when *Shelley* removed the threat of enforcement in 1948.[153] Rather than prevent racial transition, petition covenants merely put it off. The delayed (but inevitable) result was often a chaotic tip from white to black occupancy and a cycle of predatory arbitrage (sometimes abetted by intentional blockbusting) that eroded housing values at the expense of white sellers and black buyers alike.[154] More broadly, the conclusion here is clear. While public policies such as zoning, subsidies for suburban development, and neighborhood redlining sanctioned and sustained residential segregation, they did not invent it. That dubious credit goes to deed-based racial restrictions and their enforcement through a combination of legal sanction and local violence and intimidation.

CHAPTER 5

Dress Rehearsal for *Shelley*: Private Restrictions and the Law

THE LONG LEGAL battle against private race restrictions, culminating in the Supreme Court's 1948 *Shelley v. Kraemer* decision, is a well-documented episode in civil rights history and civil rights jurisprudence. In its review of covenant cases originating in St. Louis and Detroit, the Court concluded that "in granting judicial enforcement of the restrictive agreements in these cases, the States have denied petitioners the equal protection of the laws."[1] The decision erased the presumption, found in both a raft of state cases and in the Court's decision in *Corrigan v. Buckley* (1926), that such restrictions were private contracts immune from equal protection.[2] And it expanded the narrow logic of *Buchanan v. Warley* (1917), affording the protection of the Fourteenth Amendment not just to white property owners but to prospective black owners and tenants as well.[3] At the same time, the decision also confined its attention to "state action" in support of private restrictions and affirmed that "private agreements, standing alone, do not violate any rights guaranteed by the Fourteenth Amendment"—a distinction that would last until 1968, when *Jones v. Mayer* (another St. Louis case) and the Fair Housing Act finally prohibited racial discrimination in private realty and lending.

Shelley is an important milestone in the legal history of civil rights, punctuating a string of midcentury victories that stretched from *Missouri ex rel. Gaines v. Canada* (1938) to *Brown v. Board of Education* (1954). But its immediate importance, in the context of private racial restriction and residential segregation, is less clear. While the NAACP leaned on the logic of state action to question the constitutionality of racial covenants, such restrictions did not actually rely extensively on judicial enforcement. Instead, they operated and succeeded largely as a social norm—as a set of expectations that guided the assumptions and behavior of both those upholding the restrictions and those targeted by them.[4] This was true in the half century before *Shelley*, an era in which racial restrictions were largely enforced through private censure, solidarity, intimidation, and violence. And it was true in *Shelley's* wake, at least partially accounting for the collective shrug at the ruling from those (ranging from local real estate agents to the leadership of the FHA) who had always understood private restriction as an essentially private mechanism of exclusion or closure.

Our understanding of the legal history of private restriction necessarily begins with the observation that the enforcement of racial restrictions fell largely outside the law. Violence and intimidation were (and remain) central aspects of racial segregation in the urban North, featuring prominently in battles over private housing and public space. The principal agents of violence and segregation were the police and individuals, mobs, and local organizations (especially neighborhood "improvement" associations) abetted by the police. Such violence was especially intense at neighborhood boundaries—often defined, as we have seen, by a patchwork of private restriction. It was both a mechanism for enforcing such restrictions and, after dramatic public violence as in east St. Louis in 1917 and Chicago in 1919, a motivation for creating new ones. "Negro housing segregation has been enforced by economic necessity, by law, contract, gentlemen's agreements, and by brute force," as one observer noted in 1931. "Where laws and private contracts have failed, mobs have attempted to maintain the racial integrity of neighborhoods."[5]

This systematic violence is well documented.[6] "Probably the chief force maintaining residential segregation of Negroes has been informal social pressure from the whites," as Gunnar Myrdal observed in 1944. "Few white property owners in white neighborhoods would ever consider selling or renting to Negroes; and even if a few Negro families did succeed in getting a foothold, they would be made to feel the spontaneous hatred of the whites both socially and physically."[7] This "spontaneous hatred" is especially prominent in the history of Chicago in the half century after 1919, from the famous citywide riot of that year through the many smaller-scale and locally strategic episodes of intimidation that buttressed the "second ghetto" created by public housing and redevelopment policies in the decades after World War II.[8] Detroit's signature civil rights litigation before World War II was the acquittal of Ossian Sweet, an African American accused of murder after defending his family's residence in a restricted neighborhood from a violent white mob that resulted in the death of a white participant.[9] In St. Louis, the assemblage of petition covenants around the Ville was accompanied by a pattern of petty violence and intimidation—including stink bombs, vandalism, and bricks wrapped in threatening notes.[10] African American families venturing into the Minneapolis suburbs between the wars were met with similar tactics.[11] Drawing on this history, Massey and Denton attribute the "construction of the ghetto" largely to the "tide of violence" that swept over northern cities during the First Great Migration.[12]

This violence—and its chilling effect—did much of the work of enforcing racial restrictions. Indeed, considering their ubiquity in interwar housing markets, private racial restrictions were not widely challenged or contested in the courts.[13] In Minnesota, the only disputes involving restrictive covenants to reach appellate courts were a scattering of cases concerning either the scope of an agreement or the precise definition of "residential use."[14] None raised the question of racial restriction.[15] The only race-restrictive covenant case to reach the Iowa Supreme Court, *Rice v. Sioux City Memorial Parkway Cemetery* (1953), involved a contract for a cemetery plot that specified that "burial privileges accrue only to members of the Caucasian race." The court upheld the contract on the grounds that it was a private agreement and that legislative or judicial indifference to the restriction did not constitute state action. When the NAACP surveyed the range of state-level litigation in late 1947, it found just eighty-one cases across the previous half century. Almost a quarter of these (seventeen) were from California, where the variety of restriction (targeting African Americans, Asian Americans, and Latinos) generated ongoing controversy. And almost half of the remainder (twenty-nine) were from the three jurisdictions—Michigan, Missouri, and the District of Columbia—represented in the 1948 Supreme Court cases.[16]

Across these settings, the predominant controversy was not the constitutionality of race restrictions but their failure. Most pre-*Shelley* challenges—as likely to come from white owners looking to sell as from those "restricted" looking to buy—focused on either the failure of private instruments as valid contracts (due to, for example, missing signatures, vagaries of language, or undue constraints on property rights) or on their failure to achieve their stated purpose. Much of the litigation, accordingly, arose in racially contested or transitional neighborhoods where owners, tenants, real estate agents, and neighborhood "protective" or "improvement" associations were invested in holding the line—or moving it.[17] And much of it concerned the validity of petition covenants (like the ones at issue in *Shelley*); their assembly, coverage, and unreliable presence in the chain of title made them more vulnerable to legal challenge than other forms of restriction. Indeed, across this history, the most prominent form of racial restriction—the meticulous and sweeping subdivision restrictions found in settings like Hennepin and St. Louis Counties—went virtually uncontested.

This uneven legal history involves not just the backstory to *Shelley* but the sentiments and arguments of an array of interests—homeowners, landlords, real estate agents, and civil rights and housing advocates—in local and state courts. At issue here was more than just the validity of a given restriction: it also involved the persistent tension between property rights and restrictive constraints, the collective action challenges posed by restrictive agreements, the legal meaning or codification of often vague restrictive terms, and the ongoing effort to steer a parade of contractual disputes into constitutional territory. Focusing on St. Louis and Missouri (the setting of both the original *Shelley* case and a long local history of covenant litigation), I draw on these cases—against the backdrop of other local and state cases—to tease out the important controversies and arguments, the legal strategies pursued by both sides, and the limits of the law in shaping housing opportunity.

Litigating Race Restrictions in St. Louis

If private racial restrictions were especially pronounced in St. Louis, so too was popular and legal opposition to their constraint on housing opportunity and equal protection. The local NAACP cut its teeth on organizing opposition to the 1916 racial zoning ordinance.[18] Local civil rights activists and African American realty interests—sometimes in cooperation with the NAACP, sometimes independently—had a long history of challenging racial restrictions, especially those on the borders of the Ville. These same realty interests were central to the *Shelley* litigation and its place (alongside the cases from Detroit and the District of Columbia) in the NAACP's national legal strategy.[19]

The local legal history of racial restriction, however, is best captured in a little-known predecessor to the *Shelley* case, *Dolan v. Richardson* (1944). The plaintiff, Scovel Richardson, was born in Nashville in 1912, graduated from the University of Illinois in 1934, and from law school at Howard University three years later. In 1939, he was appointed to the inaugural faculty of Lincoln University Law School in St. Louis, where he served as dean from 1944 to 1954.[20] The move to St. Louis confronted Richardson with the harsh realities of systematic segregation in a border state, of which Lincoln University itself was a glaring example. When the Supreme Court held in *Missouri ex rel. Gaines v. Canada* (1938) that the state of Missouri was required to offer African Americans equal access to law school, the legislature—rather than open admission to the University of Missouri—hastily appropriated $200,000 to convert a shuttered beauty college in north St. Louis into a segregated alternative.[21]

Alongside the ignominy of "separate but equal" education, Richardson also confronted St. Louis's architecture of residential segregation when he set out to tackle the "acute housing problem of the colored people within the ring of steel thrown around them by so-called restrictive agreements."[22] His challenge began with the strategic purchase of 4635 North Market Street, located at the western edge of the Ville, in a neighborhood restricted to Caucasian occupancy by one of the many restrictions imposed in the early 1920s.[23] In assembling the restriction, officers of the Real Estate Exchange had collected signatures from seventy-three property owners, representing seventy-nine of the eighty-three parcels fronting the 4600 block of North Market and both sides of Wagoner Place between Easton (now Martin Luther King) and North Market. The agreement followed the language of the exchange's template. A preamble announced the goal of preserving "the character of said neighborhood as a desirable place of residence for persons of the Caucasian race," and the body of the agreement prohibited two nuisance uses of property: the erection, maintenance, or operation of "any slaughterhouse, junk shop, or rag-picking establishment," and the sale or conveyance to, or occupancy by, "a negro or negroes."[24]

In July of 1941, Richardson engineered the sale of 4635 North Market to a straw party—a tactic for transferring title used to sidestep legal restrictions on sales—breaking the chain of title to the original signatory of the restriction; he and his wife Inez then purchased the property in early October.[25] The reaction was swift. On October 18 and again in early November, stench bombs were thrown onto the Richardsons' front porch and onto the porches or through the windows of the Richardsons' few African American neighbors.[26] The Real Estate Exchange, a party to the underlying restriction (alongside the buyer and seller), immediately filed suit in the St. Louis Circuit Court in January 1942 to enjoin the sale—and the case was heard in March of that year.[27] The arguments made by Richardson and his colleagues at trial captured the legal status of race restrictions in the early 1940s and, at the same time, pushed the argument toward the more robust equal protection challenge that would eventually prevail in 1948.

Private Property and Its Limits

For Richardson and others challenging private restrictions, the most obvious and promising tack was to leverage the veneration and solicitude in American law for property rights. "Property is more than the mere thing which a person owns," as the Court underscored in *Buchanan*. "It is elementary that it includes the right to acquire, use, and dispose of it."[28] Agrarian at its roots, the close connection between property rights and citizenship was—by the early twentieth century—most fervently expressed in the context of homeownership.[29] At trial, Richardson cast racial restrictions as an invasion of the civil right to acquire, enjoy, and use property, invoking both the burden on potential (black) buyers and on willing (white) sellers, especially in transitional neighborhoods. Such restriction, he argued, imposed an "unconscionable, oppressive, and iniquitous" burden on prospective African Americans buyers and renters, especially given the acute housing shortage of the war years.[30] But it was also destructive of the rights of all who lived in the restricted area. "The property owners on whose behalf this action is alleged to be instituted will be deprived of their property rights," as Richardson underscored, noting that the "alleged restrictive agreement . . . destroys the marketability of land, interferes with the free sale and use thereof, prevents improvements to land and property, [and] encourage waste and disuse of property."[31]

This argument, in *Dolan* and other cases, found little traction. Indeed, as Robert Fogelson and others have suggested, the willingness of homeowners in restricted subdivisions or neighborhoods to relinquish or constrain their property rights was starkly at odds with the contemporary history of land-use regulation and property law.[32] In part, the attraction of private restriction reflected the limited protection offered by conventional legal remedies. The law allowed owners to sue their neighbors for nuisance uses of property, but this was a blunt and often ineffective tool. Nuisance law rested on individual claims and demonstrable harm; it lacked the scale to control behavior across an entire neighborhood or subdivision and was ill-suited to sustain the finer aesthetic and behavioral expectations of restricted subdivisions. More to the point, state courts—even in the South—had been reluctant to consider the mere presence of nonwhite occupants as a nuisance under the law.[33] Private restrictions—which set the rules for broad swaths of development and did not hesitate to list "sold or rented to negroes" as a nuisance use alongside junkyards and glue factories—overcame the problems of both scale and the interpretation of nuisance law.

In turn, private agreements accommodated property rights concerns by placing limits or constraints on the terms of restriction. "It is the rule that an absolute restriction in the power of alienation in the conveyance of a fee simple title is void," as the Missouri Supreme Court put it in *Koehler* (1918), "but it is entirely within the right and power of the grantor to impose a condition or restraint upon the power of alienation in certain cases to certain persons, or for a certain time, or for certain purposes."[34] In California, Michigan, West Virginia, Pennsylvania, and Ohio, the courts held that private agreements could be used to regulate racial occupancy but not the sale or disposition of property.[35] This was not the case in Missouri, and the language of St. Louis covenants often went to great lengths to clarify this point: "No lot, house or improvement of any kind in said Subdivision, or an interest therein," as an early St. Louis restriction put it, "may be sold, leased, rented, conveyed or transferred, willed, devised or in any way or manner given, granted or disposed of to, or occupied by any person or persons not of the Caucasian Race."[36] Private racial restrictions also generally respected the rule against perpetuities in property law and adopted time limits. (In St. Louis most petition covenants used a term of fifteen or twenty years.)[37]

More broadly, advocates of private restriction argued that restraints on use or alienation were a small price to pay for security, permanence, and a solution to the collective action challenges posed by unfettered private ownership. They were, in effect, negative easements: "Each lot relinquishes some portion of the free use which would normally accrue to its owner," as Monchow noted in her 1928 review of the practice, "and in return benefits from a similar relinquishment by other parcels in the tract."[38] Such agreements, especially in real estate marketing, were often trumpeted as "protective" restrictions. In *Porter v. Johnson* (1938), the Missouri Court of Appeals upheld a petition covenant on the grounds that signatories "should have confidence in the power and willingness of the courts to protect their investment in happiness and security."[39] In this view, the protection afforded by restrictive agreements *enhanced* underlying property rights. "There can be no doubt, indeed, that the now quite common provision that no liquor shall be sold or used in a limited area or subdivision has a marked and beneficial tendency to attract purchasers to a residential district," as one legal commentator argued in 1928, "there can also be no doubt that the fear of a negro invasion materially interferes with the profitable sale of almost every homesite. These restrictions, therefore, aid rather than restrict, free alienation."[40] The same logic held two decades later. "The avoidance of unpleasant racial and social relations and the stabilization of the value of land which results from the enforcement of the exclusion policy," as a New Jersey court concluded in 1945, "are regarded as outweighing the evils which normally result from a curtailment of the general power of alienation."[41]

Finally, such restrictions were seen as compatible with private property rights because they too were private. Property owners who railed against the threat posed by municipal zoning (often crafted to accomplish similar ends) defended their right (as the purchaser in a subdivision or the signatory to a petition) to voluntarily enter into restrictive agreements.[42] And until the *Shelley* decision, this, of course, was the basic presumption that shielded such restrictions from constitutional scrutiny. "The restraints of the Fifth and Fourteenth Amendments are directed to coercive policies formulated by the government, whether judge-made or legislated," as one observer underscored in 1928, "and not to voluntary undertakings."[43]

Defects and Flaws

The relentless emphasis on restrictions as "private agreements, standing alone" left one primary line of attack—to challenge their validity as private contracts. While Missouri courts upheld the right of property owners to enter into and enforce restrictive agreements, they increasingly scrutinized the instruments themselves and the terms under which they were drafted. These challenges focused on flaws in the original agreement, including invalid signatures, misrepresentation of the agreement to those who did sign, and failure to attach the agreement to the chain of title of restricted properties.[44] Drawing on recent decisions in St. Louis and anticipating the trial strategy in *Shelley*, Richardson leaned heavily on these arguments in his own case. "A large number of property owners in the alleged restrictive area did not sign said alleged restrictive agreement," he pointed out, adding that "plaintiffs have acquiesced in numerous breaches and violations of the alleged restrictive agreement, and in the ownership by colored persons within the alleged restrictive area."[45] At trial, Richardson grilled the notary who had drawn up the agreement regarding missing signatures and brought in a handwriting expert to bolster his claim that some owners had signed for others. Indeed, the bulk of Richardson's case hinged on his denial "that there ever was in existence at any time or is now in existence any duly executed or valid instrument . . . which gives plaintiffs authority to prosecute this action."[46]

Calling out composition or execution defects in race-restrictive agreements was a staple legal strategy. Even as it sought a firmer equal protection constitutional foothold, the NAACP devoted much of its 1945 Chicago conference on restrictive covenants to enumerating the defects and flaws that could be pointed to in order to undermine the validity of an agreement.[47] Also in 1945, Richardson penned a short note for the *National Bar Journal* that drew on his own experience to argue that restrictive agreements were so riven with errors and lapses in documentation that they were both an offense to equal protection and "a fraud upon the persons who sign."[48] And, of course, this was the opening gambit a year later in the first *Shelley* case. As George Vaughn, the St. Louis attorney who would argue *Shelley* from its inception in St. Louis, underscored at the NAACP's 1945 conference, "We always look for defects in the execution of the covenants."[49]

Across local and state case law, challenging the contractual validity of restrictions was often an effective argument. But given the issues at stake (such as coverage or signatories) that argument found purchase primarily in challenges to petition restrictions, which rested on collective agreement among residents of hastily composed neighborhoods—their boundaries defined largely by the willingness of residents to sign the petition or by the looming threat of African American occupancy. In local and Missouri law, there was no consensus (or consistent legal standard) as to the share of participating neighbors needed to execute or sustain an agreement. And enforcement of such restrictions required vigilance, on the part of the Real Estate Exchange or local neighborhood improvement associations, against encroachment or defection.[50]

The first issue, in this respect, revolved around the nature of the original petition. What share of owners needed to sign an agreement to make it valid? Were only signatories bound by the agreement?[51] Many jurisdictions settled informally on a signature threshold for petition covenants that was high enough to make a restriction viable without expecting unanimity.[52] But some practical and legal confusion remained between large-scale community-level schemes of restriction (such as those that prevailed in Chicago), and the more compact neighborhood schemes pursued in St. Louis. The former assumed a threshold of support (75 percent of residential frontage was the standard for most Chicago covenants). The latter, at least in their scale and logic, assumed universal agreement—but this was rarely accomplished and therefore a constant source of dispute.[53] Whether any less-than-unanimous agreements applied to property owners who had not signed was unclear. Could a neighborhood bound by an agreement invoke a principal of majority rule and restrict all properties within its fungible boundaries? Did a duly executed agreement constitute a negative easement binding signatories and abstainers alike?

In his own case, Richardson cited the agreement's failure to follow usual standards for witnessing signatures and its failure to achieve full coverage—especially because it had been represented to each signatory that the agreement would not be recorded unless all owners in the platted area had signed.[54] This was a point of considerable confusion. Local litigation, most notably in *Mueninghaus v. James* (1930) and *Pickel v. McCawley* (1931), commonly raised this issue, but it was unclear across such decisions whether the defect lay in the share of signatures needed to make an agreement stick or in the representations made to those who did sign.[55] Along with a demonstrable threshold of support, such agreements also rested on some form of public imprimatur: witnessed signatures, notarization, and a filing with the recorder of deeds. One St. Louis restriction fizzled when the agent charged with collecting signatures absconded with his fee and never filed the petition at City Hall.[56]

The absence of full and clean participation, in turn, raised the issue of who was actually bound by an agreement. In *Mueninghaus v. James* (1930), the Missouri Supreme Court upheld a lower court ruling that a restriction near Fountain Park in St. Louis could not be enforced because the original owner of the property had not signed the agreement. Neither he nor his African American buyer could be bound by a contract that neither was a party to.[57] Missing signatures and uneven participation were also cited to invalidate entire agreements. In *Thornhill v. Herdt* (1938), owners of properties that were original signatories to an agreement argued successfully that they should not be bound by it on the grounds that eighteen of the forty-six owners had signed improperly and another seventeen had not signed at all.[58]

Similar issues arose when the Real Estate Exchange pushed to renew the first generation of petition restrictions (most of them imposed in the early 1920s with twenty-year terms) in the early 1940s. In one such case, on the 4500 block of Enright, 95 percent of the owners had signed the original agreement in 1923. But, in the face of the Second Great Migration and the erosion of agreements all around them, barely half agreed to renew the agreement in 1938. The local courts declined to enforce the new agreement, noting that it fell short of the assumption "that these covenants must be universal and reciprocal."[59] In the first *Shelley* decision, the courts struggled to reconcile the logic of a restriction that purported to rest on the consent of all property owners (who "did not intend to be bound unless the purpose was accomplished") with the fact that its coverage—even at the outset—was so spotty.[60]

At issue here was not just the status of properties belonging to those who had declined to sign but how the commitment represented by the original signatory was sustained. In the original *Shelley* trial, the restriction was understood to "bind the signatories, their heirs, assigns, legal representatives, and successors in title to restrict the property . . . against sale to or occupancy by people not wholly of the Caucasian race." The property on Labadie Avenue changed hands six times between the original restriction in 1911 and the Shelley family's purchase in 1946, and the use of a straw party (a tactic also used by Richardson) at that last sale suggested a conviction that the tie binding "successors in title" could be broken.[61] This strategy rested on another peculiarity of petition covenants. Because such agreements were not imposed in the context of a sale or transfer, they were sown through the recorder's records as "wild deeds" that were unattached to the chain of title for any given property.[62] In many cases, sellers, purchasers, or renters had no knowledge of a restriction until the Real Estate Exchange threatened to evict tenants or enjoin a sale.[63] In *Shelley*, neither the 1945 sale nor any in the chain of transfers extending back thirty-five years to 1911 (more than some 2.6 million deed book pages) made any formal reference to a restriction—a fact that did not trouble the Missouri courts, even as it undercut a basic premise of property law.[64]

Subdivision restrictions largely escaped this tangle of challenges. Imposed by original developers or by subdivision governing bodies of their creation, such restrictions were both universal to the development in question and usually firmly attached to the chain of title of each of its lots or properties. In turn, developers and subdivision trustees could rely on the Sanborn rule, which assumed all such agreements to be universal in coverage and agreement.[65] Under this rule, restrictions were valid and enforceable on all lots as long as they were imposed by a single grantor (the developer) and laid out as a general scheme of restriction of which all buyers were deemed to have "constructive notice." The general scheme created a "negative reciprocal easement" binding on all lots and owners.[66] "If the general plan has been maintained from its inception and has been understood, accepted and relied upon by all in interest," as one 1947 opinion put it, "it is binding and enforceable on all *inter se* and runs with the land, binding all purchasers equally."[67] This binding provided cover when subdivision restrictions were sloppily worded or inadvertently omitted some properties. This logic frayed a little, as in a scattering of instances in the City of St. Louis, when trustees imposed racial restrictions years after development and asserted that they were retroactive, or when the buyer or seller of lots within a subdivision imposed a restriction and claimed it applied to all lots.[68]

Changed Conditions

A more fundamental challenge to private restrictions—in part because it was raised by both prospective black buyers and white homeowners—was their failure to stem African American occupancy or racial transition.[69] In *Thornhill v. Herdt* (1938), a case that influenced both Richardson and the *Shelley* lawyers, the circuit court voided a restriction on Vine Grove Avenue in St. Louis on the grounds that it had failed in its purpose. The Missouri Supreme Court upheld the ruling but crafted its own reasoning, arguing that the point of the agreement was not just to bind its signatories but to attract enough signatories for the agreement to succeed as a neighborhood scheme of restriction. "While it is true that covenants or agreements creating racial restrictions of the kind in question are generally sustained by the courts as against objections going to the validity of instruments of such character," the court noted, "this can only be so where they are entered into in such a manner and with such completeness as to give them force and effect."[70] Anything less than universal agreement, in the court's view, doomed a restriction to failure. Even one or two holdouts could invite racial transition.[71] As the decision concluded, "This Court, and every other resident of the City of St. Louis knows that it is impossible to secure a white tenant of respectability when negroes live on each side of the premises. The only white tenant who will ever be procured for respondent's premises is some person who is hiding from the police or seeking to cover his tracks in some way."[72]

Across a wide range of covenant cases, in the Missouri courts and elsewhere, the most persistent point of evidence used to challenge such agreements was the mere presence of African American owners or tenants on or near the footprint of the restricted area.[73] "The property hereinabove mentioned and surrounding the same," as the appellants argued in *Thornhill*, "is completely occupied by Negroes as owners, occupants, or tenants"—adding that "when there are upwards of eighteen negro residents in the block now, one more or less will not affect the comfort or safety or happiness of any white resident."[74] Or as a 1942 District of Columbia case (*Hundley v. Gorewitz*) put it bluntly: "the purpose has been essentially defeated by the presence of a Negro family now living in an unrestricted house in the midst of the restricted group, and as well by the ownership by another Negro of a house almost directly across the street. And this is just the beginning." Sometimes (as in *Shelley* and *Dolan*) this evidence took the form of a house-by-house canvas noting "holes" in the original agreement. Pockets or instances of established African American occupancy were used to argue that an injunction against sale or eviction of a tenant was arbitrary or unfair.[75] More often, some degree of African American occupancy was offered as evidence that the agreement had failed; that neighborhood conditions had changed enough to invalidate the restriction in question.[76] "Some of the restricted homes have non-restricted property on both sides which may be occupied by Negroes," as one reporter characterized a contested covenant on Enright Avenue. "The situation found here defeats the very purpose of the neighborhood scheme—to limit the use and occupancy of these homes to members of the Caucasian race."[77]

Such cases rested on the balance of benefit and harm that might follow from upholding or sustaining a restriction. "The conditions surrounding the neighborhood had so changed that the reasons for inserting that clause in the deed had ceased to exist," as the plaintiffs in *Koehler v. Rowland* (1918) argued, "therefore the consideration for such stipulation had wholly failed, and the plaintiffs were not damaged by the breach of the condition."[78] Since original agreements were premised on their mutual benefit to all owners or signatories, challenges often focused on the evaporation of that benefit under changing conditions—arguing that, especially for white owners unable to sell to black buyers, that benefit had actually become a liability. Such agreements should not be enforced, as one of the District of Columbia cases put it, when "enforcement would substantially lessen the value of the property, or, in short, that injunctive relief would not give a benefit but rather impose a hardship."[79]

This calculus of benefit and harm was often raised by white owners in transitional neighborhoods, especially in settings like St. Louis or Chicago where third parties such as the St. Louis Real Estate Exchange or the Real Estate Board in Chicago sought to sustain restrictions on principle and in defense of broader social norms. In *Pickel v. McCawley* (1931), the Missouri Supreme Court let stand a ruling voiding a restriction on Finney Avenue in north St. Louis. The lower court had found that the original agreement was defective. The supreme court dismissed that finding but agreed with the assessment that "conditions in the neighborhood" had changed radically and that "the essential object of the covenants were then totally destroyed. Negroes were at liberty to buy and did purchase and occupy many homes . . . within the proposed restricted district. There is no valid reason why the restrictions should be saddled upon plaintiffs in this case. They are living under the very conditions and surroundings against which the proposed covenant was to protect them."[80] Or, as Emma Pickel herself testified: "If I look out my back window I see negroes, and the front door it is negroes. . . . I am tied up in my own house."[81] In Chicago, a group of white owners in the Washington Park neighborhood made a similar case, reasserting their property rights and arguing for "relief from the glaring inequity of this existing 'restrictive agreement' upon the undeniable grounds of repeatedly proven Abandonment, Impracticability [*sic*] to further Enforce, Public Policy and to reassure our members the restoration of their inherent American right to again freely exercise, within their discretion, adequate safeguards toward the vital protection of their financial investments herein."[82]

As much as prospective black buyers and anxious white owners raised the issue, the legal assessment of "changed conditions" was complicated. Courts were sporadically sympathetic to legal arguments that focused on dramatic changes in racial occupancy within the footprint of a given restriction but were reluctant to void agreements based on changes at its edges.[83] "The possibility of an infiltration of Negroes into adjacent areas," as one commentator noted, "is not only foreseen, but probably the moving cause of the contract."[84] In the Kansas City case *Porter v. Johnson* (1938), the Missouri Supreme Court sustained a restriction that had been filed in 1921 in the face of changed conditions on the grounds that "property owners, in 1921, anticipated these very changes in the surrounding neighborhood, and believed that unless they protected themselves against it the block would be invaded by colored residents."[85] Petition covenants, in settings like Waterloo and St. Louis, were assembled in neighborhoods threatened by racial transition; that threat—even if it had grown—could not then be used to dismantle the same agreement. "There must always be some property which, by reason of its location on the very threshold of the restricted district," as the court reasoned in *Thornhill*, "is forced to bear the brunt of the thing or condition against which the restriction is directed."[86]

In St. Louis and elsewhere, challenging the defects and flaws in these agreements, or establishing that they had failed in their purpose, proved an unevenly effective strategy. But, of all the issues raised by Richardson at trial, this was the one that stuck: "Defendants established to the Court's satisfaction, and it would appear almost somewhat to the point where plaintiffs could not refute," as the trial decision concluded, "that in the original execution of the alleged restriction there had been several defects."[87] But, as Richardson and his colleagues recognized, such arguments were also inherently limited. Almost all the flaws and defects that lay behind these challenges (such as missing signatures, incomplete coverage, failure to attach restrictions to the chain of title, or changes in neighborhood conditions) were particular to petition-based restrictive agreements. They did little to challenge the larger scale, more carefully drafted racial restrictions routinely attached to new subdivisions—which accounted for over 40 percent of restricted parcels in the City of St. Louis and for virtually all the restricted parcels in suburban St. Louis County, Black Hawk County, Johnson County, and Hennepin County.[88]

While challenging the veracity of signatures might void a given restriction, it did little to chip away at the larger injustice of segregation. The NAACP eagerly cataloged these strategies but also grew frustrated with the ways in which they allowed courts and judges to duck the larger constitutional question of equal protection.[89] For their part, the champions of restriction were unfazed. In none of these cases "did the court raise any question about this method of control as such," as one commentator noted. "The potentialities of the device, therefore, not only for negative control by restriction as in the instant cases but also for positive control by establishment of neighborhood standards, should be explored by those seeking to promote the stability of real estate development and property values."[90]

Who Is Caucasian?

Alongside the documentation of individual agreements' flaws and failures, Richardson and his colleagues also raised more fundamental objections. One argument, following the lead of the NAACP, challenged the racial categories at the core of restriction. At the NAACP's 1945 Chicago conference, Charles Houston recommended challenging the practical or legal meaning of white, Caucasian, or Negro, or what we would today call the social construction of race. "One technique is to start out denying that the plaintiffs are white," he suggested. "There has been a past tendency to draw clear cut lines admitting that the plaintiffs are white and the defendants are Negroes. The first thing I recommend is to deny that the plaintiffs are white and the defendants are Negroes."[91] Here, the NAACP lawyers were tapping into a broader contention—evident in immigration law, in shifting census definitions, and elsewhere—over the very meaning of racial identities or categories.

The designation of Caucasian, as we have seen, was an ambiguous foundation for exclusion. It had a more capacious, albeit more contested, meaning in the eugenics-inspired rankings of the first generation of restrictions.[92] But even as these lists of excluded racial categories were gradually displaced by inclusive agreements with the single category of Caucasian, the term lacked clear definition. While understood as synonymous with white, especially in the distinctly biracial Midwest, Caucasian was inconsistently applied to national and religious minorities, including Jews.[93] It was not clear, in a strictly legal sense, what "pure Caucasian blood or descent" (as some Hennepin County restrictions read) really meant.[94] The shifting and varied identification of

African Americans—colored, Negro, African, African blood, Ethiopian—
was also a source of contention and confusion. Some restrictions, as we
have seen, invoked a blood-quantum hierarchy (as in the St. Louis County
restriction targeting "any person having one thirty-second part or more
negro blood"), but the meaning or precision of these labels was belied by
their logic and administration. The Chicago Real Estate Board appended
to its one thirty-second rule the assurance that the restriction applied to
"any appreciable admixture of negro blood, and every person who is what
is commonly known as a colored person."[95] The South Richmond Heights
restriction allowed that "the Court or jury trying any case . . . may determine the proportion of negro blood in any party who may be in possession of the property by the appearance of such person."[96] When an African
American couple in Michigan claimed that a restriction against "people of
the African race" did not apply to them, the court brushed the objection
aside: "The language employed in stating the restriction is to be taken in its
ordinary and generally understood or popular sense, and is not to be subject
to technical refinement."[97]

Richardson put his own spin on this logic at trial. He was "willing to
stipulate that he is a member of the colored race, and a colored American,
but not as to the term 'negro.'" For Richardson, the former was a racial classification and the latter a social and political one. "As a defendant I cannot
help but have personal feelings about it," he continued, "and the word
'negro' to my mind denotes something black and despicable, and if I am
to be classified as a negro, according to this agreement along in the same
category with slaughterhouses, junk-shops, rag-picking establishments, it is
impertinent and scandalous to me. I have always stated that I am a colored
person and an American citizen."[98] With this line of argument, Richardson
underscored both the ambiguity of racial categories such as Caucasian and
the slippery legal logic of racial identification and self-identification.

Public Policy and State Action

The central goal of the legal campaign against racial restriction, of course,
was to get the courts to see racial restrictions as a matter of public policy
rather than as private agreements. The *Civil Rights Cases* had determined in
1883 that the Fourteenth Amendment applied only to state action and did
not protect against discriminatory acts by private individuals.[99] And *Plessy v.*

Ferguson in 1896 had opened the door to the "separate but equal" provision of public goods and services.[100] This was the strained logic behind the Supreme Court's claim that it lacked jurisdiction in *Corrigan v. Buckley* in 1926 and the state precedents (in Missouri and elsewhere) regarding race restrictions on property. And this was the logic that the NAACP, after its 1945 conference on restrictive covenants, was so intent on overturning. "We argued the question of public policy," as William Hastie recalled of the unsuccessful effort to get the Court to take up the District of Columbia case *Mays v. Burgess* in 1945, "presented the contention that this was not a case of requiring a person to fulfill his promise because the grantor had not signed the covenant; called it state action by the Court in enforcing court-made rule of property law; tried to show that this state action was a denial of equal protection."[101] For the NAACP, and for local challengers like Richardson, this broader argument consisted of two lines of attack. The first was to establish that private restrictions were "contrary to public policy"; the second was to establish that some element of private restriction constituted "state action," exposing the practice to the equal protection clause of the Fourteenth Amendment.[102]

The "public policy" argument was a difficult one. It was commonly (and successfully) invoked when private agreements—such as the sale of illegal drugs or an employment contract paying less than the minimum wage—clearly violated the law. But it was "an unruly horse" when used, as in the restrictive covenant cases, to make the fuzzier argument that private contracts ran contrary to a broader definition of the public good or welfare.[103] In *Koehler*, the Missouri Supreme Court had not only underscored that "the restriction was one which the vendor had a right to make" but held that such agreements *complemented* public policy, "as the purpose was to preserve the segregated nature of the property, and such discrimination was recognized in other matters." In what would become a powerful and controlling precedent well into the 1940s, the court concluded:

> There is nothing against public policy in inserting a condition in a deed that the property shall not be sold or leased to colored people. Such restrictions, tend to promote peace and to prevent violence and bloodshed, and should be encouraged. The courts have sustained laws providing for separate schools for negroes and separate coaches on railroad trains, and even in street cars, and laws prohibiting negroes from attending theatres attended by white

people and segregating negroes and whites in cities. The covenants contained
in this deed are perfectly reasonable, lawful and binding.[104]

In response, the NAACP drew on social science research to demonstrate
the impact of such restrictions on African American citizens and communities.[105] Such an approach aimed to bolster and expand the notion that
private restrictions were "contrary to public policy," not on legal grounds
but on evidence that the enforcement of race restrictions ran counter to
or frustrated other policies—such as improving housing availability and
conditions or protecting public health and welfare. The NAACP's litigat-
ing position intended to flip the script on the prevailing assumption that
African American occupancy was a nuisance that destroyed property values.
Instead, Weaver and others argued that restrictive covenants distorted the
natural trajectory of neighborhood transition and, by choking housing supply,
created the very conditions they purported to combat.[106]

Richardson echoed these arguments in *Dolan,* contesting the notion that
African American occupancy hurt property values and emphasizing the
negative role that racial restrictions had played during the wartime housing
crisis. Even if the agreement were valid, in Richardson's view, its enforcement would "strike a severe blow to the public health, morals, safety, and
general welfare of St. Louis." Enforcement would not just limit the housing
options available to African Americans, he continued, but "would compel
their increasing population, due both to the increase in the birth rate and
migration from the South, to live in an overcrowded and slum-ridden section of the city. This situation would breed disease and develop criminals."[107]
Restrictions were not a *response* to housing conditions and property values
in African American neighborhoods but their proximate *cause.* Indeed, in
the months between the first *Dolan* trial in 1942 and the appellate decision in 1944, local courts increasingly recognized not just "changed conditions" but persistent housing shortage yielded, at least in part, by racial
restriction.[108]

The larger goal, of course, was that of equal protection. To make the
legality of racial restrictions a *constitutional* question, rather than one that
hinged on the arcane details of state-level contract or property law, the
NAACP needed to press the argument that private restrictive agreements,
in some manner or form, depended on "state action." Civil rights leaders—
horrified by the willingness of federal authorities to sanction and even

encourage racial restrictions in federal housing policy—recognized that such willingness further implicated state actors and state agencies in the maintenance of segregation. The NAACP hoped to link the impact of racial restriction to federal policies—especially urban renewal and public housing—to bolster this reasoning.[109] The strongest argument in this respect, which would eventually prevail in *Shelley*, was that the enforcement of private agreements constituted state action.[110]

During the *Dolan* trial, Richardson argued that restrictive agreements violated the privileges and immunities and due process clauses of the Fourteenth Amendment and infringed on the freedom of contract of white property owners and prospective black buyers alike. Such restrictions, Richardson underscored, "expressly contemplated and provided for state action and the use of state agencies, its courts and its public officers in the enforcement of said alleged restrictive agreement in violation of the Fourteenth Amendment of the Constitution of the United States of America." In his questioning of the Real Estate Exchange's Ray Dolan, Richardson expanded on this point, arguing that the Real Estate Exchange had no standing under its charter to enter into such restrictive agreements and that, because "the Real Estate Exchange gets its authority from the State of Missouri," the corporate charter implicated the state in any actions taken by the exchange.[111] "The Exchange is a corporation obtaining its existence from the State," Richardson reasoned, "and being the creature of the State, it can have no greater power than its creator. No state can grant to a corporation power to do that which the federal constitution forbids it to do itself. . . . What a state is forbidden to do directly, it may not do by indirection."[112] In making this argument, Richardson reached back to the logic of Justice John Marshall Harlan's dissent in the *Civil Rights Cases*, which held that the common carriers and inns at issue in those cases occupied "a sort of public office" or provided a "quasi-public service."[113]

One lasting irony of this story is that it was *Dolan* (rather than *Shelley*) that most closely resembled the test case that civil rights leaders were looking for. Richardson's presentation at trial hewed closely to the position then being refined by the NAACP, but the case itself ended with a whimper. In 1944, noting that the restriction covering 4635 North Market had expired in December 1942, the appellate court declined to proceed with the "empty formality" of rendering a decision where "no actual controversy exists between plaintiffs and defendants."[114] It was a hollow victory.

The Richardsons were able to keep their house, but the court had declined to weigh in on any of the issues raised by the case. All that was left was the circuit court's original determination that the restriction was unenforceable because it was so sloppily executed—a ruling implying that, had the Real Estate Exchange been more attentive in collecting signatures, the restriction would have been perfectly valid. "The sooner those who persist in restrictive covenants against colored American citizens in St. Louis can prepare a covenant which meets the technical requirements of the law," as Richardson reflected in 1945, "the sooner we can go to the United States Supreme Court and obtain the ruling we are entitled to as American citizens."[115]

This was precisely the strategy of the NAACP when the plaintiffs in *Shelley* forced its hand a few years later.[116] The NAACP wanted a case that would rest solely on equal protection, distinct from the scattering of victories in state and federal courts that had been won on technical grounds.[117] At trial, the Shelleys' lawyers had gestured at equal protection (citing the long-ignored 1892 *Gandolfo v. Hartman* precedent)[118] but, in both the initial circuit court decision and the Missouri Supreme Court's reversal, the case focused narrowly on the defects in (and the failure of) the original restriction.[119] Without consulting the NAACP, George Vaughn appealed to the Supreme Court, which then agreed to hear the St. Louis case alongside one from Detroit, as well as a parallel federal case from the District of Columbia.[120] At the hearing, Vaughn bucked the NAACP's strategy and based his argument on the Thirteenth Amendment's prohibition of slavery. The case did not get off to a good start. "He didn't cut through the underbrush," one of the solicitor general's lawyers recalled, "he got caught in it."[121] NAACP stalwarts Charles Houston, Thurgood Marshall, and Loren Miller argued the other two cases, and it was Marshall and Miller's invocation of the Fourteenth Amendment in the Michigan case—and their reasoning that enforcement of restrictions constituted clear state action—that carried the day.[122]

Shelley and After

For Richardson, the NAACP, and the Shelley family and millions like them, it was a victory that was at once momentous and fleeting. The prohibition on state enforcement of private racial restrictions, like the blow to "separate but equal" won in *Brown v. Board of Education* six years later, transformed the meaning of the law, but the decision could neither undo the damage that had been done nor stem the determination of state and private actors alike to evade its clear intent. In St. Louis, some restrictions recognized the legal uncertainty created by *Shelley* and other litigation, while still doubling down on their exclusionary efforts. "No lot or lots, parts of lots, shall be sold, leased, rented to, or used by persons other than of the Caucasian race," read the 1947 agreement covering May Acres in St. Louis County, adding the provision that "if at any time it shall be held by any court that this restriction taken in its entirety is invalid than so much of it as prohibits the use of any lot or lots, part or parts of lots, by persons other than Caucasian blood shall remain and shall be in force."[123]

Private housing interests, of course, had other means of accomplishing and sustaining segregation. Race restrictions, in this respect, formalized— even made respectable—other private strategies of racial exclusion and subordination that had predated the use of deed covenants and remained very much in place after 1948. Such strategies included opportunities for racial discrimination at every stage of the process of buying or renting a home: uneven access to credit and home insurance, racially disparate property appraisals, neighborhood steering by real estate agents, the recalcitrance of developers, and move-in violence and other forms of intimidation.[124] In the wake of *Shelley*, the St. Louis Real Estate Exchange bluntly reaffirmed its expectations that "no Realtor may sell to Negroes, or finance any transaction involving the purchase by a Negro of any property north of Easton Avenue and west of Marcus Avenue nor elsewhere outside of the established unrestricted districts."[125] Private assumptions about housing value and African American occupancy, as we shall see, also continued to shape public housing policies—including the FHA's immediate and infamous response that it would not "fail to recognize the validity of such restrictions and the right of . . . private individuals" to use them.[126]

Real estate agents and developers floated other mechanisms of enforcement, including country club memberships, first right of refusal or repurchase options, and ownership structures (such as housing cooperatives) that distanced restrictive practices from the point of sale.[127] One such option— as we have seen—was a reversionary clause, by which the original developer retained a property interest and sales could be forfeited if restrictions were violated. Some Hennepin County restrictions, for example, included the provision that "any breach of any or either thereof shall work a forfeiture of title, which may be enforced by re-entry" or simply "if breached property reverts to grantor."[128] However, this was not a common strategy. It was only possible in subdivision restrictions where an original grantor (the developer) could assert such a claim—and even then, reversionary clauses were rare. In the City of St. Louis, they seem to have been favored by a few large developers—including Fillmore, who included them in the indentures for every stage of St. Louis Hills from 1929 to 1950. In St. Louis County, they appeared infrequently and were as common before 1930 as they were after 1940. Of the eighty-eight county subdivision restrictions put in place after *Shelley*, only one (Yorkshire #3) included a reversionary clause, which—as with St. Louis Hills—reflected the persistence of one developer rather than a response to the *Shelley* decision. When the same developer completed the next two stages of the Yorkshire subdivision in 1949, the racial restriction was dropped.[129]

A more promising tactic, at least in the short term, was to evade *Shelley* by moving the target of legal action from the black buyer to the white seller. *Shelley* made it clear that enforcement in equity, when judicial action upheld a restriction and voided a sale or lease, put the burden on the prospective buyer or tenant and denied them equal protection of the laws.[130] The narrowness of the ruling invited other strategies, including suing the white seller for damages—on the grounds that sale to a restricted party came at demonstrable cost to others "protected" by the restriction.[131] Developers and subdivision trustees experimented widely with damage suits, but the tactic was upheld by just two state court decisions: *Corell v. Early* (1951) in Oklahoma, and *Weiss v. Leaon* (1949) in Missouri. The argument, in both cases, was twofold: Since *Shelley* had held that such agreements allowed "voluntary adherence to their terms," as *Weiss* put it, damage suits did not constitute state action. The fact that one remedy "is ruled out because of constitutional reasons," the case argued, "need not necessarily affect the remedy by way of damages." In addition, the equal protection standard no longer applied—requiring a white owner to pay damages, as *Corell* put it, "would not constitute any act of discrimination by the state against a Negro citizen."[132]

These thin distinctions were quickly punctured by the Supreme Court. In *Barrows v. Jackson* (1953), the Court held that allowing damages was no different from judicial enforcement—that "the action of a state court at law to sanction the validity of the restrictive covenant here involved would constitute state action as surely as it was state action to enforce such covenants in equity of a restriction." *Barrows* also dispensed with the assumption that, by effectively relegating restricted classes to third-party status, the injury or the denial of equal protection somehow disappeared. Leaning on *Shelley's* admonition that the "Constitution confers upon no individual the right to demand action by the State which results in the denial of equal protection of the laws to other individuals," *Barrows* concluded bluntly that allowing damages was a poorly camouflaged gambit "to punish respondent for not continuing to discriminate against non-Caucasians."[133]

Coda

"If the Court should follow up its action of declaring all local laws to segregate Negroes unconstitutional by declaring illegal also the private restrictive covenants," Myrdal argued hopefully in 1944, "segregation in the North would be nearly doomed."[134] He was wrong. In this respect, Richardson's occupancy of 4635 North Market and the NAACP's triumph in *Shelley* were hollow victories. The covenant cases—culminating in *Barrows*—removed one mechanism of segregation, but both Myrdal and the legal strategies of the 1940s underestimated the durability of private restrictions—and the ease with which they would be adapted to other domains and emulated by other actors, and their outcomes institutionalized by public policies.[135]

As options for formal enforcement of private racial restrictions evaporated, their influence lingered. The Supreme Court decisions in *Shelley* and *Barrows* closed off judicial enforcement (in law or equity), but this was never—in practice—the primary way to make private restriction work. The threat of injunction, damages, or forfeiture served primarily to signal the seriousness of social norms. Such threats continued to serve that purpose—in part because of the segregation they had already accomplished, in part because the restrictive language remained without correction or comment—"singularly unpleasant ghosts of the past" in the words of Brooks and Rose—in the property records.[136] The legal and legislative advances that rendered private racial restrictions unenforceable and then prohibited them outright provided no mechanism for removing or redacting those that were enshrined in title abstracts, property records, and the bylaws of subdivisions or homeowners' associations. Indeed, the prevailing logic of property law—sustained by the courts and by thousands of county recorders and assessors—was that property records were assembled and maintained as a cumulative record of transactions (and any accompanying conditions or restrictions), which was indexed by grantor and grantee and which established title by documenting and resolving competing claims.[137] County recorders, in this process, were neutral archivists without the authority or inclination to remove any provision, clause, or document. Almost two decades after *Shelley*, a standard property law text (West Publishing's *Modern Legal Forms*) blithely sanctioned the use of private racial restrictions, doubling down on the Court's distinction between judicial enforcement and "voluntary adherence."[138]

In the wake of the Fair Housing Act (1968), federal housing agencies and the courts pushed to get county recorders and title companies to remove or redact racial covenants—based on the act's provision that it was now illegal to "make, print, or publish, or cause to be made, printed, or published any notice, statement, or advertisement" that discriminated against protected classes.[139] This push yielded one significant victory: *Mayers v. Ridley*, a 1972 decision by the District of Columbia Court of Appeals holding that the mere recording of a restriction constituted a fair housing violation. Racial restrictions were commonly buried in abstracts or (as in the case of petition restrictions) filed elsewhere; current deeds had simply referenced and deferred to "restrictions of record." *Mayers* addressed not only the presence of racial restrictions but their often-veiled inclusion in the record.[140]

But, in a recording system governed by 50 states and 3,141 counties (or county equivalents)[141] neither the Fair Housing Act nor *Mayers's* more restricting interpretation of "publication" made much of an impact. Only recently, as a result of innovative local documentary projects such as Mapping Prejudice (Hennepin and Ramsey Counties in Minnesota) and Segregated Seattle, as well as the new politics of racial equity that followed the police killings of Michael Brown (2014) and George Floyd (2020), have race restrictions—and their lasting implications—received renewed attention.

Since 2014, many states have revised or reaffirmed their fair housing laws, most of which echo the provisions and protections of the federal law. Some have addressed racial deed restrictions specifically, by underscoring or restating that they are void and unenforceable, by making it easier for interested parties to discharge or renounce them (or sever them from other restrictions of record), or even by requiring their removal.[142] The most common tactic (pioneered in California, Washington, and Minnesota) is a streamlined process by which owners, buyers, title companies, or attorneys can easily discharge a racial restriction—often with a common form and a minimal filing fee.[143] In California, a 2022 revision now requires all title abstracts to include both a cover page disclaiming any illegal restrictions and a copy of the state's "Restrictive Covenant Modification" form.[144] A few states (including Washington, Missouri, Kansas, and California) require homeowners' associations to revise and remove racial restrictions.[145]

The states represented in this study offer a sense of the range and concerns of current state law. In Minnesota, the Mapping Prejudice project spurred substantial legislative reforms and local action. Minnesota code reiterates the illegality and unenforceability of racial restrictions, lays out a process for discharging or releasing restrictions, and provides a standard form for doing so.[146] While the state law requires standard filing and recording fees, the Just Deeds project offers homeowners free title assistance, and some jurisdictions (including Hennepin) have waived the fees.[147] The Missouri legislature affirmed the illegality of race restrictions in 1993 and required homeowners' associations to remove them in 2005. In 2022, the state passed a basic discharge bill and provided a boilerplate form.[148] Iowa housing law reiterates basic fair housing provision, but the only mention of race-restrictive covenants is the legislative response to the 1953 Sioux City case, which added a prohibition on race restrictions to the Iowa Cemetery Act.[149]

Targeting the remnants of racial restriction in property records is a delicate task. Enabling homeowners and others to renounce or discharge such restrictions runs the risk of removing them from the historical record. In this respect, Missouri's 1993 law averring that racial restrictions "shall be void and unenforceable, and shall be ignored, *as if the same never existed*," strikes the wrong chord. Here, the protocols of property recording—in which new documents (such as discharge forms) are added to the stack, but old documents are never removed—offers some protection. In Washington in 2021, a homeowner tried to have an old racial restriction expunged entirely. Recognizing "the delicate balance required in addressing the elimination of morally repugnant covenants and the preservation of the documented history of disenfranchisement of a people," the state supreme court held (in *May v. Spokane County*) that, if and when covenants were removed from a chain of title, they needed to be maintained elsewhere in the public record.[150] This concern also shaped an affirmative response: that same year, the Washington state legislature funded teams at the University of Washington and Eastern Washington University to research the extent of racial restriction across the state's thirty-nine counties and report the results to affected property owners and county officials.[151] In 2023, the Washington legislature adopted a compensatory program, providing down payment and closing cost assistance (financed by recording fees) to low-income, first-time home buyers who were subject to such restrictions before the passage of the Fair Housing Act in 1968 (or who were descendants of those subject to restrictions).[152]

Current campaigns to document and release race-restrictive agreements or covenants underscore both their ambiguous status in property law and their tenacity in private realty and public policy. Local legal battles eventually pressed the issue of equal protection but, in getting there, also touched on the foundational dynamics and elements of racial segregation: How did private interests reconcile collective action and individual property rights? What constituted a "failure" of local restriction? How did white realty interests sustain agreement or manage defection? What did the racial categories used in restrictive agreements mean in practice? Did private restriction complement public policies or defy them? The *Shelley* decision truncated the practice of private restriction but—because the motives and assumptions of racial exclusion were not confined to property deeds or subdivision indentures—left the broader questions unanswered.

The persistence of the records, in this respect, echoes the persistence of their impact on housing opportunity and the built environment. Documenting the extent and pattern of local restriction is not an archaeological exercise, excavating curiosities—unenforceable for more than half a century—from another time. Rather, it establishes and quantifies the damage done when private restriction was routine and legal.[153] And, as we turn to in the next chapter, it reveals the foundation for a tangle of durable racial and spatial inequalities that have long outlasted the enforceability or legality of private racial restriction in the courts.

CHAPTER 6

Long Shadow: The Durable Inequalities of Private Restriction

FOR THE FIRST half of the twentieth century, private racial restrictions systematically excluded African Americans from many developments and neighborhoods and exploited them—through predatory rents and lending terms on often substandard housing stock—in those areas left unrestricted. Such restrictions were rendered unenforceable by *Shelley* in 1948 and, after a flurry of interest in evading the "state action" logic of the Court's decision, the practice quickly faded. A few developers (in settings like St. Louis and Hennepin Counties) continued to include racial restrictions in new subdivision indentures, but this seems to have been more of an inertial business practice than anything else. In 1968, *Jones v. Mayer* extended the principle of equal protection to private real estate transactions, and on the heels of that decision, the Fair Housing Act prohibited racial restriction outright.

But while *Shelley* closed off one important mechanism of racial segregation, it could do little to challenge either the scale of segregation that had already been accomplished by private restriction or the assumptions—about property values, about neighborhoods, and about the people that lived in those neighborhoods—that accompanied, justified, and sustained that segregation. The consequences of private restriction, as a result, proved intractable and persistent. Rates of racial (black-white) residential segregation in most metropolitan settings reached their highest measured levels at the 1970 or 1980 census, but dipped only slightly across the next half century, particularly in the Midwest.[1] Job and capital mobility hardened the concentration of poverty and disadvantage.[2] Segregation shaped not just residential options and opportunities but all the advantages or disadvantages that accompany spatial concentrations of wealth or poverty.[3] Pervasive neighborhood effects exaggerated local risks and undermined the policies and institutions that might mitigate them—affecting the health, safety, cognitive development, and civic engagement of neighborhood residents.[4] In struggling neighborhoods, predatory finance and declining property values eroded (or destroyed) any financial returns to homeownership.[5] These cumulative and compound disadvantages curtailed social mobility, sustaining neighborhoods that effectively penalized and imprisoned the people who lived in them.[6]

How and why did such inequalities endure and even flourish in the face of legal and political challenges? Charles Tilly's framework for understanding durable inequality posits two sources of original inequality (exclusion and exploitation) and two sources for its durability (emulation and adaptation).[7] This is a structural and stylized account, focused on the creation and persistence of inequality in organizational settings. It is not well-equipped, without specification or modification, to capture the unique constellation of intentional, ecological, and cultural mechanisms that have sustained racial inequality in the United States.[8] Drawing on Tilly, as well as Anderson's adaptation of his framework to the case of racial segregation, I trace six mechanisms that carried forward the intent and impact of private restriction and allowed the practice to cast such a long shadow.[9] My interest here lies less in distributional outcomes than in the processes that allowed discriminatory intent to migrate from one set of social, political, and legal circumstances to the next.[10] I begin with a brief sketch of these mechanisms; the bulk of the chapter traces how these played out in private realty and public policy.

First, following Tilly, root inequalities are sustained through *emulation*, the replication or transplantation of practices and assumptions from one domain or arena to another.[11] The spread of racial restriction in the first half of the twentieth century, in this respect, was itself a pattern of emulation—from single sales (parcels) to larger-scale subdivision and petition restrictions, from one development (or developer) to the next in suburban settings. And, as we have seen, the core assumptions of private restriction were emulated by other actors—homeowners, private appraisers, and local planners—in ways that not only reinforced and sanctioned them but ensured that they would last.

In practice, emulation was often shaped by private (market) or political power—by the willingness and capacity of some actors to drive the expansion of exclusionary practices or policies. This can be understood (following Anderson) as *leverage*, or the ability to use dominance in one set of relations to exert it in another. Leading developers used their prominence in professional networks like the NAREB to promote and disseminate restriction, and they harnessed their privileged position in local growth politics to ensure local planners fell in line.[12] New actors did not just replicate established categories and categorical assumptions; they embraced and embedded them as organizational conventions and social norms.[13] Conversely, just as political or economic circumstances afforded some actors leverage, they also marginalized others—making it more difficult or more costly for them to combat the original inequality.[14]

Disparities in political power, in turn, were both a cause and consequence of the *institutionalization* of categorical inequalities. Institutionalization is itself a particular form of emulation or leverage, in which original inequalities are sanctioned and solidified by public authority.[15] Across jurisdictions, policymakers routinely deferred to the architects of private restriction and dismissed the lonely advocates of equal protection. As a result, they embedded private restriction and its assumptions in local, state, and federal policies—both reinforcing private restriction in its heyday and extending its impact forward in time. This deference, as I trace later in this chapter, was most evident in local zoning and in federal housing policies—each of which, in their own ways, embraced the premises of private restriction. Once cemented into policy and policy design, these premises magnified the benefits of sustaining segregation, while raising the costs of challenging it.[16]

Inequalities are often sustained by *adaptation*: by the tendency of all involved—including those exploited or excluded—to accept categorical relations as given or inescapable, and to navigate them by doing what is necessary to live under their circumstances.[17] The African American residents of St. Louis, Minneapolis, and Waterloo fully understood the injustice of segregation and exclusion—and they fought back whenever the opportunity presented itself.[18] But they also adapted to or *accommodated* segregation, investing in parallel local institutions when access to broader public and private goods was denied or constrained.[19] More broadly, the characterization of neighborhoods (and neighbors) at the root of private restriction became widely accepted as spatial markers of security, opportunity, and risk.[20]

Adaptation also captures the ways in which the original terms of exclusion could be *adjusted* to allow the privileged to sustain their advantages.[21] This was a dismal undercurrent of the Great Migrations: as African Americans moved north for better employment and housing opportunities, the white reaction often moved that opportunity elsewhere.[22] In northern cities, racial exclusion migrated from the central city–suburb divide created in the first wave of white flight, to one separating cities and their inner (or second hand) suburbs at one end, and gated exurban bastions at the other.[23] Increasingly, this divide was both racial and economic—marked by increased economic segregation and large swaths of suburban poverty.[24] And, as the suburbs became poorer and more diverse, affluent whites shifted the categorical goalposts again, rediscovering, recasting, and gentrifying urban pockets they had long disdained as irretrievably blighted.[25]

The durability of the spatial and racial inequalities generated by private restriction also rested on the *inertia* of the original exclusion. Private restriction was no mere contractual commitment, the impact of which evaporated once declared unenforceable by the courts. Exclusion and exploitation in housing markets, as Melvin Oliver and Thomas Shapiro argue, widened the racial wealth gap and created a "sedimentary" inequality that was both profound and generational.[26] Distributional outcomes observable at a given point in time—including the wealth gap, as well as concentrated neighborhood poverty—were also *processes*.[27] They shaped racial segregation and housing opportunity by setting an original condition of exclusion or disadvantage. But that original condition entailed significant investments—and disinvestments—that compounded over time and across generations. Even as (or if) the elements of the original disadvantage were addressed—as the half century since the Fair Housing Act underscores—its momentum propelled that disadvantage forward.[28]

Private restriction was also a brick-and-mortar form of discrimination: it inscribed segregation in urban space. In this respect, *Shelley* slowed construction but did nothing to disassemble what had been built. "The constellations of land uses we confront today are the consequences of countless decisions made decades (even generations) ago," as Eduardo Peñalver underscores,

Figure 6.1 Mechanisms of Durable Inequality

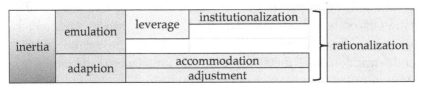

Source: Author's compilation.

"and the decisions we make today will reverberate through the same mechanisms into the future."[29] The physical remnants of such decisions—the width and orientation of streets; the location of schools, transit stops, or highway interchanges; the spatial pattern of new development or of land clearance and redevelopment—serve as a reminder of past patterns of segregations and at the same time ensure their persistence.[30]

Finally, each of these mechanisms depended on a set of assumptions, prejudices, and stereotypes that made the original exclusion seem just and prudent.[31] As people make sense of the world and their place in it, cognitive and cultural processes justify, legitimize, normalize, and naturalize background inequalities.[32] This process of *rationalization* willfully confuses cause and effect, attributing the consequences of exclusion and exploitation—crowding, concentrated poverty, declining property values, and the like—to the behavior of those excluded or exploited.[33] Neighborhood perceptions rest heavily on racial stereotypes and associations, so that areas with significant black populations are routinely interpreted as poorer and riskier—regardless of actual incomes or crime rates.[34] Such "narratives and causal attributions," as Lauren Valentino and Stephen Vaisey underscore, "are important pathways by which inequality becomes ossified, and in fact, these justifications may be increasingly salient as inequality worsens because it comes to be seen as normal."[35] These narratives and causal attributions framed original inequalities with powerful assumptions about who was deserving and who was not.[36] In this respect, perhaps the signature "neighborhood effect" of suburban white affluence was the conviction that any accompanying advantages were fairly earned.[37]

These mechanisms—emulation, leverage, institutionalization, adaptation (accommodation and adjustment), inertia, and rationalization—overlapped, infused, and reinforced one another (see figure 6.1). The broad category of emulation encompassed both leverage (affirmed by actors in positions of power) and institutionalization (affirmed specifically by state power); adaptation encompassed accommodation by those targeted by unequal relations, as well as adjustments by those benefiting from them. Emulation and adaptation, in all their variations, were simultaneous and intertwined processes. Given the material and physical investments in residential housing, each of these variations carried with it an inertial resistance to change or reversal. As original inequalities were entrenched and institutionalized, adaption became more urgent and any challenge more costly. And these sources of durability shared a common language and logic, a set of assumptions or rationalizations that both bound them together and propelled them forward.

Taken together, these mechanisms ensured that early private innovations in exclusion would continue to shape housing outcomes and opportunities well after their fate was decided in the courts. *Shelley* shifted the means but not the ends of racial segregation. The resulting economic disparities and opportunity gaps were willfully employed to confirm the wisdom or logic of exclusion.[38] "These are the practices which during the past decade have come to be regarded as expedient and profitable," as the head of the Minneapolis Urban League argued in late 1944. "These are also the practices which if endured for another decade will reap for Minneapolis a sorry harvest."[39]

Private Restrictions and Private Realty

Racial property restrictions must be situated in the history of capitalism, as the product of markets and market actors.[40] The language and logic of restriction, including the conviction that African American occupancy destroyed property values, was invented and elaborated by white developers, real estate agents, and homeowners in response to the First Great Migration. Local and national realty interests did not simply respond to white interest in segregation, they cultivated it and made it an article of professional faith and ethics.[41] The growing scale of subdivision development, the emergence of trade associations like the NAREB, and the professionalization of urban planning and property appraisal all contributed to the emergence of metropolitan "growth machines" focused—above all else—on attracting and sustaining enough private investment to boost property values and property tax revenues.[42] Local homeowners, whose assessed values determined the quality of local public goods (especially schools), were likewise fixated on sustaining property value—and warding off threats.

Private restriction infused the practice of private realty in ways that buttressed the practice before 1948 and ensured its impact long after. Private real estate agents were the most important enforcers of private restriction, and the task of assembling and promoting restrictive agreements was a key organizational impetus for the professionalization of realty.[43] Local realty boards were largely responsible for the profusion of neighborhood agreements, which were often (as in St. Louis) reinforced through professional codes and state licensing. "The restriction against selling property in this block to Colored expired in September," as one St. Louis real estate agent advised a seller, "but the agent who has your property in charge being a member of the Real Estate Exchange will not sell to Colored."[44]

Restricted subdivisions, in turn, relied heavily on the ability and willingness of real estate agents to steer clients to "race appropriate" developments— a well-documented practice uninterrupted by *Shelley*.[45] St. Louis real estate agents responded to the Court's decision by continuing to enforce existing agreements and restrictions and doubling down on the exchange's long-standing rule "that no Realtor may sell to Negroes, or finance any transaction involving the purchase by a Negro . . . outside of the established unrestricted districts."[46] Housing rights advocates documented systematic steering in greater St. Louis into the 1960s and 1970s.[47] Black homeowners displaced by highway construction in the 1960s in Minneapolis–St. Paul reported both the refusal of real estate agents to offer relocation options outside established black neighborhoods, and their own reluctance to cross the boundaries established by private restriction.[48]

At the same time, of course, real estate agents were instrumental in flipping neighborhoods from white to black. Blockbusting created or exploited the "changed conditions" that undermined the legal status of restrictive agreements and encouraged the defection of white homeowners.[49] In St. Louis, given the iron hand of the Real East Exchange, it was mostly black real estate agents who initially challenged north-side covenants. The *Shelley* decision, in St. Louis and elsewhere, changed the calculus and encouraged white real estate agents to flip blocks they had long "protected."[50] For its part, the NAACP pragmatically and briefly accepted the practice—or at least recognized its utility in breaking down restrictions and opening neighborhoods to African American occupancy.[51] More broadly, the willingness of white realty interests to "protect" neighborhoods from racial transition and then (after 1948) hasten that transition and reap the gains confirms the assessment (underscored by Weaver and others at the time) that private restrictions curtailed African American housing opportunities when they succeeded and continued to do so when they failed.[52]

The premises behind private restriction were also baked into the practice of private appraisal. Restrictive practices sought "to stabilize land values, it may be, to enhance land values," as Monchow emphasized in 1928, adding that such "results are obtained through a form of restraint which establishes the character of a given area."[53] Real estate agents, lenders, and insurers embraced the assumption that black occupancy threatened property values and dutifully incorporated "negro encroachment" and "presence of deed restrictions" into their assessment and valuation of property. Restrictions were a key metric in private appraisal, inflating values in "protected" neighborhoods and discounting them where restrictions were absent or soon to expire—in turn sustaining the conviction that African American occupancy (or even proximity) threatened property values. Over time, as Clarissa Hayward suggests, the narratives constructed by real estate agents, developers, and other local interests "linked the physical deterioration of the central city, not to the age of its housing stock, or to overcrowding, or to dearth of resources for renovation or repair, but rather to the race of its new inhabitants."[54] The standard appraisal form used in St. Louis into the 1950s included fields for "racial influence," "% negro population," "nearby adverse influence," and "encroachments"—the latter commonly listing "colored people" or the distance to the nearest "negro colony." The form also specified any constraints or regulations affecting land use, noting approvingly both single-family residential zoning and the presence of deed restrictions.[55]

Property appraisal was—and remains—firmly rooted in a hierarchy of racial valuation developed during the era of private restriction. Early social surveys of urban neighborhoods, the emerging discipline of land economics, and professional realty all reinforced the view that segregation was both natural and an essential guarantor of white property investments.[56] Segregation, as well as segregated property values, was sustained by the widespread adoption of "sales-comparison"—a value deduced from recent transactions and buyer and neighborhood characteristics—as the "scientific" standard for appraisal. In turn, the classification, description, and mapping of neighborhood characteristics—which began as computational shortcut—was embraced as a predictive model of neighborhood risk and value.[57] In this process, as Frederick Babcock (who would go on to direct the underwriting division at the FHA) argued in his 1924 treatise *The Appraisal of Real Estate*, "attention is directed upon the home as an entity and its desirability as a home, its newness, its prettiness, the neighbors, [and] the district." Of course, "any menace or improvement affects value, but in general the neighborhood elements are considered as having been reflected in the prices of properties recently solid in the district." The result was a process that accepted as given the racial logics of property value: that appraisal should "correspond to the market in which the property would be sold."[58]

These appraisal standards persisted, largely unquestioned, as the core conventions of private realty, private credit, and public policy. Surveying the sorry catalog of professional and academic appraisal literature in 1955, Charles Abrams marveled at the uniform willingness of "FHA zone managers, presidents of real estate boards, officials of the HOLC, and college instructors" to "parrot the theories and often the same dogma on the need for racial and social homogeneity if value is to be maintained."[59] Indeed, the FHA, for its part, embraced the sales-comparison method—uncritically sustaining and recycling housing values that were first established under starkly and explicitly discriminatory terms.[60] Appraisers and real estate agents conjured value from a tangle of assumptions about demand, appreciation, and the self-fulfilling risk of investment in African American neighborhoods.[61] By the second half of the twentieth century, as Paige Glotzer concludes, "a commercial logic binding real estate's profitability to racial segregation" was firmly established and standardized.[62] And it remains so. By one 2022 estimate—focusing on metros with a population of 500,000 or more and controlling for both housing characteristics and the quality of local public and private goods—location in a white neighborhood more than doubled the appraised value of comparable homes.[63] In the third decade of the twenty-first century, residential home appraisals are still too often determined by the race of those who populate the photographs on the mantel.

Adding insult to injury, private appraisals based on place and race in the twentieth century were reflected in the provision of a wide array of public and private goods. The same assumptions that dampened the value of houses in African American neighborhoods also raised the costs of financing or insuring them.[64] Risk-rating in private insurance, deeply rooted in early twentieth-century eugenics and calibrated to placed-based actuarial assumptions, raised the costs of basic economic security.[65] The tyranny of the zip code that devalued investment in African American neighborhoods—marked by scarcity of public and private goods and predatory forms of retail and credit—also raised the relative costs of living in them.[66]

Local Zoning

Land-use zoning was closely entangled with the history of private restriction. Private restriction filled the breach left by the *Buchanan* decision in 1917, which prohibited racial zoning; ran alongside early local zoning efforts that followed *Euclid* in 1926; and was subsumed by the flurry of municipalization and local zoning that followed *Shelley* in 1948. Across this era, private restriction not only stood in for formal zoning when the latter's legal status was uncertain, but also fundamentally shaped and legitimized principles and practices of land-use regulation—including constraints on use, the definition and regulation of "nuisances," and the discretionary use of such regulations to protect some neighborhoods and neglect or displace others.[67]

Early land-use zoning in the United States was unequivocally and unapologetically a handmaiden to racial segregation, crafted and pursued, under the guise of the "general welfare," to protect some urban and suburban neighborhoods from the encroachment of "nuisances" or "inharmonious use."[68] The first municipal zoning ordinances were, with few exceptions, explicitly racial—their sole concern the formalization and enforcement of racial boundaries threatened by rapid demographic change and the inability of conventional methods (that is, social norms and violence) to contain it.[69] Beginning with Baltimore, twenty-one cities (including St. Louis) adopted racial zoning ordinances between 1910 and 1917.[70] *Buchanan* prohibited the practice in 1917, but it did so on narrow "property rights" grounds—inviting local officials to float variations on zoning-based segregation (almost all of which would be struck down by local or state courts) and to experiment with broader comprehensive zoning as an alternative.[71]

The segregationist impulse was central to the invention and articulation of modern zoning. *Buchanan* prohibited comprehensive zoning from adopting explicitly racial criteria, but zoning had already easily and routinely relied on thinly veiled racial surrogates such as density, inharmonious use, property value, and tax capacity.[72] The result, as Christopher Silver and others have suggested, was a "racially informed" planning process that utilized land-use zoning, public housing placement, and comprehensive planning toward the same ends.[73] At the core of the new zoning regime was the goal of "protecting" certain neighborhoods—specifically high-end homes in central cities, white working-class neighborhoods facing racial transition, and restricted developments spilling out into the suburbs.[74] The "general welfare," in this respect (especially after *Euclid*) was reliably confined to, and defined by, white neighborhoods. As early as 1918, the developer Frederick Law Olmsted Jr. (son of the famous urban planner, and eldest of the Olmstead Brothers) justified and promoted single-family residential zones as "more or less coincident with racial divisions."[75] St. Louis City engineer Harland Bartholomew advocated zoning as a means of protecting property values in established urban neighborhoods, stemming encroachment, and checking the flight of "our people" to the suburbs.[76]

Comprehensive zoning's embrace of spatial hierarchy and spatial separation echoed and extended the "separate but equal" logic of racial zoning.[77] It did so primarily through two mechanisms—both of which emulated, supported, and sustained the premises of private restriction. First, zoning set standards for residential density. While routinely defended as a "general welfare" protection of residential areas from overcrowding, zone plans reliably downzoned white neighborhoods and upzoned black neighborhoods. Downzoning meant not just protecting existing patterns of low-density single-family development, but often setting lot, building, and use standards that were more exclusive than current footprints. By the same token, upzoning was employed to increase density in African American neighborhoods and stem their expansion.[78] Second, zoning sought to reshape cities and push out African American residents by inviting commercial or industrial use in and around African American neighborhoods. Such "expulsive zoning," anticipating the era of urban renewal, defined both mixed-use neighborhoods and African American occupancy as variants of "blight" to be remedied or removed.[79]

Across this early history, the practice and assumptions of zoning dovetailed with those of private racial restriction. Some developers argued that zoning and private restriction served similar ends by complementary means and that the latter should be "carefully coordinated with municipal zoning regulations."[80] Zoning, in this view, might set broad controls over land use and planning, while private restrictions filled in the details or invited greater exclusivity on the floor set by public policy.[81] Others viewed zoning as a logical and necessary successor to the "dress rehearsal" of private restriction, arguing that it was more permanent and less capricious than private contracts, it could accomplish restrictions on land use at a more efficient and effective scale, and its rules were easier to enforce.[82] "The administrative aspects of zoning on the whole possess more advantages than those incident to restrictions in deeds," as one observer noted in 1928, "namely, protection for the community as a whole, systematic control, greater flexibility, and official as against individual enforcement."[83] Realty interests could be found in both camps. Elite champions of restriction (including Olmsted, Nichols, and Edward Bouton of Baltimore's Roland Park) led the charge for comprehensive zoning.[84] Others preferred private contracts to the heavy hand of the local state and dug in against zoning ordinances that imposed any constraints on land use *other than those on racial occupancy*—an exception they viewed as necessary and prudent.[85] In any case, private agreements served as a template for public zoning and, over time, encouraged property owners to accept constraints on private property rights.[86]

St. Louis, Minneapolis, and Waterloo all pursued comprehensive zoning during the era of private restriction. In St. Louis, the 1916 racial zoning ordinance was a response to the expansion of African American occupancy beyond the borders of the Ville—and, as we have seen, it was accompanied and succeeded by a flurry of private restriction. The conventional zone plans of 1918 and 1925 quite candidly use private streets and subdivision-based racial restrictions to set the boundaries of the most exclusive "first residence" districts. "In practically all cases," as Bartholomew conceded, "the first residence districts are areas that have restriction in the deeds," adding that exclusive zoning was intended as insurance "against the day when private restrictions expire."[87] This was the general pattern on the south side, where "first residence" districts closely tracked the geography of racial restriction.[88] On the north side, the logic of emulation was quite different: restrictions north of Delmar were less sources of protection or exclusion than they were markers of threat and racial transition. Throughout the 1920s and 1930s, city planners increased density by systematically under zoning some north-side neighborhoods and inviting industrial and commercial redevelopment in others they deemed blighted.[89] In Minneapolis, similar activities prevailed—albeit in the absence of well-established African American neighborhoods. Local planners identified "invasion of the residential areas" by multiple dwellings between 1918 and 1924 as the "predominating impetus" behind the city's 1924 zone plan.[90]

Most central cities had already been substantially developed before the adoption of zoning. Early ordinances were often animated by the desire (but not the means) to sort out the chaos of unplanned development. In the suburbs, by contrast, zoning was seen as a means of cementing the exclusive uniformity of private residential subdivision. Here too, the pace and timing of development often ceded land-use decisions to private developers. In St. Louis County (maps 3.1–3.4), much of the race-restricted development (especially in the central and north areas of the county) was in unincorporated areas. The absence of building or zoning codes gave private developers wide license to plan for exclusion.[91] "It is the Realtor subdivider who is really planning our cities today," as one planner noted in 1925, "who is the actual city planner in practice."[92] Private development, in this respect, invited developers to experiment with strategies of exclusion—including both racial restriction and the building and use regulations that would succeed it. "Where a very substantial area has been set aside for a high type through the medium of deed restrictions," as one observer noted in 1928, "officials ordinarily recognize the character of the development and classify that section accordingly, so that the objectives of statutory and deed restrictions are the same. . . . The zoning ordinance is not intended to abrogate or supplant restrictions privately imposed, except that where the legislation lays down the more restrictive requirements, those regulations shall control."[93]

The congruence of private restriction and public zoning was evident in the postwar housing boom, before and after *Shelley* rendered the former unenforceable. Municipalities, especially in the suburbs, increasingly used large-lot single-family zones and prohibitions on multifamily housing as economic surrogates for racial exclusion. While less direct than the blunt "Caucasians only" terms of private restriction, size and use thresholds effectively leveraged the penalty of private restriction and private discrimination to accomplish the same ends.[94] In the bargain, race-blind zoning provisions effectively camouflaged racial restriction with a rhetoric of harmonious neighborhoods, property values, and good schools—inviting those who benefited to deny any advantage or responsibility.[95]

In Minneapolis, postwar planning replicated the exclusion of the city's suburbs by reorganizing "shoestring" commercial development into compact shopping malls, closing a loophole that allowed some duplexes in single-family zones, and inviting neighborhoods to further restrict use or raise lot thresholds. The 1947 rezoning plan argued that "the general boundaries of original residential areas be not encroached upon for any less restricted use and that these areas, community by community, be allowed insofar as is practicable, self determination as to the intensity or density of residential use."[96]

In greater St. Louis, local elected officials and planners quite candidly viewed the strategy of patchwork municipal incorporation and exclusive large-lot single-family zoning as the logical successor to private restrictions.[97] The first five years after the war (maps 3.3–3.4) saw a flurry of new incorporations, annexations, and local zoning. Increasingly, subdivision developers adopted leaner indentures and deferred instead to local zoning. The 1946 restrictions on Fourland Place, for example, simply held that "no building or premises shall be used for purposes prohibited by law or ordinance."[98] The 1948 indenture for Bayless Place included the usual restrictions on non-residential use but allowed that "if a commercial building or a commercial building with dwelling shall be erected with the approval of St. Louis County or other authority having jurisdiction and regulation of building permits than this restriction shall not apply."[99] The plat for Regina Gardens (1949) simply struck through the reference to private restrictions and deferred to local zoning: "All lots in this subdivision ~~shall be subject to further conditions and restrictions affecting same as set forth in an instrument filed simultaneously with this plat, in the office of the Recorder of St. Louis County, Missouri~~ shall be subject to any such conditions and restrictions as may be imposed by the Council of the City of Florissant, Missouri."[100]

After 1948, local zoning became the most common mechanism of exclusion and segregation. Explicit racial zoning was prohibited (by both *Buchanan* and the "state action" logic of *Shelley*), and municipal zoning regulated land use but not (as had private covenants) occupancy or alienation.[101] Under zoning, exclusion was accomplished through density controls and prohibited uses.[102] Unsurprisingly, the footprint of private race restriction in St. Louis, Minneapolis, and Waterloo was echoed and succeeded by large-lot single-family zoning (maps 6.1, 6.2, and 6.3). More broadly, the "general welfare" premise of local zoning was rendered ludicrous by zone plans increasingly designed to hoard housing opportunity and property tax revenues.[103]

Map 6.1 Private Restriction and Single-Family Zoning, St. Louis, circa 1968

▓	Restricted by subdivision
■	Restricted by petition
☐	Zoned for single-family housing

Source: Gordon 2008; Gordon 2023e.

Map 6.2 Private Restriction and Single-Family Zoning, Hennepin County, circa 1973

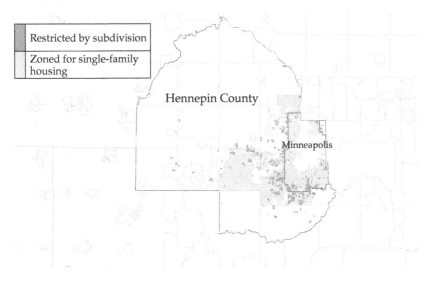

▓	Restricted by subdivision
☐	Zoned for single-family housing

Hennepin County

Minneapolis

Source: Zone maps for Minneapolis (1940), Brooklyn Center (1959), Edina (1973), Minnetonka (1963), Richfield (1973), and St. Louis Park (1973) from John R. Borchert Map Library, n.d.; Ehrman-Solberg et al. 2020.

Map 6.3 Private Restriction and Single-Family Zoning, Waterloo, 1948

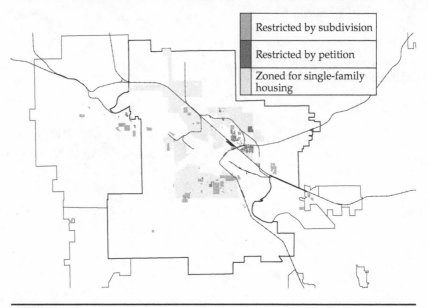

▨	Restricted by subdivision
▨	Restricted by petition
▨	Zoned for single-family housing

Source: Waterloo zone map (1948) from Iowa Digital Library, n.d.; Gordon 2023c.

Between 1950 and 2020, while median family size shrank, the average size of a new single-family home nearly tripled, from 841 to 2,473 square feet.[104] "The preservation of expensive homes . . .," as one critic noted in 1953, "apparently becomes a proper function if suitably dressed up as a zoning ordinance."[105]

Local zoning fragmented the idea of the general welfare, inviting suburban municipalities to pursue local gains at the expense of neighboring municipalities, central cities, and the larger metropolitan region.[106] The spread—and exclusivity—of local zoning was enabled by the *Euclid* decision in 1926, but it was animated largely by demographic change and the threat posed by African America occupancy. Cities at the receiving end of the Great Migrations adopted zoning earlier, and their land-use plans were more restrictive, featuring both larger lot sizes and tighter prohibitions against multifamily units.[107] Between 1940 and 1955, the share of jurisdictions imposing minimum lot sizes nearly tripled (from under 20 percent to almost 60 percent), and the share imposing minimums greater than 10,000 square feet grew from 15 to 40 percent.[108]

Locking It Down: Federal Housing and Mortgage Policies

The most important emulation and institutionalization of private restriction came in the form of federal housing policy—from the onset of the New Deal, through the *Shelley* decision, and for decades after. Public housing, federal mortgage and insurance programs, and federal subsidies for urban renewal and redevelopment all leaned heavily on the premises of private restriction, and all accepted—without significant dissent—the landscape of stark racial segregation and yawning spatial inequalities that private restriction had crafted. Federal policies, for reasons endemic to policy design under democratic capitalism and particular to housing policy, systematically deferred to local and private interests. In some respects, federal policies simply amplified well-established private strategies of exclusion and segregation with state power and state resources. This institutionalized and legitimized private practices, locked down the segregation and inequality they had already accomplished, and enabled their persistence at an unprecedented scale.[109]

The motives and consequences of federal redlining reflect the mechanisms that connected federal policies to both the patterns of private restriction that preceded redlining and the persistent patterns of spatial and racial inequality going forward.[110] The sin of such policies—captured in primary colors by the HOLC's infamous "residential security" maps and sustained by the FHA well into the 1960s—was not that they "segregated America" but that they failed to challenge, and even invested in, *existing* patterns and practices of segregation. This raises three important and intertwined questions: What was the relationship, over time and across metropolitan settings, between private restriction and public policy? What was the relative impact of private restriction and the policies that followed? And how do we account for, or explain, public deference to private exploitation and discrimination?

Across its formative years—from the tentative initiatives of the Hoover administration in 1930 and 1931 through the Housing Act of 1949—federal housing policy systematically deferred to private interests, their prejudices, and their assumptions about real estate markets. Local politicians, their regulatory and taxing powers constrained by the "home rule" provisions of state law, viewed economic growth and property valuation (often in competition with other jurisdictions) as essential to local public policy. Federal housing agencies, hurriedly cobbled together during the Great Depression, leaned heavily on local realty interests to set the spatial criteria for mortgage insurance, public housing, and urban renewal. This effectively layered the local clout of private realty on top of its national political influence—through which the housing lobby ensured Congress would bail out struggling lenders and stimulate (through demand-side and supply-side policies) private residential construction.[111] New Deal housing policies, in this respect, were no different from those of subsequent housing crises in their willingness to secure private rewards while socializing their risks. This market deference was both instrumental and structural: It featured close reliance on realty interests in local settings and a revolving door between federal agencies and well-heeled private realty interests and their organizations. And it reflected a fundamental agreement on goals and priorities, a shared conviction that homeownership and private housing starts were the key to economic security and recovery, and a near-complete concession to private sector experience and expertise.[112]

The result was a tangle of federal policies that emulated, embedded, embraced, and exaggerated the core assumptions and practices of private housing markets. This was unconscionable—we can and should expect more of public actors—but it was also unsurprising. American social policies have always been marked by a thin commitment to decommodification, generally assuming that markets bear the first and primary responsibility for social organization and distribution, that market outcomes are natural and just, and that state intervention should be reserved for exceptional instances of market failure.[113] Market deference is underscored not just by the prevalence of direct subsidies to private interests but by policy designs (such as that of the home mortgage interest deduction) that disguise the fact of public assistance.[114] And public policies, most notoriously in the Housing Act of 1949, were routinely calibrated so as not to "compete with" or displace private investment. Large-scale public housing was primarily built to bolster market goals elsewhere (warehousing those displaced by urban renewal) and dismantled when that task was accomplished.[115]

Deference to private interests, as well as emulation of their preoccupation with race and local housing markets, was evident in the short history of the HOLC, established in 1933 to address the Depression-era foreclosure crisis. The HOLC's color-coded residential security maps are now infamous and often misinterpreted as the root cause of contemporary inequalities— a conclusion belied (as I explore later in this chapter) by the timing and dissemination of the maps and by the HOLC's actual lending patterns. At the same time, the primary documentation of the HOLC (including both the maps and the accompanying narrative descriptions) is extraordinarily rich, evocative of the deference of federal housing policy to private realty interests, and suggestive of the logic and assumptions of other local, state, and federal housing policies.

The HOLC was charged with relieving both lenders and homeowners by refinancing defaulting or foreclosed properties. The federally backed loans, in turn, were amortized over long terms at low rates, kick-starting the transition from short-term private mortgages (usually with large down payments and variable rates) to the modern conventions of home finance. The HOLC refinanced just over a million home loans between 1933 and 1936, then closed its books. After 1936, the HOLC's parent organization, the Federal Home Loan Bank Board (FHLBB) turned its attention to servicing HOLC loans and establishing more robust appraisal standards for ongoing or future federal housing programs. Toward this end, the FHLBB launched an ambitious project to appraise residential properties and neighborhoods in over two hundred cities, yielding the residential security maps prepared by HOLC field agents in close cooperation with local realty interests.[116] These maps divided cities into a tier of graded and colored zones (from A or green for most "desirable," to D or red for "hazardous") and were meant to represent, as HOLC leadership saw it, "a composite opinion of competent Realtors engaged in residential brokerage, good mortgage lenders and the HOLC appraisal staff" or simply "the consensus of opinion of four or five of the best real estate men available."[117]

The HOLC approach to risk-rating was bluntly racial. Not all redlined neighborhoods were assessed on racial grounds but, across the project, African American occupancy virtually guaranteed a red or yellow rating.[118] And while other factors—including age of housing, mixed-use zoning ordinances, and trends in home value—were often cited in the area descriptions, these were closely entangled with patterns of racial occupancy.[119] Private restriction, as we have seen, prized new construction and homogeneity of neighborhood—and relegated African Americans to residential areas marked by aging housing stock or proximity to industrial and commercial use. Low or declining values were a threat when they went "so low as to attract an undesirable element."[120] The same assumptions that deemed such areas hazardous also marked them off as the default housing option for African American migrants.[121] The HOLC, in this respect, dutifully red-lined areas of both current and future African American occupancy.

HOLC ratings also reflected the presence or absence, as well as the effi-cacy, of private racial restrictions.[122] Instructions for preparing the area description sheets that accompanied each rating asked appraisers to take note of the "absence of zoning or restrictions for [the] protection of the neighborhood."[123] The explanatory preamble to the 1940 area descriptions cites "restrictions set up to protect the neighborhood" as one of the key cri-teria used in the ratings and points to "expiring restrictions or lack of restric-tions" as an important factor driving C ratings. ("D areas," it continued, "represent those neighborhoods in which the unfavorable factors . . . have already done their work.")[124] The HOLC routinely gave its highest ratings to suburban neighborhoods well protected by restrictions, although its A and B area appraisals generally referred to neighborhood characteristics (such as "high-class area," "stability of the community," and "uniformity") rather than the restrictive agreements that yielded them.

In greater St. Louis, the relationship between private restriction and HOLC ratings reflected the two spatial logics of restriction: subdivisions on the south side of the city and in St. Louis County and petitions on the north side surrounding the Ville. On the south side and in the county, HOLC ratings corresponded closely with the geography of restriction. In 1937, HOLC A grades almost perfectly replicated the footprint of restricted subdivisions, especially in and around St. Louis Hills.[125] Where the HOLC granted an A rating in areas without formal restrictions (such as the neigh-borhoods immediately north of Forest Park), it leaned on either the exclu-siveness of the neighborhood or the presence of racial restrictions nearby. This pattern held in the 1940 revision to the ratings for St. Louis, although in many neighborhoods the HOLC downgraded the 1937 A areas to B and the adjoining 1937 B areas to C. Indeed, in the 1940 ratings a distinct pessimism regarding the long-term prospects for restriction and exclusion drove ratings down. "Zoning and restrictions still apply," as the HOLC said of one 1937 A neighborhood south of Forest Park that it had demoted to B three years later. "But transition evident in neighboring areas is taking effect," it noted, citing a "gradual shifting of population in this neighbor-hood, [with] the original owners moving westward and out of the city."[126]

Across the assessed portion of St. Louis County, the same logic prevailed. Scattered "negro colonies" were sufficient to warrant a C rating, while more established pockets of African American occupancy, like Kinloch and Meacham Park, were unequivocally stamped D. In one area near Clayton with a small pocket of African American occupancy, the HOLC counseled that there was "no likelihood of any increase or expansion of this negro section." It concluded bluntly that "although in the area are some good homes, occupied by substantial white people, location therein of a negro element . . . gives this area a fourth grade."[127]

On the city's north side, the HOLC appraised racial restrictions quite differently. In their area descriptions, the HOLC cited the same exact elements that animated the area's patchwork of petition restrictions: mixed occupancy and racial transition at the borders of the Ville. In 1937, the Ville itself received a D grade, the bordering neighborhoods were ranked C, and the neighborhoods north of St. Louis Avenue and west of Kingshighway were graded B. In 1940, virtually all of the B districts north of Delmar were downgraded to C. The HOLC often attributed these ratings to a combination of housing quality and black encroachment: "There is not much hope for betterment," it concluded for a district near Grand and Cass, "as this district is flanked on all sides by Negro, slum and blighted communities."[128] Black occupancy alone was enough to earn a D rating: "Large brick and better appearing homes are found along Enright and Taylor to Sarah Ave.," noted the surveyors of one D district, "but occupied by colored people."[129] In a few cases, HOLC ratings directly acknowledged the tension over neighborhood boundaries: "The population is very stable," as appraisers noted of a C district just northeast of the Ville. "Area's occupants are determined to keep the Negro element (D-4) (now bordering on the south boundary of area) from spreading and infiltrating into this district. (Court action now pending to seeking to enjoin further encroachment of colored)."[130]

This logic—by which subdivision restrictions protected neighborhoods in south St. Louis and in St. Louis County, while petition restrictions marked uncertainty and transition in north St. Louis—is also captured in the count of restricted parcels by HOLC grade. Of the parcels restricted by subdivision (table 6.1), fully 92.3 percent were graded A or B by the HOLC in 1937. For the parcels restricted by petition, that share falls to 42.1 percent. The relationship between anxieties over racial transition and plummeting appraisals is underscored by HOLC scoring of those parcels on which original petition restrictions were renewed. The HOLC extended A or B grades to 33.9 percent of first renewals but only 11.7 percent of second renewals.

Table 6.1 Restricted Parcels, by Type, 1937 HOLC Grade, and 2002 Vacancy Rate

1937 HOLC Rating	Subdivision		Petition		Renewals		Second Renewals	
	Number	Share (%)	Number	Share (%)	Number	Share (%)	Number	Share (%)
Total	12,877	100.0	14,043	100.0	4,693	100.0	351	100.0
A	4,479	34.8	390	2.8	250	5.3	0	0.0
B	7,411	57.6	5,536	39.4	1,325	28.2	39	11.1
A and B	11,890	92.3	5,926	42.2	1,575	33.6	39	11.1
C	797	6.2	6,224	44.3	2,972	63.3	312	88.9
D	0	0.0	1,773	12.6	145	3.1	0	0.0
C and D	797	6.2	7,997	56.9	3,117	66.4	312	88.9
Vacant in 2002	298	2.3	3,116	22.2	721	15.4	68	19.4

Source: Nelson et al., n.d.; FHLBB, Division of Research and Statistics 1940; Gordon 2023b; Gordon 2023e.

Note: Renewals are petition restrictions circulated in advance of (or after) expiration of the original restriction. A second renewal indicates a third attempt to restrict through petition.

The distinct trajectories of subdivision and petition restrictions are also evident in the count of vacated parcels. A tiny fraction (just 2.3 percent) of parcels restricted by subdivision were vacant or abandoned by 2002. Of those properties restricted by petition, nearly a quarter (22.2 percent) had, by century's end, reverted from private ownership to the city's land bank of tax-delinquent properties.

A similar pattern prevailed on a smaller scale in Waterloo, where the HOLC identified nine D areas.[131] Three of these bordered Black Hawk Creek or the Cedar River and were deemed hazardous because they were "subject to floods," one of which was further downgraded because it was populated by "poor white trash." Three others circumscribed "poor farm-land" or industrial use at the city's edge. The other three ran through the center of the north side. Area D-3, encompassing most of central Waterloo, was noted for the proximity of the Deere tractor works and the Rath Packing plant, "mixed good and bad residences," and "mixed" inhabitants. Area D-3a, spanning the border between the Triangle of early African American occupancy and the 1914 petition restriction that had attempted to set the Triangle's northern boundary, earned a blunt five-word description: "this is the colored section." Area D-4 to the north was damned by association: a "poor workingman's neighborhood close to colored section."[132] As in St. Louis, the area of petition restriction was redlined both because it demarcated a zone of racial encroachment or transition and because it had largely failed to stem that transition. The city's A and B zones, all to the southwest, made no mention of private restrictions—most of which were not put into place until the 1940s, after the HOLC had completed its appraisal.

In Minneapolis, the hierarchy of HOLC zones reflected local idiosyncrasies: most of the nonresidential (industrial and commercial) areas were not rated, and some others were oddly gerrymandered and sometimes noncontiguous.[133] Three of the city's fourteen D areas were marked off for racial reasons: In D-3, "most of the population today is of the poorer class of Jew and colored people." In D-5, there was a "considerably large negro settlement." And in D-6, appraisers noted "a considerable infiltration of negroes and Asiatics." These assumptions and anxieties carried over into the C ratings: C-4 warned of the "shifting of negroes westerly." C-8 was described as a B for dwellings but was also threatened by the "expansion of the derogatory features of D-6 into the area." And C-15 noted disapprovingly of the presence of "several colored families." HOLC confined its security mapping to

Minneapolis–St. Paul and did not rate the suburban municipalities (such as Richfield, Edina, and St. Louis Park) where private restriction proliferated. In Minneapolis, most of the fourteen A and twenty-two B ratings do not refer directly to private restrictions but routinely note favorably of "no shifting of population" or no threat of "encroachment," and unfavorably of the presence of "wealthy Jews" or "the Jewish race." Appraisers identified B-13 as "a restricted district" and noted that "a slow encroachment of negroes on the extreme easterly limits of this area threatens it"—adding the hopeful caveat that "efforts of the Nicollet Improvement Association, a voluntary organization of property owners in the district, is affording protection against much encroachment."[134]

While the HOLC's maps and area descriptions offer a stark catalog of midcentury racism in private realty and public policy, the program itself had little direct or immediate impact. The HOLC was a short-term response to the 1930s foreclosure crisis that confined its attention to refinancing existing loans and bailing out lending institutions. It did little to shape new lending or construction.[135] The HOLC completed virtually all of its loans between 1933 and 1936, *before* it undertook the appraisal project for which it would become infamous. Its red and blue pencils played no role in determining who got loans and who didn't.[136] Indeed, across the country, the HOLC did not hesitate to make loans in areas it would later designate as hazardous, and it refinanced loans held by African American borrowers at a rate roughly proportional to their share of the market.[137] Finally, the assumption that other lenders relied on these appraisals is belied by clear evidence that— with few exceptions—the HOLC kept is "City Survey" program under close wraps and made a point of not sharing its work with either private lenders or other public agencies.[138]

For these reasons, the impact of the HOLC and its appraisals has been hard to assess. Efforts to link HOLC ratings with contemporary spatial and racial inequalities often rest on unspecified causal assumptions that exaggerate the importance of the HOLC and disregard other intervening policies, mechanisms, and patterns.[139] Given the prevalence of private discrimination and restriction before 1933 and the complex history of segregation and concentrated disadvantage that followed, HOLC ratings and analogous contemporary inequalities may simply be describing the same distressed neighborhood at two different points in time—and their juxtaposition mistaken for a causal explanation.[140] There is, in this respect, a "drunk under the streetlight" fascination with HOLC maps, an observational bias that rests on their availability and accessibility rather than on their actual causal or historical importance.[141] Tellingly, the more cautious and circumspect scholarship on the links between HOLC ratings and contemporary inequalities concede that the mechanisms connecting HOLC redlining to current disparities are unclear or speculative.[142]

Perhaps the most robust findings in this literature are those that align closely with historical assessments. One of the consequences of the HOLC's refinancing focus was that it refinanced only existing loans, in the process reinforcing existing patterns of racial segregation.[143] Indeed, cities appraised by the HOLC are more segregated today than those (of similar size and original levels of segregation) that were not—suggesting both the immediate impact of HOLC loans and the institutionalization of its appraisal methods.[144] HOLC appraisals in turn, proved more a source of exploitation than of exclusion. While HOLC interest rates were set by legislation, borrowers on the private market in redlined neighborhoods paid higher interest rates.[145] Decades later, those same neighborhoods remained vulnerable to "predatory inclusion," especially through the subprime lending boom that preceded the Great Recession.[146]

In explanations of the persistence of racial segregation and its consequences, the HOLC occupies an uncertain position. It leveraged the judgment of private realty interests (who already had a clear working hierarchy of good and bad neighborhoods) into public policy, and both the threat of African American occupancy and the ability of private restrictions to meet that threat were central to its assessments. Given their timing and provenance, HOLC ratings are a sort of red-light camera snapshot of private appraisal (and of public deference to private prejudice and private priorities) at a particular moment. They document the transgression (of exclusion or restriction) but have little to say about what happened next. In another respect, HOLC ratings were a rough but well-documented proxy for the baseline assumptions of other federal agencies—especially the FHA. In this sense, the HOLC was exemplary of a broader array of public policies that legitimized and perpetuated private discrimination.[147]

If the impact of the HOLC is hard to pin down, the same cannot be said for the FHA. It was created just months after the HOLC and, while animated by the same Depression-era concerns, was crafted as a long-term guarantor of housing markets and housing security. At its creation in 1934, the FHA offered insurance for home improvement ("modernization") loans, conventional mortgages, and larger-scale housing projects. A few years later, it had also established a secondary mortgage market organized through two national mortgage associations (now Fannie Mae and Freddie Mac). These federal guarantees, in turn, made the low–down payment, long-amortization loan an industry standard.[148] Unlike the HOLC, the FHA focused increasingly on new loan origination and construction, giving it enormous influence over future spatial lending patterns, suburban development, and housing opportunity.

The FHA echoed and extended the work of the HOLC in two important respects. First, it too deferred systematically to private realty interests; from the outset, it was run "by and for bankers, builders, and brokers."[149] The FHA's primary charge was to stabilize and subsidize housing demand, and it rarely questioned private assumptions as to what constituted a good mortgage risk or a good neighborhood.[150] Indeed, in defense of its own portfolio (a revolving fund that used premium revenue to insure new loans), the FHA simply accepted and internalized those assumptions. By underwriting the purchase of single-family homes and the activities of large suburban developers, the FHA provided fuel for the national economy, as well as a reliable lubricant for local growth machines.[151] The FHA's regulatory hand, let alone its commitment to equal protection, was torpedoed by its conscious and intentional reliance—as a source of expertise and its own staff—on private realty interests. It could not reasonably challenge private restriction and racial segregation, as Weaver put it bitterly in 1948, "once the government had turned the agency's operations over to the real estate and home finance boys."[152]

Second, in support of its programs, the FHA launched its own appraisal project based on exhaustive "real property surveys" of cities and neighborhoods that collected information on "average rent, total number of residential structures, and percentages of residential structures under 15 years of age, of dwelling units owner occupied, of residences needing major repairs, of units without private baths, of commercial buildings, and of race other than white."[153] In its 1935 annual report, the FHLBB took note of the HOLC's "exchange of appraisal information and technical personnel data with other Federal agencies active in housing construction, insurance, and finance."[154] Todd Michney's examination of the HOLC's correspondence files confirms close and open communication between the HOLC and the

FHA.[155] Whatever the lineage, the FHA (as its few surviving maps under-score)[156] operated from the same assumptions and adopted essentially the same standards as the HOLC.

This shared worldview, of course, centered on the FHA's notorious embrace of racially restrictive private deed restrictions. While the HOLC factored private restrictions (and their effectiveness) into its security ratings, the FHA actively encouraged their use. "Deed restrictions are apt to prove more effective than a zoning ordinance in providing protection from adverse influences," as the FHA counseled in its first (1936) *Underwriting Manual*, specifying those adverse influences as "infiltration of business and industrial uses, lower-class occupancy, and inharmonious racial groups."[157] In 1938, the FHA refined its criteria and held to the view that private restrictions were the only means of accomplishing "prohibition of the occupancy of properties except by the race for which they are intended."[158] After the *Shelley* decision in 1948, the FHA deferred immediately to its private patrons, famously informing the NAACP that it "could not fail to recognize the validity of such restrictions and the right of . . . private individuals" to continue to use them.[159]

What made this stance so damaging, even as the FHA slowly and begrudgingly revised its underwriting standards to conform to *Shelley*, was the agency's influence on the spatial organization of subsidized lending and new construction. The FHA's pursuit of scale (both to address the World War II–era housing shortage and to prime the national economy), alongside its eagerness to mitigate risk in its portfolio, harnessed its programs to large-scale suburban development—or precisely the corner of the market in which racial restriction was most firmly embedded.[160] This emulated, leveraged, and institutionalized the practice of private restriction in myriad ways. Builders often interpreted the FHA's encouragement to incorporate private restriction as a requirement (or at least a benefit). Because developers were eager to build to FHA standards, they pursued conditional commitments from the agency that generalized its criteria across the private market.[161]

The FHA's centrifuge, pushing housing opportunity and resources to the suburban fringe, was accompanied and exaggerated by policy neglect of central cities. The formalization of federal lending standards and criteria did more than just favor new suburban construction—it displaced or discouraged private lending in the urban core. While the HOLC had propped up lenders and borrowers in place, the FHA created vast investment deserts in central cities where neighborhoods were marked by all the threats—inharmonious use, encroachments, age and obsolescence—the FHA sought to avoid.[162] Indeed, federal agencies increasingly focused on clearing those neighborhoods under the auspices of urban renewal (dubbed "Negro removal" by critics at the time),[163] a program largely entrusted to local boosters and developers whose pipe dreams displaced residents and deepened metropolitan segregation.[164]

Private restriction—and its legacy of segregation—decisively shaped federal housing policy. Federal agencies accepted the premises of private restriction, including the reality of racial segregation, without significant dissent. This created a powerful eddy in the uneven current of postwar civil rights policy and jurisprudence, serving—as Arnold Hirsch has suggested—as a reactionary counter to *Brown* determined to sustain residential segregation in the face of school integration.[165] Federal policy did not just subsidize the private housing market (and defer to its core interests), it transformed it. The low–down payment, long-term mortgages crafted by the HOLC and FHA both expanded the scale of private restriction and discrimination—offering racial protection, as Myrdal noted to "areas and groups of white people who were earlier without it"[166]—and rationalized it as sound public policy.[167]

The FHA, in sum, embraced, accommodated, and even promoted private restrictions on racial occupancy. Its deference to private realty interests and their practices was disappointing yet unsurprising. And the durability of local spatial and racial inequalities rested, in no small part, on the institutionalization of restriction and exclusion by federal policy. But, before the post-1946 housing boom, the FHA's direct role in segregating local housing markets was dwarfed by private action. As of 1940, the FHA insured mortgages on less than 3 percent of all homes in the St. Louis, Minneapolis–St. Paul, and Waterloo metropolitan areas; only in greater St. Louis did its share of new homes (built between 1930 and 1940) exceed 10 percent. In 1940, FHA mortgages (both new and refinanced) numbered just under 11,000 in the St. Louis metro area—whereas nearly 91,000 homes in the same area were race restricted by private agreement.[168]

The importance of the FHA (both directly and as a benchmark for private lenders) grew after the war and through the *Shelley* decision in 1948. Even as the FHA (and other federal agencies) came around to prohibit racial restriction on the basis of equal protection, the institutionalization of private

Figure 6.2 The Timeline of Private Restriction

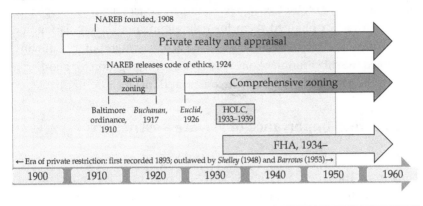

Source: Author's compilation.

restriction was and could be maintained by federal policy through omission (such as a failure to enforce fair housing laws)[169] or "policy drift" (the failure to adapt or update fair housing protections to changes in urban form or housing markets).[170] The local and federal administration of affordable housing programs—including big-box public housing, low-income home-ownership programs, and scattered site (Section 8) subsidized housing—all betrayed practical, if unspoken, commitments or deference to prevailing patterns of segregation and prevailing assumptions about race, neighborhoods, and housing.[171]

Over time, private restriction was crucial to the invention, elaboration, and durability of local racial disparities (figure 6.2). In private realty, the practice ran alongside the emergence of the modern real estate profession and neatly captured its anxieties and assumptions about racial occupancy. The segregation created by private restriction only confirmed those anxieties and assumptions—and ensured their persistence after *Shelley*. In local zoning, private restriction effectively bridged the gap between *Buchanan* (1917) and the post-*Euclid* (1926) emergence of comprehensive zoning, which was clearly designed to sustain segregation by other means after 1948. In federal policy, private restriction established the baseline criteria for public appraisals of property value and neighborhood risk. At their origins, federal programs explicitly embraced the language and logic of private restriction;

after 1948, the outcomes of private restriction were sustained by policies that lavished steep subsidies on new suburban development and neglected central cities—or blighted them for redevelopment. The emulation and adaptation of private restriction occurred across contemporary domains. It enabled the substitution of one mechanism of segregation for another; it pressed the practice (and its operative assumptions) forward in time.

The Lasting Importance of Private Restriction

In August 2014, Michael Brown was killed by police in Ferguson, a struggling inner suburb of St. Louis County—a zone of racial transition, collapsing public services, and local fiscal crises. Six years later, in May 2020, George Floyd was killed by police at the corner of 38th Street and Chicago Avenue in Minneapolis—at the border between the largely Latino and African American near south side and the overwhelmingly white (and formerly restricted) neighborhoods further south.[172] The deaths, and the social movements they inspired, reflected a long history of police brutality in African American communities as well as the painful legacy of private racial restriction in settings (such as St. Louis and Minneapolis) where local policing was animated in large part by the desire to regulate the boundaries between white and black neighborhoods and to discipline or sanction those deemed out of place.[173]

What connects private racial restrictions in the first decades of the twentieth century to persistent racial disparities in the first decades of the twenty-first is racial segregation.[174] Segregation is "a principal cause of group inequality," as Anderson reminds us. "It isolates disadvantaged groups from access to public and private resources, from sources of human and cultural capital, and from the social networks that govern access to jobs, business connections, and political influence. It depresses their ability to accumulate wealth and gain access to credit. It reinforces stigmatizing stereotypes about the disadvantaged that cause discrimination."[175] Private restriction was largely responsible for the segregation of Northern and border cities before 1950—and for the vested interests, public policies, and prevailing assumptions that would sustain that segregation well after 1950.

At the same time, the connections between the history of private restriction and contemporary patterns of segregation are not clean nor linear. In some settings, trajectories of segregation, concentrated poverty, or housing

Map 6.4 Segregation in Hennepin County, 2020

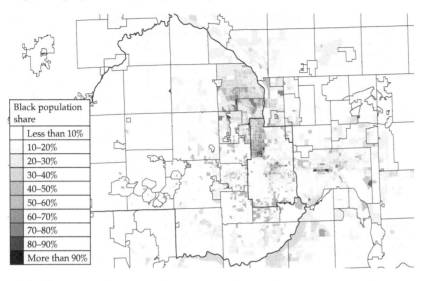

Black population share
Less than 10%
10–20%
20–30%
30–40%
40–50%
50–60%
60–70%
70–80%
80–90%
More than 90%

Source: Census 2020 (block group data) via Ruggles et al. 2022.

value run unbroken to the present; in others, early spatial disadvantages are interrupted by redevelopment, gentrification, or compensatory programs. Just as private restriction took many forms and strategies, it also yielded uneven consequences.[176] In Hennepin County, where private restriction largely preceded the arrival of African Americans, suburban restrictions traced zones of exclusion along the southern and western borders of Minneapolis and out into the more distant western suburbs; they also defined an unrestricted area in the city's northwest corner (map 3.8). It was there, in neighborhoods identified by the HOLC as "declining" or "undesirable," where most of the new migrants would settle (map 6.4). Local economic and racial segregation was intensified in city and suburban schools.[177] By the 1990s, Minneapolis's north-side neighborhoods—overwhelming nonwhite in a city that was overwhelmingly white—were increasingly marked by concentrated poverty and disadvantage, a pattern exaggerated and accelerated by the siting of public housing.[178] When Minneapolis moved to disperse the concentration of public housing on the north side, its profile of the residents to be displaced was telling: 93 percent were African American or South Asian,

Map 6.5 Segregation in Waterloo, 2020

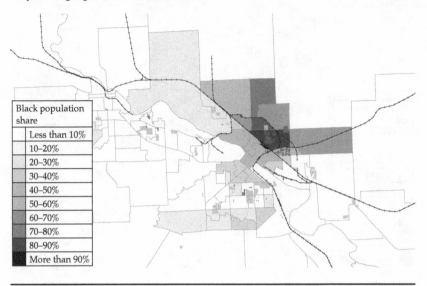

Black population share
Less than 10%
10–20%
20–30%
30–40%
40–50%
50–60%
60–70%
70–80%
80–90%
More than 90%

Source: Census 2020 (block group data) via Ruggles et al. 2022.

median income was one-third that of the City as a whole, and 73 percent lived below the poverty line. In the southern and western suburbs, by contrast, private restrictions yielded high and exclusionary property values.[179]

In Waterloo (map 3.11), scattered suburban restrictions south of the Cedar River played a similar exclusionary role. Conversely, the early petition restrictions on the north side—hastily assembled in the face of racial threat—failed to stem racial transition in the long term. But by confining early African settlement to the neighborhoods immediately north of the Illinois Central railbed, they cemented and sustained a stark pattern of local segregation (map 6.5). That segregation proved remarkably resilient. "Negro housing" in Waterloo, as a local civil rights commission understated in 1967, "is a highly segregated affair."[180] Fully a century after the first wave of African American migration to Waterloo, high levels of black-white residential segregation—and the concentration of African American occupancy in the blocks surrounding the railbed on the north side—persist as central features of local demography.[181] The concentration of African American occupancy in and around the Triangle was echoed by school segregation and yielded a familiar cascade of place-based inequalities and

Map 6.6 Segregation in Greater St. Louis, 2020

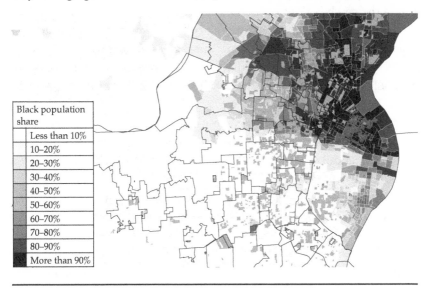

Black population share	
	Less than 10%
	10–20%
	20–30%
	30–40%
	40–50%
	50–60%
	60–70%
	70–80%
	80–90%
	More than 90%

Source: Census 2020 (block group data) via Ruggles et al. 2022.

disadvantages.[182] "No U.S. metro area," as one survey noted glumly in 2018, "has larger social and economic disparities along racial lines than Waterloo-Cedar Falls, Iowa."[183]

In St. Louis (maps 3.4, 6.6), this same pattern of uneven results played out on a much larger scale. As in Waterloo—and as with patterns of local zoning and HOLC appraisals—petition restrictions were expressions of anxiety and panic in the face of an imminent threat of racial transition. Their "protective" capacity and efficacy were short-lived. They were contested by civil rights advocates and white defectors even as they were being assembled, and they collapsed quickly after the *Shelley* decision. In the short run, white homeowners and tenants were replaced by black homeowners and tenants. In the census tracts north and west of the Ville, the white population fell by over 80 percent between 1930 and 1970, from 236,677 to 38,610, while the black population grew from 5,208 to 114,254. In the long run, virtually all the white residents fled, and the overall population plummeted: by 2010, the total population of these tracts (80,334) was less than a third of what it had been in 1950, and the white population accounted for just over 2 percent of that total.[184]

Over time, the collapse of private restriction on the north side compromised the patchwork of restriction in north St. Louis County—much of which had been imposed relatively early and on modest housing stock—especially when black flight from north St. Louis neighborhoods picked up in the 1970s.[185] This pattern effectively extended the Delmar Divide west into St. Louis County, cleaving University City in two and hastening rapid racial transition in the inner suburbs. Where the African American share of the population grew, private investment retreated, property values fell, and public services (except policing) contracted. The early and isolated concentration of African American occupancy in the Ville and the Mill Creek Valley became a single contiguous boundary extending well into St. Louis County.[186]

North of the Delmar Divide, racial exclusion from housing markets was simply accompanied or displaced by exploitation within them. Between 1940 and 1980, the number of African American homeowners in St. Louis increased more than tenfold from 2,108 to 25,984, and the African American home-ownership rate jumped from 7.2 to 38.6 percent.[187] But declining property values, predatory lending, and discriminatory patterns of zoning, property appraisal, and code enforcement meant that increasing rates of home-ownership were met with diminishing returns.[188] This pattern repeated itself, a generation later, in north St. Louis County.[189] South of the Delmar Divide, by contrast, private subdivision restrictions map cleanly onto current demographic patterns.

As the patterns in Waterloo and St. Louis both suggest, restrictions were important when they worked but also when they failed—in their wake, rapid racial transition, falling property values, and neighborhood disinvestment and decline followed.[190] The conviction that black occupancy destroyed property values became self-fulfilling. "Whites sharply constrained black residency and homeownership," as Hayward notes, "and then racialized those failures—citing low rates of homeownership or the conditions in necessarily overcrowded black neighborhoods as evidence for the black threat to neighborhoods and property values."[191] Across the urban Midwest, the upshot was the stubborn persistence of segregation and a steady widening of the racial wealth gap, even as civil rights jurisprudence chipped away at the formal mechanisms of discrimination or exclusion.[192]

The long-term and varied impact of private restrictions is evident in current home values and homeownership rates (table 6.2). In settings where private restriction yielded mostly exclusion such as Hennepin and Johnson

Table 6.2 Homeownership Rates and Median Homes Values by Race, 2016–2020

	City of St. Louis	St. Louis County	Hennepin County	Black Hawk County	Johnson County
Black homeownership rate	43.5%	55.0%	37.5%	38.4%	16.1%
White homeownership rate	66.1%	85.4%	78.4%	79.1%	74.7%
Homeownership gap (white-black)	22.6%	30.3%	40.9%	40.8%	58.6%
Black median home value	$ 75,000	$ 95,800	$230,000	$ 87,700	$196,100
White median home value	$166,700	$260,000	$308,600	$154,500	$248,000
Home-value gap (black as share of white)	45.0%	36.8%	74.5%	56.8%	79.1%

Source: American Community Survey 2016–2020 via Ruggles et al. 2022.

Counties, racial disparities are most evident in the white-black homeownership gap. In St. Louis and St. Louis County, by contrast, private restrictions are implicated more in exploitation: the homeownership gap is narrower, but the home-value gap (the returns on that ownership) is much wider. In Black Hawk County, exclusion and exploitation operate in equal measure—yielding wide racial gaps in both homeownership and housing value.

The resulting inequalities were solidified not only by the private and public policies of restriction but by a wide array of institutions, practices, and policies that raised the costs of private goods and diminished the provision of public goods. Disparate access to housing meant disparate access to public goods—especially schools—that followed residential patterns and were financed by local property taxes.[193] It also meant disparate access to public goods—such as sewers, streets, and potable water—that were increasingly provided and paid for through private residential development and private housing investments.[194] The racialization of space, as Charles Mills observes bluntly, marked "the geographic boundary of the state's full obligations."[195] And disparate access to housing also meant disparate access to private goods, the sellers of which flocked to wealthy neighborhoods and avoided (or charged a premium in) poor ones.[196] Private racial restriction, alongside occupational discrimination and policing, punctured much of the promise of the Great Migrations.[197] Private racial restrictions—and the segregation they invented and sustained—curtailed more than just housing options. They curtailed opportunity.

APPENDIX: NOTE ON METHODS

THIS STUDY RELIES on original datasets derived from the archival property records of five Midwestern counties; four were collected by the author and colleagues, the fifth (for Hennepin County) by the "Mapping Prejudice" Project in Minnesota. Despite the immediate and longer-term influence of private racial restrictions—as a mechanism of segregation and root cause of lasting spatial and racial inequalities—their inaccessibility *as data* has confounded efforts to document their adoption, diffusion, and impact; it also has encouraged reliance on other sources (such as the HOLC security maps) that distort the causality and timing of racial segregation in the urban North. The accessibility of the (now fully digitized) HOLC maps has yielded an explosion of interest, while more important causal actors or forces—the private agreements that preceded the HOLC and the FHA policies that succeeded the HOLC—linger in the shadows.[1]

The documentary evidence of private restriction is entombed in local property records, which are vast (the deed books for St. Louis from 1900 to 1950 run over 3.5 million pages; for Cook County, the county seat of Chicago, over 4 million pages), largely handwritten, indexed primarily by grantor and grantee, and organized by the daily traffic in the office of the county recorder or assessor. In most settings, restrictive agreements are interspersed with bills of sale, sewer liens, utility easements and other routine business of those offices. For these reasons, our understanding of private racial restrictions (and access to them) has been largely confined to legal disputes, or to their use by a few elite developers.[2] When Long and Johnson studied racial restrictions in Chicago and St. Louis in the late 1940s, they concluded quickly that a comprehensive accounting of racial covenants was out of the question and opted instead to "employ short cut methods in finding the restrictive agreements, because of the large number of deed and tract books to be covered."[3] A half century later, Fox Gotham reached the same conclusion, arguing for the importance of such restrictions but conceding that "there is no systematic evidence" as to their scope.[4]

In recent years, academic and community researchers have begun assembling that "systematic evidence," employing a variety of strategies to identify, catalog, and map private race restrictions in a number of border and northern cities.[5] This research presents both significant promise and significant challenges. The promise lies in the ability, working from a complete local record of private restriction, to document in time and space—and in granular, lot-by-lot detail—a crucial mechanism of racial segregation. The challenges lie in the uneven accessibility of local property records and in the need to create or leverage the digital infrastructure for mapping restrictions once they are identified. Here I touch on both promises and challenges, drawing on experience researching racial restrictions in a wide variety of settings, but especially in the five counties featured in this book.

County Deed Records

The infrastructure of U.S. property records is shaped by early patterns of dispossession and delineation under settler colonialism (that is, the task of surveying and parceling out "open" land for private ownership),[6] as well as by the ongoing importance of private property rights in American law and political culture. Rather than a single official record of title and ownership, most property records are assembled as a cumulative account of claims made by buyers and sellers (grantors and grantees).[7] These include both transactional documents and commitments such as easements or covenants. "Covenants running with the land are perpetuated through the recording process upon which the whole system of land titles and conveyances has rested for many years," as Monchow noted in 1928. "The purposes of the recording statutes are to preserve the 'muniments' or evidences of title and to give the community notice of all changes in the ownership of property and the circumstances accompanying such change of owner-ship. The theory underlying the recording acts has been to place on anyone dealing in land the legal obligation of consulting the records and acquaint-ing himself with their contents."[8]

Property records are maintained by counties (or their equivalent), an early and stable spatial jurisdiction. Deeds and other documents relating to property ownership, use, value, or boundaries are filed chronologically by the county recorder and the county assessor and indexed by grantor and grantee.[9] The record for a given property is keyed to the most recent transaction, and a chain of title is assembled by following the documentary trail back to the original platting or subdivision. The stable identifier for each parcel is not an address but usually either a legal description based on the original platting (such as "the eastern 30 feet of Lot 4 and the western 20 feet of Lot 5 of McBride's Addition to Cedar Heights subdivision") or a "metes and bounds" description based on distance and direction from a nearby landmark (such as a river, a street intersection, another property parcel, or a survey stake).[10] The recording system establishes title by docu-menting and resolving competing claims.[11]

These records are usually collected in a chronological run of deed books, each running 500 to 700 pages. The City of St. Louis Recorder of Deeds processed just over 100 deed books a year (totaling more than 3.5 million pages) between 1900 and 1950; the Johnson County, Iowa, Recorder pro-cessed roughly 100 deed books total (about 65,000 pages) over the same span. Individual records or documents are identified by a "book and page" number indicating the deed book in which they are located, and the page number on which the record begins. Each new document, designated by a line drawn across the page, begins with a legal description of the parcel or parcels in question and ends with the recorder's seal, signature, and date. The chronological run of recorders' deed books is usually accompanied by a parallel set of records (or a unique index to the same records) maintained by the county assessor and a run of large-format plat books documenting subdivisions, infrastructure, and easements.

In recent years, many county recorders have begun to digitize their records, a development spurred by both private title companies (who assem-ble chains of title or title abstracts for buyers, realtors, and lenders) and recorders' offices themselves. Most recorders have transitioned to electronic filing and storage for recent transactions, but—given the chain-of-title logic of the records—a full electronic record encouraged digitization of older records as well. In most settings, digitization has been undertaken by private vendors; Laredo and Tapestry are two of the largest. High-resolution scans of the original documents are available on-site in the recorder's office and online for both pay-as-you-go users and institutional subscribers such as title firms, realtors, and mortgage companies.[12]

Digitization opens up new avenues for access and historical research. It transforms the records into big data and facilitates searches (using optical character recognition) or analysis beyond the conventional grantor and grantee index.[13] But that access has its limits. In many settings, the digitized scans of the original property documents are treated as proprietary commercial property, not public records. Given the costs of digitization and the lighter demand for older records, many records are only partially digitized. In the City of St. Louis, for example, current (born digital) property records extend back into the early 1990s; from there back to the late 1930s, records are available on a Laredo server; earlier records are available only on archival microfilm. In turn, many of the early records are handwritten—limiting their utility for "distant reading" or searching via optical character recognition (OCR) even if they are digitized.[14] In St. Louis County, local land records were handwritten into deed books by the recorder's staff well into the 1950s. Unfortunately, property records that are at once typewritten, digitized, and accessible to researchers for the full span of years (1910–1950) in which racial restrictions were employed (such as those of Hennepin County that facilitated the Mapping Prejudice project) are relatively rare.

Racial Restrictions in the Deed Records

Racial restrictions are not neatly and consistently attached to the core chain-of-title property records, in part because of the different forms that such restrictions take. Restrictions placed by sellers, buyers, realtors, or small-scale developers on individual parcels were imposed at the time of sale and are clearly laid out in the record of that transaction and in the chain of title. In Iowa City (Johnson County), one realtor made it a practice of adding racial restrictions at each sale, creating a scatter of restricted parcels across the city's east side.[15] Parcel restriction was common practice early on, but—in settings like St. Louis—was subsumed by larger-scale restrictive agreements in the 1920s and 1930s.[16]

Racial restrictions in subdivisions—the most common form of restriction accounting for virtually all the restrictions in Hennepin, Johnson, and St. Louis Counties—typically accompanied a long list of constraints on use, imposed—in the interests of promoting exclusion and sustaining property values—by the original developers.[17] Some subdivision restrictions, in turn, are the product of subdivision governance. In St. Louis County, many subdivisions established trusteeships or other mechanisms by which buyers could impose, extend, or modify restrictions. When racial restriction was not specified by the original developer, it was often the first legislative act of such bodies. In Seattle (King County) and other settings, restrictions were often embedded in the bylaws of homeowners' associations that policed local restrictions after development.[18]

In areas experiencing significant African American migration, especially older neighborhoods adjacent to African American neighborhoods or pockets of African American occupancy, realtors or homeowners assembled petition restrictions by collecting signatures door-to-door. These restrictions were less aspirational exclusions than they were defensive responses to the threat (or reality) of racial transition. In most settings where petition restrictions were found (including Chicago, the District of Columbia, St. Louis, and Waterloo), they were responses to the first wave of African American migration, or efforts to contain an already established African American neighborhood. Petition restrictions typically had terms of fifteen to twenty-five years (in order to accommodate the "rule against perpetuities" in American property law). They could be structured as small-scale neighborhood agreements (with the expectation that all owners signed the agreement) or as broader community agreements based on a threshold (usually 75 percent) of participation.[19]

Such distinctions are important, not only because different modes of restriction reflect different motives and have disparate impacts, but because they show up in different ways (and in different places) in the recorder's records. Because they are attached to a particular property at sale, parcel restrictions are embedded in the chain of title. Subdivision restrictions are often filed as separate indentures, articles of incorporation, or "declarations of restrictions," and the records for individual properties may cross-reference this document (and its book and page number) or simply declare that a transaction is "subject to restrictions of record." In Johnson, Black Hawk, and St. Louis Counties, early (pre-1929) subdivisions often recorded their restrictions in the margins, or on the reverse, of the original plat maps. Petition restrictions can be more difficult to track down, because (unlike parcels, or the initial sales of subdivision properties) they are not imposed at sale. As a result, they are likely to exist as wild deeds, interspersed in the property records with all the other routine business of the recorder's office—restricting use and alienation, but neither attached to, nor often even referenced in, the actual chain of title of any of the restricted properties.

Tracking Down Racial Restrictions

The organization of property records, their uneven digitization, and the varieties of restriction (by type and by jurisdiction) require a careful and calculated research strategy. The range (both state to state and county to county) of recording conventions and practices necessitates familiarity with the records themselves. One way to do this is to select a single deed book from the era in which racial restrictions were most commonly recorded (roughly 1920–1950) and simply leaf through the records. This offers a sense of the distribution and range of the records, their organization, and the administrative cadence of individual entries. But, given the scale of the records (even for a small county), this is not an efficient or effective strategy for tackling the full corpus of restriction. Navigating and managing the sheer quantity of the records requires either an efficient means of searching them or some sort of key to their organization other than the conventional grantor and grantee index.

Fully Digitized Records

In cases where the full run of records is available in digital *and* machine-readable form (such as Hennepin and Johnson Counties), researchers can employ "distant reading" and OCR to identify records containing racial restrictions. This iterative process requires developing a working knowledge of the common restrictive conventions and terms and fine-tuning the search parameters accordingly. For Hennepin County, the Mapping Prejudice project used OCR to identify a subset of records (from the full property records for 1900 to 1960) that contained at least one instance of a predefined list of key words and word stems that might indicate the presence of a racial covenant. Deeds containing at least one of the key words were uploaded to the crowdsourcing platform Zooniverse, where volunteers read the flagged deeds and transcribed the relevant attribute information. As a robustness check, each deed had to be transcribed by five unique volunteers and meet a statistical measure of volunteer reliability.[20]

We employed a similar strategy for the Johnson County research, which was of a much smaller scale and was designed as a research workshop exercise for undergraduates. The recorder's office provided us with original high-resolution page scans (prepared by a private vendor who set up subscription-based access to the dataset), which we used to assemble digital PDF deed books matching the original organization of the records. We then used the search function in Adobe Acrobat to convert images to text and search key terms, words, and word stems. This, again, is an iterative process. We began with the terms commonly used in other settings (such as "colored" and "Caucasian"), then built out a working list of search terms—including those identifying excluded groups, those identifying included groups, and those that might be found in the title or headnote to a restrictive agreement or document. To minimize misses caused by stray or misread characters, we searched, for example, on "restrict" and "restr," "Caucasian" and "Cauc," "colored," and "Negro." Such basic OCR searching is always imperfect, and the results should be understood as a lower bound of "hits."[21] We confirmed all the restrictions that we found but had no way of knowing how many we might have missed. In a few deed books that contained multiple restrictions, we checked the search strategy with a page-by-page review—and found no further restrictions. Since Hennepin and Johnson County restrictions were overwhelmingly subdivision-based, results were also confirmed by multiple hits (as the restrictions often appeared in both subdivision documents and warranty deeds for individual properties).

Relatively complete temporal runs of digitized records are unfortunately rare. In many settings (including St. Louis and Black Hawk Counties), recorders have digitized recent records (often from 1970 or 1980 onward) but not those spanning the era of restriction. In the City of St. Louis, digitization has proceeded haltingly, requiring researchers to consult both digitized and microfilmed records across the 1900 to 1950 era. In other settings, digitization and typed originals cover only a window of records that limit access to deeds or indenture records at either end of the era of private restriction.[22]

Sampling

When the full corpus of records is not searchable, some sense of the scope, timing, and form of restriction can be deduced from a sample of relevant records. Monchow first sketched the use of deed restrictions in suburban development in 1928 by surveying eighty-four deeds provided to her by the Home Building and Subdividers Division of the National Association of Real Estate Boards and the Chicago Real Estate Board and by selected developers (including the Olmsted Brothers).[23] This, as Monchow acknowledged, yielded a sense of the kinds of restrictive provisions employed by exclusive developers but not of their scale, scope, or diffusion in any given setting. A number of studies have similarly sampled subdivision documents in particular jurisdictions.[24] Others have focused on restrictions put in place by leading developers.[25]

Another research and sampling strategy is to crowdsource the property research by asking homeowners to look for restrictive language in their own title abstracts, a strategy that has been used to complement research efforts (and engage the public) in a variety of settings. In the absence of a more systematic investigation or approach, such samples are illustrative but unreliable. They are likely to engage those already invested in racial equity and involve only the subset of homeowners in possession of their abstracts. (In many jurisdictions, such documents are no longer provided to homeowners or are in the custody of the lending institution holding the first mortgage.)

Subdivision Documents and Master Agreements

In most settings, the primary mechanism of racial exclusion was the subdivision, which opens up a number of possibilities—outside the drudgery of leafing through deed books—for discovering and documenting restrictions. Many recorders maintain a separate index or catalog of subdivisions, often compiled with funding from state or federal sources. The City of St. Louis, for example, has an index of all subdivisions dedicated between 1876 and 1935, prepared in 1935 by the New Deal's Works Progress Administration. The St. Louis County subdivision index, prepared by the Missouri Department of Agriculture Land Survey program in the early 1990s, runs over 2,500 pages and 22,000 entries. Unlike the subdivision indices in the City of St. Louis and the Iowa counties (as discussed later), the St. Louis

County index records every legal subdivision of land—a list that included many nonresidential developments (including cemeteries), infrastructure (such as sewer, street, and gas) plats and easements, and adjustments (replatting or resubdivision) of commercial and residential footprints.

Johnson and Black Hawk Counties in Iowa both maintain working in-house lists of subdivisions. These indices cross-reference subdivisions to their original plat or deed book entries, which allowed us to zero in on the documents containing restrictions or conditions. In most settings, this search can be narrowed chronologically: racial restrictions were not common in subdivisions before 1910, and new residential development slowed dramatically during the Great Depression.[26] As a result, most subdivision restrictions were enacted in the decade after World War I and in the early 1940s, in response to the second wave of the Great Migrations.

Such restrictions can also be discovered—regardless of whether a subdivision index is available—by working through the plat maps for the relevant years. In most counties, subdivision plats are filed chronologically in large-format plat books. These encompass all variety of subdivisions, so they often include maps of utility easements, street layouts, and minor revisions to earlier subdivisions. But most entries are architectural renderings of new residential developments. The plat books allow the researcher to move quickly and efficiently through these developments and to identify restrictions attached to them. In St. Louis and Black Hawk Counties, many restrictions were recorded on the plats themselves. In the former, it was common practice, especially in the 1920s, to include restrictions (and other details regarding dedication or incorporation) in the margins of the map. After the early 1930s, the plat maps were less likely to contain the restrictions themselves, but often referred to the deed book entry where they could be found. For this reason, we first worked from the full catalog of plat maps (fifty-two volumes spanning 1890 to 1950) before (as discussed later) moving onto the county's cross-index of restrictions. In Black Hawk County, the recorder often appended restrictions to the plat book entry, sometimes by simply pasting the relevant document to the back of the map. When restrictions are not recorded with the maps, plat book entries often include a reference or marginal notation to a book and page number—which allowed us to quickly match the subdivision with its original deed book entry.

For researchers, the plat maps provide several distinct advantages. As a chronological run, they effectively zero in on large-scale (and often restricted) residential development, uninterrupted by other routine business (such as quit claims and sewer liens) that clogs the deed books themselves. Subdivision by subdivision, plat maps enable researchers to document dozens, sometimes hundreds, of restricted properties at once. And they facilitate mapping the results. The plat maps themselves make it easier to match historical records with the current parcel database, either by simple visual correlation or by matching the subdivision name with a corresponding field ("subdivision" or "legal") in the current parcel database.

Restriction Registers or Indices

Given the importance of restriction to private realty and residential development in the first half of the twentieth century, and its elusiveness in the conventional run of deed records, county recorders and private title companies often maintained their own catalog or index of property restrictions. In their 1947 work on St. Louis, Long and Johnson relied on a list of restrictions provided to them by the St. Louis Real Estate Exchange. In our own research, we discovered a detailed register of St. Louis restrictions, recorded over the last century by one of the city's major title and abstract firms. This register catalogs almost 2,000 restrictive covenants between 1850 and 1950, 840 of which (nearly double the number found by Johnson and Long) included restrictions on racial occupancy. The register lists restrictive agreements by the recorder's book and page number and the date recorded, and indicates the presence of a racial restriction, a reversionary clause, or an expiration date. Because the "Yes/No" recording of racial restrictions was incomplete, we examined every deed record in which that field was marked "Yes" or left blank. Of the full catalog, 414 were originally coded as racial restrictions, and 426 of the 584 restrictions in which this field was blank were found to have racial restrictions.[27] Working from the register, we were able to find needles in a haystack—some 800 documents in a run of over 1 million deed book entries. Of the 840 racial restrictions identified in the original register, 72 were duplicates (or filings that merely added signatories to existing restrictions) and 5 rescinded standing agreements—leaving a total of 763 unique restrictive covenants or agreements encompassing some 30,000 residential parcels.

In St. Louis County, the recorder's office itself maintains such an index, although it is more elaborate and cumbersome. A vertical card file of restrictions, organized alphabetically by subdivision, records every constraint on property use. There are multiple entries for each subdivision, including restrictions established at dedication or incorporation and any revisions or additions over time. Some cards include a brief notation (such as "rules on location of gas stations") but most just reference a book and page number. Our strategy here was to work back and forth between the detailed subdivision index and the restrictions file: we pared the subdivision index to those developments platted between 1900 and 1950 (still over 8,000 entries), then checked each against the restrictions file. This yielded a list of deed book or plat book entries for over 2,000 subdivisions developed before 1950, which each had at least one restriction of record. These entries were then checked for racial restrictions. Not counting duplicates or renewals, we found 1,043 unique racial restrictive agreements covering about 76,000 parcels.

The Black Hawk County Recorder maintains a different kind of index. In the first half of the last century, the recorder (more so than those in other jurisdictions) acted as a sort of public notary—registering and recording a wide range of documents, including rental leases, draft deferments, agricultural contracts, and the like. Rather than muddy the run of property records with such documents, the recorder maintained a separate chronological series of "Miscellaneous Records." When developers and homeowners began drafting racial restrictions (the first in 1914), they were filed in this series. The Miscellaneous Records have their own index, which records the parties to the agreement, the date, the "character of the instrument," and an identifying book and page number. The index for 1910 to 1950 runs six large bound volumes, making it a relatively easy task to scan the "character of instrument" column for "restrictive agreement." Similarly, petition restrictions in Washington, D.C., are indexed and classified as "Agreements" in the land records database.[28]

Such catalogs or indices are crucial to identifying and documenting racial restrictions, especially when no digitized, searchable record exists. They provide either a shortcut to finding the most common and sweeping form of restriction (subdivisions), or a key to bypassing the chronological, grantor-grantee logic of the original records.[29] Even when such direct indices are not available, near-equivalents may be cobbled together. In Seattle, researchers have assembled a surrogate index using the digitized plats, which identify the original developers, who can then be searched in the conventional index of grantors. When the blanket subdivision restriction is not readily accessible, a cluster of sales (with restrictions attached to each deed) from a particular grantor may be enough to identify a subdivision restriction.[30] In Cook County, the grantor and grantee index itself contains clues to racial restriction: restrictive agreements (by subdivision or petition) are often identified by a marginal notation labeling them as such; in addition, the identification of a grantee as "[name] et al.," indicates a single conveyance from one grantor (a developer) to a large number of grantees (original purchasers or signatories to a petition restriction).[31]

This sketch of research methods across different settings raises a few important points. First, the data collected by the Mapping Prejudice project differed from that collected in the Missouri and Iowa counties in one fundamental respect. In Hennepin County (as in many other states and counties), master agreements—including subdivision indentures and neighborhood petitions—were not filed as public documents with the county recorder. The Hennepin County data, as a result, is assembled from a distant reading of individual parcel records; the existence of restrictions covering entire subdivisions can only be assumed or estimated based on the timing of development and the share of lots within a subdivision that are confirmed as restricted. This almost certainly results in an undercount, based on the absence of direct and specific restrictions in some property records (a sale or transfer may simply note the presence of "restrictions of record") and the likelihood that optical character recognition—due to uneven image quality—failed to catch all restrictions present in the digitized record.

Second, research in any given setting is likely to involve a combination of these methods, depending on the accessibility and organization of the records. The St. Louis County research is a case in point. As detailed earlier, the research workflow began with refining and culling a master subdivision register. A systematic survey of plat books enabled us to narrow that list to conventional residential subdivisions and identify the first run of restrictions: about 500 subdivision plats included racial restrictions. The county's internal restrictions file yielded another 450 racially restricted subdivisions, and about 160 restrictive agreements that did not include a racial clause. I then sampled the daily books and deed books for subdivisions platted between 1890 and 1950 but not listed in the restrictions file. The search hits were few and far between, suggesting that the county index was relatively complete. This sampling added about another 100 restrictions—for a total of 1,043 restricted subdivisions. This estimate, again, is a lower bound: it includes all confirmed restrictions but undoubtedly misses some. The daily book index, for example, provides the only available cross-reference for subdivision documents in the deed records, but the pre-1925 volumes have been lost—making it impossible to spot-check those records for restrictions not listed in the county index. Given the temporal pattern of restriction and the practice of recording early restrictions directly on the plat, this cataloging gap probably includes only a few restrictions.

Third, there are over 3,143 counties or equivalent jurisdictions in the United States.[32] The conventions for recording property (set by state law) have a few baseline uniformities (such as the grantor and grantee index) but otherwise vary from state to state and from county to county. Some of this variation is generated by the uneven and inelastic size of counties, which range in current population from over 10 million (Los Angeles County) to 86 (Kalawao County, Hawaii), and the different logics for county organization from one state to the next: Kentucky has 125 counties for a population of under 4.5 million, while Arizona has just 25 counties for a population nearly twice that size; Delaware has 3 counties for a population of just under a million; South Dakota has 66 counties for a similar state population.[33] The underlying organization of the records (whether restrictions are recorded on plat maps or in document series other than the deed books, for example) and the availability or the form of other indices (such as for subdivision or restriction) will vary according to state code and to the administrative idiosyncrasies and capacities of individual county offices.

Analyzing and Mapping the Restrictions

Once a body of racial restrictions is identified in the county records, the relevant information from each restriction must be extracted in order to draw patterns and conclusions as to its intent, diffusion, and scope, as well as to draw comparison with the practice and pattern of restriction in other settings. The key elements of that record are as follows:

Date: Most records will include both the day on which the restriction or agreement was signed and the day on which it was filed with the recorder's office. Because some agreements may have otherwise been undated, the recorder's date is the most reliable and consistent metric. Dates can establish the trajectory of restriction (and of different types of restriction) in a given jurisdiction and the influence of other factors, such as legal decisions or patterns of migration.

Type: Restriction took the form of parcel restrictions imposed at time of sale; subdivision restrictions including in new developments, and petition restrictions cobbled together in older neighborhoods. Some records might be duplicates (filed more than once for the same parcels), and some might be renewals (drafted and filed near the date when the original restriction is set to expire). Less commonly, homeowners may have filed notices rescinding or modifying an existing agreement, usually in response to a failure to stem racial transition. We found five formal rescissions in the City of St. Louis and one in Black Hawk County.

Source: The source of a restriction allows us to identify local motives and actors. Parcel restrictions may have originated with the buyer or seller, or less commonly with the realtor or lender. Subdivision restrictions were almost always crafted by the developer, although sometimes this was done with the cooperation—or cover—of subdivision trustees or homeowners' associations. Petition restrictions could have been assembled by any interested party; in all the settings covered in this book, local realtors played a major role.

Terms: Restrictions included three important and variable terms: the length of the agreement, the penalties for violation, and the procedure for rescission or renewal. As documented in chapter 3, many agreements followed the rule against perpetuities in property law, but some extended out over fifty or even one hundred years; sometimes restriction did not specify a term at all. In some settings, petition restrictions required a threshold of support (such as 75 percent of property owners on a restricted block). Parties to any restriction could have pursued breaches of the contract in civil court; some subdivision restrictions contained a reversionary clause, which returned the property to the original developer if restrictions were violated.

Scope: Restrictions varied considerably in their scope, from single parcels to sprawling multistage developments totaling hundreds or thousands of new homes. The scope of petition restrictions is reflected in both the area being restricted and the number or share of property owners signing onto it. In St. Louis, such agreements were generally smaller (most encompassed twenty-five to sixty parcels).

Language: The language of restriction varied by time, place, and region. As documented in chapter 1, the early language of exclusion often used elaborate taxonomies but over time drifted to a single marker ("Caucasian") of acceptable residents. Lists of excluded classes were often regionally or locally specific, although sometimes large developers used the same boiler-plate restriction wherever they did business.

Location: All property records include a legal description of the location and boundaries of the property in question (be it a single lot, a subdivision, or the scope of a petition). Such spatial information may include the name of a subdivision, the lot or lot numbers in a subdivision or city block, the street frontage or city blocks covered by a petition restriction, or a metes and bounds description relative to other properties, streets, or local landmarks.

This spatial information is crucial, as it allows researchers to map the trajectory of restriction in time and place. This requires matching locations and boundaries to their current equivalents, a process that depends on the history and pattern of land development in any given setting, the form and conventions of the spatial information in the original restriction, and the form and conventions of the digital assets used to map them, typically a current parcel database and shapefile (a vector data format for storing the location, shape, and attributes of geographic features).

Patterns of urban development vary considerably across the United States. In many settings, the division of land was influenced by its colonial roots and by the use of survey grids to establish private property boundaries and ownership. The Land Ordinance of 1785 systematized these methods west of Pennsylvania and north of the Ohio River, where land was demarcated by a nested grid of territories or states, counties, and townships—the latter then divided into lots of one square mile each.[34] In urbanized or urbanizing areas, this approach to the division of land persisted in patterns of street grids, subdivision, and lots.[35] American cities are not markedly influenced by pre-urban influences (such as fortifications), although there are significant variations driven by colonial histories—including river-based seigneurial holdings in the lower Mississippi and pueblos oriented around central plazas in the Southwest.[36]

In the Midwest, the survey system of demarcation and dispossession, as well as the speculative patterns of early urban development, led to the early subdividing of land and the platting of lots often long in advance of residential development.[37] While lots were often rearranged at the point of development, the original subdivision metrics were usually maintained. As a result, legal descriptions of such land often describes partial lots, such as "the western 10 feet of Lot 2 and the eastern 40 feet of Lot 3." In older settings with longer histories of urbanization, both organic patterns of urban development and an early reliance on metes and bounds parcel descriptions make the matching of restricted parcels with current records much trickier.[38]

In mapping racial restrictions, we began with the current recorder's or assessor's records, usually a geographic information systems (GIS) shapefile, the underlying database of which includes a wide range of parcel-specific information—including owner, assessed value, zoning, other jurisdictions (such as school districts), land use, property and building square footage, year built for the most recent structure, subdivision, and legal description. While current property records rely on street addresses and unique parcel IDs, several fields in the current database enable matching historical restrictions to current parcel data. For subdivision restrictions, parcels can be matched using the subdivision listed under the legal descriptors (for example, "Claggets's 3rd Addition"). Since a subdivision restriction covered all properties, the database can be sorted by this field, and the details of the restriction (that is, its type, date, and book number) entered for all properties with this descriptor. For petition restrictions, identification will follow the convention of the restriction—which could be a city block (or partial city block), a given street frontage (even-numbered addresses in the 4600 block of Labadie Avenue, for example), or a range of lots. In any case, the property descriptors in the restriction can usually be found in one or more of the fields in the current database.[39]

Assigning historical values or designations to current parcels is the simplest mapping strategy, and the current database—at least for the settings covered here—is a surprisingly accurate template for mapping historical restrictions. Major redevelopment projects in St. Louis, for example, occurred primarily downtown and in neighborhoods dominated by rental housing, leaving original patterns of residential development in those neighborhoods where restrictions were imposed largely undisturbed. Where a shift in land use had taken place—such as with the commercialization of a formerly residential street frontage—the original lot and subdivision descriptors remain in the record: the site of a big-box store, for example, might be assessed as a single parcel but will retain the legal description (such as "Lots 12-27, Burn's Addition") corresponding to the original platting or development. Historical descriptors and plat maps allowed us to map just over 70 percent of St. Louis County parcels restricted before 1950 directly to a current parcel. Almost all of the remaining 30 percent could be matched (using the subdivision descriptor) to a redeveloped footprint.

In this respect, there are three important differences between the historical residential footprint (the aggregate of thousands of platted subdivisions) and the current one. First, the premise of early suburban development was the construction of bedroom communities within commuting distance of the central city—but isolated from the nonresidential and mixed land use that prevailed there. Private development and municipal zoning often prohibited most commercial use of property. Over time, however, this premise shifted. As central cities like St. Louis continued to decline, suburban employment (or suburb-to-suburb commuting) became more common. After the 1960s, state and local constraints on the taxation of residential property pressed suburban interests to seek more retail and commercial development.[40] For these reasons, suburban developers and municipalities carved out more commercial use, especially along arterial streets and in shopping malls. Such developments often replaced all or part of some older, small-lot subdivisions.

Second, much of the early suburban footprint was redeveloped over time to accommodate larger lots and more robust infrastructure. This displaced some early subdivisions, but more commonly it yielded an ongoing pattern of redevelopment. Resubdivision plats and amended plats document the reconfiguration of older residential developments. In many cases, the racial restriction attached to the original development was simply carried over onto the new footprint. In other cases, resubdivision became an opportunity to attach a racial restriction for the first time.

And third, some early subdivisions were wholly or partially displaced by urban highway construction, redevelopment, or new environmental regulations or underwriting standards. In older cities, urban highway construction displaced homes and often split neighborhoods (a history notorious for its segregationist motives and consequences); in the suburbs, highway construction generally bypassed residential development. In St. Louis County, for example, we had to re-create one small subdivision, and restore portions of others, that had been erased by urban highway development. In Hennepin County, the Mapping Prejudice project had to recreate the restricted subdivision of "New Ford Town," (erased by expansion of the Minneapolis airport) from its original plat.[41] In city and suburb, an early penchant for crowding new housing onto lakefronts and riverbanks gradually retreated. Some of the older residential development missing from the current records shows up as floodplains or gravel pits.

In making these adjustments, mapping needs to be attentive to both changes in land use and changes in the size and count of residential lots. Across a county and in any given subdivision, the mapping workflow yields two counts of restricted lots: the first derived from the original subdivision of land (as represented on the historical plats); the second derived from the current GIS database. The current GIS count—reflecting a general pattern of redevelopment for either larger lots or nonresidential use—is generally smaller: in St. Louis County, for example, the plat book count was about 73,500 parcels, whereas the current GIS count was about 64,500. In most cases, the original plat offers the most reliable count of restricted parcels. The only exception to this rule (and adjustment of the lot totals) occurred when the original plat recorded a preliminary subdivision of land into large undeveloped lots. In such cases, we used the current parcel layer and records of housing construction to estimate the number of developed lots.

In all, and accounting for the adjustments described earlier, the current property database is a convenient and accurate base for the mapping of historical restrictions. The retention and consistency of original legal descriptors (such as subdivisions or city blocks) offers a precise crosswalk between historical and current property records. It is relatively easy to make the necessary corrections or adjustments, such as restoring the original parcels when they have been erased or distorted by subsequent development. And the ability to map historical restrictions onto contemporary platforms makes the history and impact of racial restriction more accessible and palpable to public audiences; assigning historical values or designations to current parcels allows contemporary homeowners (and others) to see the history of restriction underlying local properties.

Documenting racial property restrictions yields a precise and telling portrait of the geography and the timing of this crucial mechanism of housing patterns and opportunities. Mapped to the parcel level and to the date of restriction, these data add an important (if largely descriptive) dimension to our understanding of the broad patterns and local mechanisms of urban segregation. Temporally, the restriction data bridge the decennial postholes of the census and document the creation of a strategic patchwork of neighbor-hood restrictions and neighborhood boundaries. Spatially, the restrictions data can be overlaid and analyzed alongside other parcel or neighborhood measures such as housing prices; policy interventions such as urban renewal, federal housing policies, and local zoning; and the finer-grained local demographics unlocked by full-count census data and enumeration districts. This data and the work based on it afford a deeper understanding of the complex connective tissue between historical practices and current patterns of segregation, neighborhood risk, and housing value. It enhances both public awareness of past practices of racial discrimination and segregation and their current reflection or persistence in our public policies and built environment.

NOTES

Chapter 1: Introduction

1. City of St. Louis Recorder, Deed Book 1121-525 (1893); 1148-106 (1893).
2. Indenture provided to author by Spoede Hills resident Timothy McBride.
3. These restrictions, most commonly referred to as restrictive covenants, took a variety of legal forms. They could be added to deeds by the buyer or seller, drafted by home-owners as distinct agreements apart from the chain of title, or imposed at develop-ment in the form of a restrictive agreement or subdivision indenture. Almost all took the form of covenants, or voluntary contracts that ran with the land binding both the original signatories and future grantors and grantees. Many imposed restrictions on use or occupancy other than racial ones. Except where the form of restriction is important to the argument, I use the generic terms "restriction" or "restrictive agree-ment" to refer to any racial constraints on the sale or occupancy of residential property. See Brady 2021, 1614; Glotzer 2020, 8; Vose 1959, 7.
4. These calculations used the 1950 count of "owner occupied" homes as a denominator.
5. Sterner 1943, 208; Weaver 1948, 231–32; Thurgood Marshall, "Memorandum to Members of the National Legal Committee" (June 13, 1945), Group II, Series B, Legal File, Restrictive Covenants; Chicago, Illinois, Conferences [Conferences on Restrictive Covenants of NAACP National Legal Committee], 1945–1946, Papers of the NAACP, Part 05: Campaign against Residential Segregation, 1914–1955 [microfilm]; Vose 1959; Gonda 2015.
6. Brooks and Rose 2013; Glotzer 2020; Hayward 2013, 111–50; Rothstein 2017; Gotham 2000a; Rose 2022.

7. Radin 1982; Peñalver 2009.
8. Frug 1998.
9. Marshall 1950, 6; Somers 2008.
10. Rose 2022, 248; Mills 2017.
11. Bruch, Rosenthal, and Soss 2019.
12. Committee on Negro Housing 1931, 19.
13. Rusk 2001; Cutler and Glaeser 1997; Committee on Negro Housing 1931; Oliver and Shapiro 1995; Howell 2006.
14. Bruch and Gordon 2019; Kucheva and Sander 2014; Akbar et al. 2020.
15. Weaver 1948, 234.
16. Brubaker 2015; Sharkey and Faber 2014; Sharkey 2013; Sampson 2012; Anderson 2010, chapter 2.
17. Brubaker 2015, 9; see also Sampson 2012; Sharkey 2013; Massey 2020; Massey and Rugh 2021.
18. Lamont, Beljean, and Clair 2014; Valentino and Vaisey 2022.
19. Tilly 1998; Anderson 2010; Massey 2007; Lamont, Beljean, and Clair 2014; Valentino and Vaisey 2022.
20. Massey 2020.
21. Brady 2021, 1613.
22. Gotham 2000b, 617–8. In 1947, Herman Long and Charles Johnson argued that a comprehensive accounting of racial covenants was out of the question. Their research instead "employ[ed] short cut methods in finding the restrictive agreements, because of the large number of deed and tract books to be covered." See Long and Johnson 1947, 12.
23. Brooks and Rose 2013; Vose 1959; Gonda 2015.
24. Gordon 2008; Plotkin 1999, 2001; Stach 1988; Chase 1995; Gotham 2000b.
25. Cutler, Glaeser, and Vigdor 1999, table 1; Massey and Denton 1993, table 2.1. See chapter 4 for a fuller discussion of these measures.
26. Weiss 1987; Gordon 2008; Gordon 2019a.
27. Mills 2017; Rose 2022.
28. Fiel 2022; Bruch, Rosenthal, and Soss 2019; Bell and Willis 1957.
29. Logan et al. 2023.
30. On elite developers see Gotham 2000b; Glotzer 2020; Fogelson 2005. Classic accounts of suburbanization often touch on race restrictions in passing. See Hayden 2003; Fishman 1987; Jackson 1985.
31. Hayden 2003, 66-69; Slingsby 1980, 112–22.
32. Mills 1997, 52–53, 118–19.
33. Loren Miller in Survey Graphic, General [Restrictive Covenants; Violence and Intimidation], 1947–1950, Group II, Series B, Legal Files, Restrictive Covenants, Papers of the NAACP, Part 05: Campaign against Residential Segregation, 1914–1955 [microfilm].
34. Kahen 1945; Abrams 1955, 217.
35. Wimmer 2013, 68.
36. Block 2018.

37. Fields 1990, 110; see also Holt 1995.
38. Tilly 1998, 102; see also Anderson 2010; Hayward 2013; Valentino and Vaisey 2022.
39. Brady 2021, 1676.
40. Hochschild and Weaver 2007.
41. Du Bois 1923, 60.
42. Freund 2007, 99–116; Jackson 1985, Gotham 2000a; Hirsch 2000b.
43. Bateman, Katznelson and Lapinski 2018; Katznelson, Geiger, and Kryder 1993.
44. Gordon 2019c.
45. Abrams 1955, 229.
46. Weaver 1948, 211.
47. This follows the lead of Tilly (1998), focused and refined by Anderson (2010) to capture the durability of racial inequality and segregation in the United States.
48. Brady 2021; Godsil 2006.
49. Korngold 2001; Revell 1999.
50. Gibson and Jung 2005; Boustan and Margo 2013.
51. Gregory 2005; Boustan 2017.
52. Brooks and Rose 2013, 25.
53. Spear 1967; Muhammad 2010; Balto 2019; Derenoncourt 2022.
54. Muhammad 2010, 4.
55. Nightingale 2012.
56. Bell 1954; Meyer 2000; Massey and Denton 1993; Spear 1967; Hirsch 1983; Jones-Correa 1999.
57. Fisher 1990, 131.
58. Troesken and Walsh 2019.
59. Troesken and Walsh 2019; Silver 1991; Whittemore 2018, 2020.
60. Flint 1977; Weiss 1987.
61. Godsil 2006.
62. Address of Loren Miller (June 1947), Part 1, Reel 12: 0167, Papers of the NAACP, Part 05: Campaign against Residential Segregation, 1914–1955 [microfilm]; Gotham 2000c, 623.
63. Stach 1988; Fogelson 2005, 81–95. Brooks and Rose 2013, 48-49; Brady 2021. "Elements of effective restrictions include a declaration of intent and a clear legal description. Restrictions fall into the following categories: prohibited and permitted uses; approval of plans and building placement; prohibitions on resubdivision; cost and size of improvements; streets, easements, and rights-of-way; limits on occupancy; signage; Maintenance and upkeep; duration and terms; and declaration of right to enforce." Mott and Wehrly 1947, 4.
64. *Corrigan v. Buckley,* 271 U.S. 323 (1926).
65. Monchow 1928, 42–68; Fogelson 2005, 36.
66. Monchow 1928, 1; Fogelson 2005, 56–57.
67. Monchow 1928; Brooks and Rose 2013; Quinn 1979, 6; Zile 1959; Jost 1984.
68. Fogelson 2005, 121–22, 187–93.
69. See Philpott 1978; Fisher 1990.

70. Jost 1984; Monchow 1928.
71. Fogelson 2005, 96–99.
72. Monchow 1928.
73. Gordon 2023a; Long and Johnson 1947; Spear 1967; Weaver 1948.
74. Weaver 1948, 232.
75. Gotham 2000b; Glotzer 2020; Fogelson 2005, 59–69.
76. Gotham 2000a; Weiss 1987; Glotzer 2020; Michney and Winling 2021; Korver-Glenn 2021.
77. Nightingale 2012; Freund 2007, 54–66.
78. Gotham 2000b, 617–19; Jones-Correa 2000, 543.
79. Monchow 1928, 8; Stach 1988; Chase 1995; Weiss 1987.
80. Plotkin 2001, 30–36, 41–42; Garb 2005, 2006; Shoenfeld and Cherkasky 2016; Gordon 2023a, Long and Johnson 1947; Quinn 1979.
81. Quinn 1979; Zile 1959; Delegard 2016.
82. In New York City, petition-based racial restrictions were used briefly (before World War I) to "protect" blocks or buildings in Harlem. See McGruder 2015, 68–96. In his work on Philadelphia, Larry Santucci (2020) found just under 4,000 restricted properties in the deed books spanning 1920–1932 (roughly 1 million unique entries).
83. Horiuchi 2007.
84. Dawson 2019.
85. Fisher 2008; Redford 2017.
86. Garcia 2018; Garcia and Yosso 2013; Lieb 2019; Tretter 2012.
87. Cayton 1940; Plotkin 1999, 20–21, 45; Weaver 1948, 246; Slingsby 1980, 112–22. Varying estimates (in Chicago and elsewhere) reflect a wide array of survey methods. Some estimates are based on samples of subdivision records; some on a complete scan of the available property records. Some are "point in time" estimates of restricted property; some are estimates for a given range of years. In the research assembled for *Tovey v. Levy* (1948), estimates based on designated square mile sections, adjusted for residential and nonresidential use, found that thirty-eight of eighty-five residential sections (44 percent) were race restricted. See Slingsby 1980, 112–120.
88. Shoenfeld and Cherkasky 2016.
89. Redford 2017.
90. Freund 2007, 50–80, 94; Dean 1947; Gotham 2000b; Quinn 1979; Chase 1995, 260–64; Zile 1959. In Kansas City, estimates based on subdivision plats found about three-quarters of new development between 1930 and 1947, and fully 96 percent in suburban Johnson County were race restricted. Slingsby 1980, 112–22.
91. Governor's Interracial Commission 1947, 66–67.
92. Consigny and Zile 1958; Dean 1947; Jost 1984.
93. Santucci 2020; Gregory et al. 2016; Garcia 2018; Weaver 1948, 246; Long and Johnson 1947.
94. See, for example, U.S. News and World Report 2022.
95. See, for example, One Economy 2017, which notes for Waterloo, Iowa: "we live in a community that touts its livability for young professionals and retirees alike yet landed at #3 of the Worst Cities for African Americans just this year" (6).

96. Sauter 2017; Gordon 2019b.
97. Derenoncourt 2022; Wilson 1987; Wilson 2011; Boustan 2017; Trotter 1985; Gottlieb 1987; Grossman 1989; Gregory 2005; Phillips 1999.
98. Sugrue 1996, 143–44; Knudsen 1989.
99. Hirsch 2000a; Rothstein 2017; Sugrue 1996; Hirsch 1983; Gordon 2008; Gotham 2002; Trotter 1995; Fogelson 2005.
100. Logan and Parman 2017.
101. Vock, Charles, and Maciag 2019.
102. Jones-Correa 1999; Balto 2019; Tuttle 1970, Pacyga 1997; Lumpkins 2008; Jackson 1967.
103. Derenoncourt 2022; Phillips 1999; Boustan 2017.
104. Cayton and Drake 1945, 101.
105. Kasarda 1989; Haynes and Machunda 1987.
106. Gordon 2014.
107. Wilson 1987; Kain 1968.
108. Sharkey 2013; Wilson 1987; Chetty et al. 2020; Brady and Wallace 2001.
109. Author's calculations based on Ruggles et al. 2022.
110. Committee on Negro Housing 1931, 35–36.
111. Gordon 2008; Gordon 2023a.
112. Breaux 2002.
113. Neymeyer 1980, Jones 1997, 108ff.
114. Delegard 2016; Montrie 2022; Walker et al. 2023.
115. Fox and Guglielmo 2012.
116. Lamont, Beljean, and Clair 2014; Valentino and Vaisey 2022.
117. Gonda 2015; Vose 1959; Brooks and Rose 2013.

Chapter 2: Caucasians Only: Categories, Frames, and Narratives in Private Restriction

1. Mills 1997; Fields 1990; Hacking 2005; Gossett 1963; Wacquant 2022.
2. Anderson 2010, 9; see also Tilly 1998, 53; Mills 2019, 104.
3. Haney López 2006.
4. Hayward 2013, 63; Wimmer 2013, 63–72.
5. Mills 2019.
6. Bonilla-Silva and Embrick 2007.
7. Cayton and Drake 1945, 672.
8. Bonilla Silva and Embrick 2007; Anderson 2010, 44–66; Hayward 2013, 42–80. On the centrality of these ideas to the worldview of local property interests and professional realty, see Krysan and Crowder 2017; Helper 1969; and Glotzer 2020.
9. Rusk 2001; Weaver 1948, 261–78.
10. Gibson and Jung 2006.
11. Jacobson 1999, 78; Dillingham 1911, 3.
12. Dillingham 1911, 30–31.

13. Jacobson 1999, 41–43.
14. Grant quoted in Jacobson 1999, 82–83; Gossett 1963, 354–57.
15. Roediger 2005, 35–48; Fields 2001; Hochschild and Weaver 2007; Fox and Guglielmo 2012.
16. Hoyt 1933, 316.
17. Brady 2021.
18. Black Hawk County Reorder, Miscellaneous Records 2-232, 2-399.
19. Ehrman-Solberg et al. 2020, Walton's 6th Division of Seven Oaks, Minneapolis, 1914; Walton Hills 2nd Addition in Minneapolis, 1915. Since the Hennepin County data do not include the original master agreements, restrictions are dated to their first appearance in a subdivision or addition.
20. *Shelley v. Kraemer*, Transcript of the Record before the St. Louis Court of Appeals (1946), Supreme Court Case Files, Record Group 600, Missouri State Archives, Jefferson City; City of St. Louis Recorder, Deed Book 2400-488 (1911); 3107-125 (1912); for anti-Chinese clauses, see City of St. Louis Recorder, Deed Book 1814-547 (1905); 1817-313 (1905); 1820-317 (1905); 1854-260 (1905).
21. St. Louis County Recorder, Deed Book 168-514 (Maple Place, 1909); 1355-452 (Huntleigh Woods, 1936).
22. See St. Louis County Recorder, Deed Book 355-1 (Ames Place, 1915); 532-581 (University Park, 1922); 735-1 (University Park 2, 1925); 812-27 (Osage Hills, 1926); 911-40 (Pasadena Hills, 1928–1929); 1410-38 (Deer Creek Woods, 1935); 1598-316 (Chafford Woods, 1939); 1654-131 (Frederick Lane, 1939); 1842-312 (Parkside, 1942); 1830-394 (Belleview Park, 1942–1948); 2666-547 (Glyn Cagny, 1950).
23. See Black Hawk County Recorder, Miscellaneous Records 2-232.
24. See Ehrman-Solberg et al. 2020, Elmhurst Addition of Minneapolis, 1924; Crystal Park, Robbinsdale, 1922; Killarney Addition, Brooklyn, 1948; Solomon Gray Block, Minneapolis, 1932; Triangle Addition to Minneapolis, 1924; and Fieldstone Acres, Brooklyn, 1948.
25. McWilliams 1946, 61.
26. Delegard 2019.
27. St. Louis County Recorder, Plat Book 27-28 (Algonquinwood Resubdivision, 1928); Deed Book 2319-472 (High Acres, 1946); 1355-452 (Huntleigh Woods, 1936); 1572-24 (Quade Tract, 1939).
28. Johnson County Recorder, Deed Book 146-62 (1927); 155-7 (1929).
29. Ehrman-Solberg et al. 2020, Wooddale, 1924; Wooddale 2nd Addition, 1931.
30. St. Louis County Recorder, Deed Book 562-172 (Sunset Terrace, 1922); Ehrman-Solberg et al. 2020, County Club District Fairway Section, Edina, 1924.
31. For the earlier version, see the run of restrictions beginning at City of St. Louis Recorder, Deed Book 5247-1 (1932); for the post-1942 version, see City of St. Louis Recorder, Deed Book 6162-52.
32. See St. Louis County Recorder, Deed Book 1596-367 (Vermont Park, 1939); 2214-612 (Bender, 1946); for Hennepin County (Edina Highlands, Edina 1946);

(Countryside, Edina, 1948); (Bel-Air Addition, Robbinsdale, 1948); (Pennhurst, Minneapolis, 1946); (St. Anthony Boulevard Addition, Minneapolis, 1927).

33. St. Louis County Recorder, Plat Book 8-84 (Mortiz Place, 1909); 15-25 (Mortiz Place Addition, 1921); 17-62 (Acreton, 1924); 20-118 (Acreton Addition, 1926).

34. The Iowa City exceptions are Johnson County Recorder, Deed Book 146-62 (1927); and 155-7 (1934).

35. Gordon 2023a; Plotkin 1999; Glotzer 2020.

36. Monchow 1928; Stach 1988; Weiss 1987.

37. Brady 2021, 1624–26. Of restrictive language in Austin, Eliott Tretter (2012) notes "a noticeable shift away from using the phrase no people of 'African descent' could buy or occupy land (except, in many cases, as domestic servants) in particular neighborhoods to stating a subdivision or a property could only be inhabited by 'Caucasian' or 'white' persons."

38. Hochschild and Weaver 2007.

39. Mills 2017, 127. See also Jacobson 1999, 102–08; Roediger 2005, 11–13; Hayward 2013, 50–51; Morris 2000.

40. Muhammad 2010; Roediger 2005, 165–66.

41. Hoyt 1933, 314.

42. Roediger 2005, 157–77; and McGreevy 1996 18–21, 36.

43. Fox and Guglielmo 2012, 365.

44. Roediger 2005, 171–73.

45. Morris 2000.

46. "Housing-Cote Brilliante Ave" (June 1927), Series 1, Box 5, Urban League of St. Louis Records, Special Collections, Washington University, University City, Mo.

47. Instructions to enumerators from Ruggles et al. 2022, accessed April 19, 2023, https:// usa.ipums.org/usa/voliii/tEnumInstr.shtml.

48. Pascoe 1996; see also Hochschild and Weaver 2007.

49. Haney-López 2006, chapter 3 and appendix tables 1 and 3.

50. Sharfstein 2003; Holt 1995.

51. Plotkin 1999, 18–24, 29.

52. St. Louis County Recorder, Deed Book 343-158 (South Richmond Heights, 1914).

53. Shoenfeld and Cherkasky 2016, 37.

54. *Sipes v. McGhee*, 316 Mich. 614, 628, 25 N.W.2d 638, 644.

55. Ehrman-Solberg et al. 2020, Franklin Steeles Minnehaha Terrace Addition, Minneapolis, 1924; Bellevue Acres, Brooklyn, 1924; Dorman's First Addition, Minneapolis, 1913.

56. St. Louis County Recorder, Deed Book 1355-452 (Huntleigh Woods, 1936).

57. Ehrman-Solberg et al. 2020, Murray Heights Addition to Minneapolis, 1947; Snyders Victory Memorial Drive, Minneapolis, 1941; Park Manor, St. Louis Park, 1929.

58. St. Louis County Recorder, Deed Book 303-13 (New St. Louis Country Club, 1912); 1266-275 (Layton, 1934); 1707-50 (Monticello, 1940); 2174-248 (Green Park Hills, 1946).

59. See Ehrman-Solberg et al. 2020, Elmquist Addition, Richfield, 1946.

60. See Dawson 2019; Glotzer 2020.

61. Ehrman-Solberg et al. 2020, Thorpe Brothers Nokomis Terrace, 1913; Eastview Park, Minnestrista, 1946.

62. St. Louis County Recorder, Deed Book 181-223 (Glen Echo Park, 1906); 205-357 (West Ashby, 1910).

63. Johnson County Recorder, Deed Book 159-472 (Kirkwood Circle).

64. Brady 2021.

65. Quoted in Abrams 1955, 156, emphasis added.

66. Godsil 2006.

67. Freund 2007, 67–68; Brady 2021.

68. This example from Montgomery County (PA), Deed Book 729-578. See also St. Louis County Recorder, Plat Book1-102 (Gibson, 1902); Deed Book 154-30 (Bemis Addition, 1905); 249-426 (Forsyth Place, 1910); 534-152 (Bellevue Square, 1922); Plat Book 15-115 (Harris Place, 1924); Plat Book 22-51 (Coral Gables, 1926).

69. Bruce 1927, 716.

70. Vose 1959, 7; Brooks and Rose 2013, 49–50.

71. *Kathan v Stevenson* 307 Mich. 485 (1943).

72. See "Vandeventer Place Owners Would Bar Renting to Negroes," *St. Louis Post-Dispatch* (April 10, 1944), "Vandeventer Place Hearing Continued," *St. Louis Globe-Democrat* (April 27, 1944), "Hearing on Vandeventer Place Suit to Bar Negro Owners," (publisher not indicated; 1943), "Vandeventer Place Injunction Granted," *St. Louis Post-Dispatch* (March 5, 1943), "Vandeventer Place Residents Sue," (publisher not indicated; 1943), all in St. Louis Public Library, Discrimination in Housing, Clippings Collection.

73. Vandeventer Place Indenture at City of St. Louis Recorder, Deed Book 413-25. See Beito and Smith 1990, 265–67.

74. City of St. Louis Recorder, Deed Book 6209-104 (1943).

75. Chase 1995, 309.

76. For one of the first uses of this agreement, see City of St. Louis Recorder, Deed Book 3739-178 (1922).

77. City of St. Louis Recorder, Deed Book 3463-383 (Cleveland Heights, 1921).

78. St. Louis County Recorder, Deed Book 691-515 (Westcamp 1928); 2252-576 (Yorkshire, 1946).

79. Ehrman-Solberg et al. 2020, Winnetka, Golden Valley, 1915; Glenwood, Golden Valley, 1917; Lakeview Heights, Golden Valley, 1916. This was the general pattern in Detroit as well, especially during Prohibition. See Freund 2007, 95.

80. Johnson County Recorder, Deed Book 146-62.

81. Brooks and Rose 2013, 14, 211–30; Glotzer 2020, 5; Hayward 2013, 111–50; Gonda 2015, 25.

82. Du Bois 1925, 9.

83. Freund 2007, 8–15, 33; Morris 2000.

84. Du Bois 1899, 348; Weaver 1948, 211.

85. *Buchanan v. Warley*, 245 U.S. 60 (1917).

86. Quoted in Abrams 1955, 155.
87. Kniskern 1933.
88. American Institute of Real Estate Appraisers 1951, 51.
89. Helper 1969, 119.
90. Mott and Wehrly 1947, 7.
91. Garb 2006, 773.
92. Chilton Anderson, "Observations on the Segregation Ordinance" (1916), Rare Books Collection, SLPL.
93. William Butts to Archbishop Glennon (December 14, 1927), Box 2, folder 17, Charles Vatterott Research Collection, S1004, State Historical Society of Missouri, St. Louis.
94. City of St. Louis Recorder, Deed Book 5247-1 (1932), 6162-52.
95. Appellant's Abstract of the Record, *Thornhill v. Herdt*, Supreme Court Case Files, Record Group 600, Missouri State Archives, Jefferson City.
96. "Negro Question Causes Protest," *Minneapolis Morning Tribune* (November 16, 1920), 2.
97. Governor's Interracial Commission 1947, 52.
98. Roithmayr 2010; Weaver 1948, 234.
99. Long and Johnson 1947, 5.
100. Weaver 1948, 302. "The ill-kept and unsightly outward aspect of these areas . . . becomes associated in the minds of other city residents with the current occupants themselves, who merely inherited the area in the last stages of its usefulness as a dwelling place. The significant result is that the condition of this housing actually becomes the reason for public insistence that Negroes continue to live in it." Long and Johnson 1947, 4.
101. Shertzer, Twinam, and Walsh 2016; Flint 1977; Muhammad 2010; Balto 2019.
102. Du Bois 1925, 9.
103. Weaver 1948, 279–303, quote at 297.
104. Hoyt 1933, 314.
105. Nightingale 2012, 309–11.
106. Weaver 1948.
107. Roithmayr 2010; Sood, Speagle, and Ehrman-Solberg 2019.
108. Long and Johnson 1947, 44.
109. Committee on Negro Housing 1931, 79, 87.
110. Stone 2005, 66.
111. Mills 2017, 63–64.

Chapter 3: Dividing the City: Patterns of Private Restriction

1. The Hennepin County data, assembled entirely from parcel-level deed restrictions, strongly implies restriction through subdivision indentures or declarations of restrictions but does not actually document these. There is anecdotal evidence (see Montrie

2022, 135) that some of these may have been accomplished through petition. But given the pattern in other settings (Long and Johnson 1947; Shoenfeld and Cherkasky 2016), where petitions were used only in "threatened" neighborhoods, the assumption here is that almost all of the Hennepin County restrictions were established by developers or subdivision trustees.

2. Jackson 1980.

3. Checkoway 1980.

4. The city of St. Louis and St. Louis County are the only settings in which we have a full catalog of all restrictions, of which racial restrictions are a subset.

5. Gotham 2000c; Fogelson 2005; Monchow 1928; Weiss 1987; Checkoway 1980; Dean 1947.

6. Frug 1998.

7. Fogelson 2005; Glotzer 2020; Gotham 2000c.

8. This contrasts, for example, with settings developed by early railroad suburbs. The "Main Line" suburbs of Philadelphia, for example, were strung along the Pennsylvania RR at regular intervals in the late nineteenth and early twentieth centuries; suburban development in the 1920s and 1930s filled in the gaps. See Jackson 1980, 91–92; Fishman 1987.

9. Committee on Subdivision Layout 1931, 14–15.

10. Fogelson 2005, 81–95.

11. Quoted in Kahen 1945.

12. In Iowa and Missouri, master subdivision agreements were recorded in the regular run of deed records; in Minnesota they were held by the developer.

13. Jost 1984, 726–27.

14. St. Louis County Recorder, Deed Book 1024-22. Bellerive Acres (693-3, 1924); Richmond Hills (2166-371, 1946).

15. St. Louis County Recorder, Deed Book 552-422 (1922). See also Webster Heights (St. Louis County Recorder, Deed Book 62-163 [1893]; 563-148 [1923]); Bonita Park (162-30 [1905]; 806-65 [1926]); and Algonquinwood (Plat Book 27-28 [1928]; Deed Book 934-152 [1928]).

16. Mott and Wehrly 1947, 4.

17. In Hennepin County, subdivision restrictions can only be estimated, as the master agreements were not filed with the recorder and the data were collected at the parcel level. The Mapping Prejudice data include 582 unique subdivisions. If that is narrowed to all the platted additions with at least 10 restrictions and a restriction rate of at least one-third, that yields a count of 251 subdivisions with an average size of just under 100 parcels.

18. Jaffee 2007; *Sanborn v. McLean,* 206 N.W. 496, 497 (Mich. 1925); Zile 1959.

19. Abrams 1955, 170–71.

20. Montrie 2019.

21. Ware 2020; Stach 1988.

22. Checkoway 1980.

23. Checkoway 1980; Weiss 1987, 146–48.

24. Freund 2007, 99–116; Gotham 2000b.
25. City of St. Louis Recorder, Deed Book 5087-617; St. Louis Real Estate Exchange Restrictive Agreement, in *Dolan and Wehmeyer v. Richardson et al.*, Abstract of the Record before the St. Louis Court of Appeals (1944), Plaintiff's Exhibit "A," Supreme Court Case Files, Record Group 600, Missouri State Archives, Jefferson City.
26. Brooks and Rose 2013, 12–13, 81–82.
27. St. Louis County Recorder, Deed Book 1679-112 (Penmar, 1940).
28. City of St. Louis Recorder, Deed Book 5209-284 (1931).
29. Richardson 1945; Long and Johnson 1947, 19–20. On some forms starting in 1931, the St. Louis Real Estate Exchange filled in all property owners and then crossed off those that did not sign (see 5715-436).
30. On the Marcus Avenue Association, see Vose 1959, 100–109; for the similar pattern in Kansas City, see Slingsby 1980, 49–52.
31. Gordon 2008; Richardson 1945; Long and Johnson 1947; St. Louis Real Estate Exchange Restrictive Agreement, reprinted in *Dolan and Wehmeyer v. Richardson et al.*, Abstract of the Record before the St. Louis Court of Appeals (1944), Plaintiff's Exhibit "A," Supreme Court Case Files, Record Group 600, Missouri State Archives, Jefferson City.
32. Van Hecke 1928, 409.
33. Brooks and Rose 2013, 79–80.
34. See "History," National Association of Realtors, accessed April 20, 2023, https://www.nar.realtor/about-nar/history.
35. "Frederick Seeks Quiet: Accused St. Louis Man Defers a Promised Statement," *New York Times* (April 12, 1915), 10.
36. National Association of Real Estate Boards, 1924, article 34.
37. National Association of Real Estate Boards 1950.
38. Weiss 1987, 24–32; Glotzer 2020.
39. Helper 1969; Yinger 1995.
40. "Segregation of Negroes Sought," *Waterloo Courier* (June 29, 1916), 6.
41. See Johnson County Recorder, Deed Book 128-169; 128-550; 145-178; 146-62; 151-132; 154-81; 154-196; 154-399; 155-7; 159-56; 159-535; 160-321; 160-473; 162-491; 164-19; 164-32; 164-348; 172-187; 172-315; 175-54; 175-142; 176-114; 181-262; 187-107; 187-331; 193-343.
42. City of St. Louis Recorder, Plat Book 12-136, 1888.
43. "Chouteau Place in Fight to Halt Negro Invasion," *St. Louis Post-Dispatch* (December 2, 1914), 8; Fogelson 2005, 96–99.
44. Beito and Smith 1990; Hunter 1988, 20–24. See, for example, the original deed for West Cabanne Place (City of St. Louis Recorder, Deed Book 1896-192 [1905]) specifying racial restrictions and the addition of racial restrictions at Vandeventer Place (6209-104 [1943]).
45. City of St. Louis Recorder, Deed Book 1896-192 (West Cabanne Place, 1905); 2149-477 (Thornby Place, 1908).
46. Dawson 2019.

47. City of St. Louis Recorder, Deed Book 6209-104 (Vandeventer Place 1943).
48. City of St. Louis Recorder, Deed Book 2149-477 (Thornby Place, 1908); 3371-517 (Thornby Place 1920).
49. This as a pattern echoed in Kansas City. See Gotham 2002, chapter 4.
50. Jones-Correa 2000, 548–51, 557–58.
51. City of St. Louis Recorder, Deed Book 1963-176 (1906); 2042-245 (1907); 2319-382 (1910); 2297-534 (1910); 2332-343 (1910); 2474-164 (1911); 2490-134 (1911); 2697-512 (1914); 2878-160 (1915); 2952-22 (1916); 2956-102 (1916); City of St. Louis Recorder, Plat Book 9-4 (1913).
52. City of St. Louis Recorder, Deed Book 2330-353 (1910); 2400-488 (1911); 2660-550 (1912); and 3107-125 (1912).
53. The Mapping Prejudice data do not include master agreements, and the dating of restricted parcels does not necessarily reflect the original or first restriction of said parcel. The year-by-year calculations here assume any subdivision with at least ten restricted parcels to be covered by a master agreement and assign all restricted parcels in that subdivision to the date of the earliest recorded restriction. The conservative parcel estimate includes *only* those confirmed as restricted.
54. Snowden 2006, table Dc510-530.
55. Glotzer 2020, 137–47; Helper 1969; Gotham 2000c, 617–19, 621; Freund 2007, 51–54.
56. Snowden 2006, table Dc510-530.
57. FHLBB 1938, Exhibit 24.
58. Boone and Wilse-Samson 2021.
59. Weaver 1948, 235.
60. Vose 1959, 12; Gordon 2008, 82–88.
61. City of St. Louis Recorder, Deed Book 6879-439 (1949); 6894-410 (1950).
62. In the Mapping Prejudice data, 916 parcels in 57 subdivisions have a restriction date after May 1948. But many of these are in subdivisions where the first recorded restriction comes earlier. If we assume that the original (subdivision) restrictions in these cases were filed pre-*Shelley,* that narrows the list to 10 subdivisions in which all recorded restrictions come after May 1948.
63. See St. Louis County Recorder, Deed Book 2528-323 (Brookdale Park, 1949); 2531-99 (Forest Heights Place, 1949); 2561-78 (Champlain, 1949).
64. Leffingwells First Addition (1876-602) in 1942 was race restricted; the Second Addition (2556-70) in 1949 retreated to a general nuisance restriction. See also Woodlawn Terrace (restricted through City of St. Louis Recorder, Deed Book 2479-312, 1948; unrestricted deed book 2673-448, 1950); Hathaway Hills (restricted through City of St. Louis Recorder, Deed Book 2479-429, 1949; unrestricted deed book 2561-520, 1949); Hanley Hills (restricted through City of St. Louis Recorder, Deed Book 2654-49, 1950; 2725-386, 1950).
65. City of St. Louis Recorder, Deed Book 4941-170 (4200 block of Ashland, 1929); 5583-474 (3600 block of Finney, 1936); 5956-90 (single parcel, 1940); 6305-142 (Bayard between Page and Delmar, 1944); 6195-144 (4300 block of Ashland, 1943).

66. Black Hawk County Reorder, Miscellaneous Records 58-381; 58-384 (1948); and 62-621 (1949).

67. Given the challenges of archival research in two more counties (St. Clair and Madison) and another state, this analysis does not include the "industrial suburbs" on the Illinois side of the St. Louis metropolitan area.

68. See Wright 2001.

69. High-resolution color versions of this and other maps in the book, as well as datasets and additional maps, are available in the online appendix at https://www.russellsage .org/publications/patchwork-apartheid.

70. St. Louis Recorder of Deeds 2400-488 (1911).

71. Long and Johnson 1947, 25–30.

72. Montrie 2022, 133.

73. Brooks and Rose 2013, 72–78; Fogelson 2005, 107–10; Plotkin 2001, 41-2; Vose 1959, 11; Monchow 1928, 56. For case law, see *Queensboro Land Co. v. Cazeaux*, 136 La. 724, 67 So. 641 (1915) (twenty-five years); *Koehler v. Rowland*, 275 Mo. 573, 205 S.W. 217 (1918) (twenty-five years); City of St. Louis Recorder, Deed Book 3841-386 (1923); 30 F. (2d) 981 (App. D.C. 1929) (no time limit); *Chandler v. Ziegler*, 88 Colo. 1, 291 Pac. 822 (1930); *Lee v. Hansberry*, 372 Ill. 369, 24 N.E. (2d) 37 (1939).

74. Governor's Interracial Commission 1947, 65–66.

75. St. Louis County Recorder, Plat Book 28-52 (Hyland Park, 1930); (Belvair Place, 2208-205, 1946) St. Louis County Recorder, Deed Book 555-3 (Westmoor Park, 1922); 2208-206 (Balvair Place, 1946).

76. City of St. Louis Recorder, Deed Book 4956-390 (St. Louis Hills, 1929).

77. St. Louis County Recorder, Spoede Road; Deed Book 2166-371 (South Richmond Hills, 1946).

78. St. Louis County Recorder, Deed Book 1673-548 (Brentwood Terrace, 1940).

79. Brooks and Rose 2013. On Minneapolis, see Montrie 2022, 134–36; for St. Louis examples, see "Stench Bomb Again Hurled," *St. Louis Argus* (September 19, 1941), 1; "Harm Negro Homes: 5 Race Families Get Threats," *St. Louis Argus* (October 24, 1941), 1; "Continue N. Market Neighborhood Suits: Homes Stench Bombed," *St. Louis Argus* (November 14, 1941), 1; "More Negro Homes Stench Bombed," *St. Louis Argus* (December 5, 1941), 1.

80. Long and Johnson 1947, 66–69.

81. Vose 1959, 7–11, 110–12.

82. St. Louis County Recorder, Deed Book 175-550 (University Heights, 1906); 1633-321 (Cardinal Hills, 1940).

83. Long and Johnson 1947, 19.

84. Chase 1995, 310.

85. City of St. Louis Recorder, Deed Book 6511-557 (St. Louis Hills, 1946). See also St. Louis County Recorder, Deed Book 170-392 (Vinita Park, 1905); 2166-371 (Richmond Hills, 1946); 2252-576 (Yorkshire #2, 1946); 1507-456 (Laymont, 1939); 2309-522 (Glen Creek, 1947).

Chapter 4: Patchwork Apartheid: Private Restrictions and Racial Segregation

1. Massey and Denton 1988; Fiel 2022.
2. Anderson 2010; Charles 2003; Sampson 2009; Sharkey 2013; Massey and Denton 1993; Massey and Rugh 2021; Massey 2020; Gordon 2019c.
3. Massey and Denton 1988, 26–30.
4. Muhammad 2010; Balto 2019, Jones-Correa 2000, Spear 1967.
5. Cayton and Drake 1945; see also Spear 1967; Jones 1997.
6. Bell and Willis 1957; Fiel 2022.
7. Tilly 1998.
8. Work by Allison Shertzer, Randall Walsh, and John Logan (2016), breaking local census demographics into their original enumeration districts, provides a fine-grained picture of black and white population patterns for the years before census tract (pre-1930 in St. Louis) or census block (pre-1940) data are available. In size and population, enumeration districts are roughly equivalent to contemporary census block groups (in St. Louis, there were 478 enumeration districts in 1910 and 359 block groups in 2010). This scale offers a cleaner and more consistent surrogate for "neighborhood" than political wards, the conventional unit for indices of segregation before 1930 (Bae and Freeman 2021).
9. Lee et al. 2008.
10. Kramer 2017.
11. In his 1955 classic, *Forbidden Neighbors*, Abrams described five key mechanisms of segregation: violence, structural controls, social controls, economic constraints, and legal constraints (Abrams 1955, 77–78).
12. Ananant 2011.
13. Roberto 2018, 183.
14. Garcia 2018; Grannis 2005; Roberto and Hwang 2017.
15. Fiel 2022; Wacquant 1997; Bruch, Rosenthal, and Soss 2019.
16. Connolly 2014; Mohl 2004; Tretter 2012; Rabin 1980.
17. Glotzer 2020; Trounstine 2018.
18. Carriere 2011; Glotzer 2020; Horiuchi 2007; Winling 2011; Schindler 2015.
19. FHA 1938, 935.
20. Prener et al. 2019. The most infamous example here is Detroit's Birwood Wall, erected by developers at the behest of the FHA to insulate a new development from the risk posed by an established black neighborhood. See Dusen 2019; Sugrue 1996.
21. Davis 2006, 154–56, 224.
22. Shertzer, Twinam, and Walsh 2016; Rothwell and Massey 2009.
23. Bischoff 2008; Erickson 2016; Owens 2017.
24. Slingsby 1980, 42–43.
25. Ayers 2021; Hayward 2013; Helper 1969; Sugrue 1995.
26. Crowder and Krysan 2017, 6.

27. Quoted in Cayton and Drake 1945, 79.
28. Long and Johnson 1947, 31.
29. Gordon 2023a; Santucci 2020; Shoenfeld and Cherkasky 2016.
30. Long and Johnson 1947, 10.
31. Kahen 1945, 204.
32. Long and Johnson 1947, 23–31; Weaver 1948, 246.
33. Krysan and Crowder 2017.
34. Brooks and Rose 2013.
35. Weaver 1948.
36. DeSena 1994.
37. Bruch, Rosenthal, and Soss 2019.
38. See Logan et al. 2023; Dusen 2019.
39. U.S. Census Bureau 1953 (Part IV, Missouri, table 26).
40. Jubara and Zhang 2021; Lloyd 2013; FHA 1938.
41. The 1910 African American population totals for both Waterloo (twenty-five) and the County (twenty-nine) were inflated by inconsistent enumeration: residents of Greek and Turkish origin were coded as white, mulatto, and other. See 1910 Manuscript Census, Black Hawk County, Ward 1, Enumeration District, page 8; Ward 2, ED 16, page 1; and Ward 3, ED 23, page 1.
42. Jones 1997, 108ff; Neymeyer 1980, 108ff; "Central Adds to Police Guard," *Waterloo Courier* (October 5, 1911), 8.
43. "Waterloo I.C. Shopmen Left Places at 8 A.M.," *Waterloo Courier* (October 2, 1911), 1.
44. "Governor Wants Strike Settled," *Waterloo Courier* (February 2, 1912), 3.
45. Jones 1997, 110–11.
46. See Jones 1997; Neymeyer 1980.
47. "Negro Loafer Is Arrested; Police Watching All Idlers," *Waterloo Courier* (September 18, 1918), 7.
48. Black Hawk County Reorder, Miscellaneous Records 2-232 (1914); 2-399 (1915).
49. Neymeyer 1980.
50. Black Hawk County Reorder, Miscellaneous Records 4-539 (1922).
51. Spear 1967, Cayton and Drake 1945.
52. Harlan 2014.
53. John Clark, "Historical Sketch of Negro Housing" (1935), Box 5, Series 8, Urban League of St. Louis Records, Special Collections, Washington University, University City, Mo.
54. Barone 2018; Bartholomew 1918; Long and Johnson 1947.
55. Gordon 2008.
56. "Blocks in Which Negroes May Thereafter Take Up Residence," *St. Louis Post-Dispatch* (March 2, 1916), St. Louis Public Library, Discrimination in Housing, Clippings Collection.
57. Bartholomew 1918; Gordon 2008.
58. W.C. Bitting, "Zoning Promotes the Public Welfare," in Bartholomew 1918, 67.
59. Revell 1999.

60. Gordon 2008.

61. *St. Louis v. Evraiff,* 301 Mo. 231, 256 S.W. 489 (Mo. 1923).

62. See online appendix map 4A.1.

63. Flint 1977; Baker 1925; Gordon 2008.

64. "Recommendations for Changes in Zoning in Negro Residential Area" (1938), Series 1, Box 5, Urban League of St. Louis Records, Special Collections, Washington University, University City, Mo.

65. Shertzer, Twinam, and Walsh 2016.

66. Flint 1977; Rothwell and Massey 2009; Shertzer, Twinam, and Walsh 2016.

67. John Clark to Harland Bartholomew (December 3, 1946), Series 1, Box 5, Urban League of St. Louis Records, Special Collections, Washington University, University City, Mo.

68. Gordon 2008.

69. Flint 1977.

70. Beito and Smith 1990.

71. Bartholomew 1917.

72. "Recommendations for Changes in Zoning in Negro Residential Are" (1938) and "Proposed Zoning of Negro Residential Area West of Grand Avenue" (1938) both in Box 5, Series 1, Urban League of St. Louis Records, Special Collections, Washington University, University City, Mo.

73. "Realty Exchange Opposes West End Sales to Negroes," *St. Louis Post-Dispatch* (February 21, 1920), St. Louis Public Library, Discrimination in Housing, Clippings Collection.

74. "Plans Advanced to Solve Negro Housing Problem," *St. Louis Post-Dispatch* (August 31, 1923), St. Louis Public Library, Discrimination in Housing, Clippings Collection.

75. Gordon 2023a; Long and Johnson 1947; Vose 1959.

76. "Social and Economic Factors Involved in the Movements of Negro Families in St. Louis," (n.d.), folder 46, box 8, series, 8, Urban League of St. Louis Records, Special Collections, Washington University, University City, Mo.

77. "Enright Property Owners Organized to Oppose Sale of Property to Colored," *St Louis Argus* (January 30, 1920). See also Long and Johnson 1947.

78. Hurley and Murray 2022.

79. See *Pickel v. McCawley,* 329 Mo. 166 (1931); Appellant's Abstract of the Record, *Pickel v. McCawley, Mueninghaus v. James,* 324 Mo. 767 (1930), Supreme Court Case Files, Record Group 600, Missouri State Archives, Jefferson City.

80. Schelling 1963.

81. Ananat 2011; Boger 2009.

82. Weaver 1948, 238.

83. John Clark to Real Estate Exchange (November 1927); "Open Letter to Cote Brilliante Property Owners" (July 1927), both in Series 1, Box 5, Urban League of St. Louis Records, Special Collections, Washington University, University City, Mo.

84. "Negroes Are Moving into the 4300 Block Page," *St. Louis Post-Dispatch* (November 9, 1939), St. Louis Public Library, Discrimination in Housing, Clippings Collection.

85. Area Description D-15, FHLBB, Division of Research and Statistics, St. Louis 1940.

86. "Home Sale to Negro Arouses Page BLVD.," *St. Louis Post-Dispatch* (July 18, 1937), St. Louis Public Library, Discrimination in Housing, Clippings Collection.

87. "Negroes Are Moving into the 4300 Block Page," *St. Louis Post-Dispatch* (November 9, 1939), St. Louis Public Library, Discrimination in Housing, Clippings Collection.

88. "Renewed Restrictions on Property Urged," *St. Louis Globe Democrat* (February 2, 1943), St. Louis Public Library, Discrimination in Housing, Clippings Collection.

89. "File Suit to Enjoin Deal on Property," *St. Louis Globe Democrat* (August 10, 1939); "Realty Restriction on Negroes Upheld," *St. Louis Post-Dispatch* (May 7, 1939), St. Louis Public Library, Discrimination in Housing, Clippings Collection; St. Louis Recorder, Deed Book 3829-348.

90. See *Corrigan v. Buckley*, 271 U.S. 323 (1926); and the Missouri cases *Koehler v. Rowland*, 275 Mo. 573 (1918); *Porter v. Johnson*, 232 Mo. App. 1150 (1938); *Porter v. Pryor*, 164 S.W.2d 353 (1942); *Swain v. Maxwell*, 355 Mo. 448 (1946); *Kraemer v. Shelley*, 355 Mo. 814 (1946).

91. "Suit to Bar Renting of Property to Negroes," *St. Louis Post-Dispatch* (August 6, 1936); "Court Rules Negroes May Occupy 3019-21 Vine Grove," *St. Louis Post Dispatch* (December 7, 1937); "Court Holds Negroes May Rent on Vine Grove," *St. Louis Globe-Democrat* (December 7, 1937), all in St. Louis Public Library, Discrimination in Housing, Clippings Collection; *Thornhill v. Herdt*, 130 S.W.2d 175 (1939).

92. John Clark to Congressional Committee Investigating Housing Problems (October 24, 1947), Series 1, Box 5, Urban League of St. Louis Records, Special Collections, Washington University, University City, Mo.

93. Weaver 1944, 184.

94. St. Louis Recorder of Deeds, Deed Books 3908-408 (1923) and 5785-262 (1938); "Realty Exchange Officers Sue over Restriction against Negroes" (March 13, 1942); "Refuses Injunction Restraining Negroes from Enright Area" (September 28, 1943); "Court Finds against Old Negro Restriction on Enright Blocks" (September 27, 1943), St. Louis Public Library, Discrimination in Housing, Clippings Collection.

95. "Suit to Bar Negro Tenants on Delmar Filed against Firm," *St. Louis Globe Democrat* (April 30, 1929) St. Louis Public Library, Discrimination in Housing, Clippings Collection; Gonda 2015.

96. "More Property for Negro Use Sought," *St. Louis Globe Democrat* (December 23, 1937), St. Louis Public Library, Discrimination in Housing, Clippings Collection.

97. Bush testimony in Appellants Abstract of the Record, *Dolan and Wehmeyer v. Richardson*, No. 26502, St. Louis Court of Appeals (March 1944), 128.

98. Bush quoted in "Negroes Buying Homes Farther West on Delmar," *St. Louis Post-Dispatch* (June 24, 1944), St. Louis Public Library, Discrimination in Housing, Clippings Collection.

99. Robert Weaver, "Public Policy," in Chicago Conference on Restrictive Covenants, Group II, Series B, Papers of the NAACP, Part 05: Campaign against Residential Segregation, 1914–1955 [microfilm].

100. Bruch and Gordon 2019; Kucheva and Sander 2014.

101. See online appendix map 4A.2.
102. Gordon 2008.
103. Cooper-McCann 2016; Williams 2013.
104. Baker 2020.
105. Prener et al. 2019.
106. DeBaliviere Station Garage, Historic American Engineering Record, Mo. 6 (1983).
107. Weaver 1948.
108. Logan et al. 2023.
109. Walker et al. 2023.
110. Gordon 2019a.
111. Kucheva and Sander 2014.
112. Massey and Tannen 2018; Lichter, Parisi, and Taquino 2015.
113. Committee on Subdivision Layout 1931; Fogelson 2005; Jackson 1980; Glotzer 2020.
114. Thorpe Brothers pamphlet quoted in Montrie 2022, 133, emphasis added.
115. Walker et al. 2023.
116. Display Ad for Parkview, *St. Louis Post-Dispatch* (May 17, 1908), A14B; Display Ad for Delmar Heights, *St. Louis Post-Dispatch* (May 1, 1922), B5B.
117. St. Louis County Recorder, Deed Book 247-235.
118. Display Ad for Vinita Terrace, *St. Louis-Post Dispatch* (April 7, 1912), A15B.
119. Freund 2007; Hayward 2013.
120. Calculated from St. Louis County Recorder and St. Louis County Recorder Plat Book Records.
121. Area Descriptions B-27 and C-25, FHLBB, Division of Research and Statistics, St. Louis 1940. This expansive logic of private restriction is, I argue, a more convincing source for the popular wisdom surrounding racial exclusion often attributed to "sundown towns" (whose existence is widely rumored but lightly documented).
122. When an African American developer was offered the sale of lots in nearby Berkeley, the response was simple: "We could never use them. . . . [There are] no colored allowed in Berkeley." See Oliver Moorman to Father Provincial (July 25, 1945), Box 2, folder 17, Charles Vatterott Research Collection, S1004, State Historical Society of Missouri, St. Louis.
123. Subdivisions built by Charles Vatterott (n.d.), Box 4, folder 20, Charles Vatterott Research Collection, S1004, State Historical Society of Missouri, St. Louis; Sexauer 2003, 28–59.
124. See McGreevey 1996; Koeth 2019; Sexauer 2003.
125. Dorr 2015.
126. Sexauer 2003, 145ff.
127. St. Louis County Recorder, Deed Book 1696-453; Plat Book 37-8 (Mary Ridge, 1940).
128. St. Louis County Recorder, Deed Book 1696-453 (Mary Ridge, 1940).
129. Oliver Moorman to Father Provincial (July 25, 1945), Box 2, folder 17, Charles Vatterott Research Collection, S1004, State Historical Society of Missouri, St. Louis.

130. See Atlas of the Village of Richfield, Hennepin Co. Minnesota (1952), HCDLC; Atlas of Territory Annexed to the City of Minneapolis from Village of Richfield, 1927, Maps of Minneapolis Annexations, Minnesota Digital Library, University of Minnesota.

131. Morris Park 1911, Morris Park 4th Addition, Harriet Terrace 1911, High View Park 1912, Harriet Manor 1913, South Shore Park 1913, Ingleside 1911, Ray's Lynhurst 1916, Ray's Lynhurst 2nd 1916, Portland Avenue Acres 1920, Kavlis Lynhurst Park 1921, Kavlis Lynhurst Plateau 1921, Ingleside 2nd Addition 1921, Bachman's Lynhurst Terrace 1922, Lynwood 1922, Pennhurst 1922, Kavlis Lake Harriet 1922, Wooddale 2nd 1923, Nokomis South Shore 1923, Nokomis South Shore 2nd 1923, Edgewater on Nokomis 1923, Lyndale Shores 1923, Wood Lake Highlands 1923, New Ford Town 1923, Irwindale 1923, Fairwood Park 1925, Lynwood 1925, Girard Parkview 1925, Silverwood Addition 1925, Woodlake Highlands 1926, Nokomis Gardens 1927, Tingdale Brothers Lincoln Hills 1928, Blair's Wooddale 1931, Lyndale Shores 1937–1941, Betcher's Addition 1939, Wood Lake Shores 1939, Nicollet Terrace 1940, Nicollet View Gardens 1940, Rich Acres 1940, Rich Highlands 1940, Academy Terrace 1941, J.N. Hauser's 1941, D.L Tate's 1941, Sunland Vista 1941, Ralph Milner's 1942, Nicollet Homes 1942, Sheldon Blair's 1942, Wooddale 1942, Forest Lawn 1941–1945, J.N. Hauser's Second Addition 1945, Fairfield Addition 1945, Nicollet Garden Lots 1945, Ireland 1946, Lyndale Oaks 1946, RC Soen's 1946, Sunset Terrace 1946, Terrace Gardens 1946, Falden's 1947, Richfield Center 1947, Home Acres 1948, Penn Lake Terrace 1948, Towns Edge Village, 1948–1950. Additions dated by plat or by first instance of restriction.

132. Calculated from Atlas of the Village of Richfield (1952) and subdivision plats, HCDLC; Atlas of Territory Annexed to the City of Minneapolis from Village of Richfield (1927), Maps of Minneapolis Annexations, Minnesota Digital Library, University of Minnesota.

133. Glotzer 2020.

134. Committee on City Planning and Zoning 1931, 13.

135. FHA 1938, 934, 980(1): "Generally, a high rating should be given only where adequate and properly enforced zoning regulations exist or where effective restrictive covenants are recorded against the entire tract, since these provide the surest protection against undesirable encroachment and inharmonious use. To be most effective, deed restrictions should be imposed upon all land in the immediate environment of the subject location."

136. Massey and Denton 1988, 282.

137. Massey and Denton 1988, 281–315; Shertzer, Walsh, and Logan 2016, 187.

138. Massey and Denton 1988, 282.

139. Logan and Parman 2022; Logan and Parman 2017.

140. Lieberson 1963; Kusmer 1976.

141. Cutler, Glaeser, and Vigdor 1999; Taeuber and Taeuber 1965; Lieberson 1980; Massey and Denton 1993.

142. Cutler, Glaeser, and Vigdor 1999, 462–63.

143. Shertzer and Walsh 2019.

144. Massey and Denton 1993, 42, 31.
145. Spear 1967; Kusmer 1976; Trotter 1985.
146. Logan and Parman 2017; Shertzer and Walsh 2019.
147. Shertzer, Walsh, and Logan 2016; Bae and Freeman 2021; Logan et al. 2015; Shertzer and Walsh 2019.
148. Kucheva and Sander 2014.
149. Taeuber and Taeuber 1976.
150. Weaver 1948, 231.
151. Weaver 1948, 238.
152. Sood, Speagle, and Ehrman-Solbert 2019.
153. Kucheva and Sander 2014; Bruch and Gordon 2019.
154. Weaver 1948, 234–38.

Chapter 5: Dress Rehearsal for *Shelley*: Private Restrictions and the Law

1. *Shelley v. Kraemer*, 334 U.S. 1 (1948); Vose 1959, Gonda 2015. The Court also considered *Hurd v. Hodge* (162 Fed. 2d 233 [1947]) out of the District of Columbia as a companion case. Since *Hurd* involved federal rather than state jurisdiction, the NAACP rested its case on the due-process clause of the Fifth Amendment. In a separate opinion, *Hurd v. Hodge*, 334 U.S. 24 (1948), the Court reversed its 1926 ruling in *Corrigan* and held federal jurisdictions to the same equal protection standards underscored in *Shelley*. See Vose 1959, 187–90, 208–10.
2. *Corrigan v. Buckley*, 271 U.S. 323 (1926); Vose 1959, 15–18; Brooks and Rose 2013, 54. The *Corrigan* ruling was generally echoed by state courts—including Missouri in *Porter v. Pryor* (1942).
3. Ely 1998; Klarman 1998; *Buchanan v. Warley*, 245 U.S. 60 (1917).
4. Brooks and Rose 2013, 4–6, 14, 51–52; Brooks 2011; Jaffee 2007.
5. Committee on Negro Housing 1931; Lumpkins 2008; Jones-Correa 1999.
6. Meyer 2000; Bell 2013.
7. Myrdal 1944, 622.
8. Cayton and Drake 1945, 177–85; Spear 1967; Balto 2019; Pacyga 1997; Garb 2006, 20–24. For the "second ghetto," see especially Hirsch 1983.
9. Boyle 2005.
10. *St. Louis Post Dispatch* clipping (1937); *St. Louis Argus* (June 28, 1940), both in St. Louis Public Library, Discrimination in Housing, Clippings Collection.
11. Montrie 2019, 300–20.
12. Massey and Denton, 33–35.
13. Brooks and Rose 2013, 13.
14. *Godley v. Weisman*, 133 Minn. 1 (1916); *Klapproth v. Grininger*, 162 Minn. 488 (1925); *Cantieny v. Boze*, 209 Minn. 407 (1941); *Strauss v. Ginzberg*, 218 Minn. 57 (1944).
15. Governor's Interracial Commission 1947, 65.

16. Untitled table of cases, General [Restrictive Covenants; Violence and Intimidation], 1947–1950 and undated, Papers of the NAACP, Part 05: Campaign against Residential Segregation, 1914–1955 [microfilm]. Washington, D.C., was a special case, marked by both extensive efforts to restrict property and a prominent African American professional class. See Shoenfeld and Cherkasky 2016.

17. Slingsby 1980, 9.

18. Kelleher 1969.

19. Gonda 2015; Vose 1959.

20. Longa 2007.

21. *Missouri ex rel Gaines v. Canada*, 305 U.S. 337 (1938); Endersby and Horner 2016; Desnoyer and Alexander 2017.

22. Appellants' Abstract of the Record at 9, *Dolan v. Richardson*, 181 S.W.2.d 997 (Mo. Ct. App. 1944) (No. 26502), Supreme Court Case Files, Record Group 600, Missouri State Archives, Jefferson City.

23. Gordon 2008, 79–83.

24. City of St. Louis Recorder, Deed Book 3841-386 (1923).

25. City of St. Louis Recorder, Deed Book 1122-74 (July 1941); 1129-96 (October 1941).

26. "Law Professor Must Go to Court; Eviction Is Sought: Residential Battle Rages in St. Louis," *Atlanta Daily World*," October 29, 1941, 1; "Lincoln Professor Faces Covenant Fight: Order Teacher and Four Others out of Mo. Homes," *Chicago Defender*, November 1, 1941, 5; "Stench Bomb Again Hurled," *St. Louis Argus*, September 19, 1941, 1; "Harm Negro Homes: 5 Race Families Get Threats," *St. Louis Argus*, October 24, 1941, 1; "Continue N. Market Neighborhood Suits: Homes Stench Bombed," *St. Louis Argus*, November 14, 1941, 1; "More Negro Homes Stench Bombed," *St. Louis Argus*, December 5, 1941, 1.

27. *Dolan v. Richardson*, Circuit Court of the City of St. Louis 53039, Div. 2 (1942); Appellants' Abstract of the Record at 13, *Dolan*, 181 S.W.2d 997 (No. 26502).

28. *Buchanan v. Warley*, 245 U.S. 60 (1917).

29. Radin 1982, 957–1015; Van Hecke 1928, 531; Vose 1959, 4–5, 19–22.

30. Appellants' Abstract of the Record at 9, *Dolan*, 181 S.W.2d 997.

31. Appellants' Abstract of the Record at 9–10, *Dolan*, 181 S.W.2d 997.

32. Fogelson 2005, 21–24.

33. Brooks and Rose 2013, 32–33; Fogelson 2005, 36–39; Godsil 2006.

34. *Koehler v. Rowland*, 205 S.W. 217 (Mo. 1918).

35. *Los Angeles Investment Co. v. Gary*, 18i Cal. 680, 186 Pac. 59 (1919); *Porter v. Barrett*, 233 Mich. 373, 206 N.W. 532 (1925); *White v. White*, 1o8 W.Va. 128, 150 S.E. 531 (1929); *University of Chicago Law Review* 1940; Godsil 2006; Brooks and Rose 2013, 8, 56–62; Cohen 1921; Fogelson 2005, 46–48; Monchow 1928, 16.

36. Restriction on Oakland Terrace First Addition, City of St. Louis Recorder, Deed Book 2952-22 (1916); Fogelson 2005, 46–48; Brooks and Rose 2013, 8; Vose 1959, 4–5, 19–22.

37. Brooks and Rose 2013, 75–77.

38. Monchow 1928, 23.

39. *Porter v. Johnson* 232 Mo. App. 1150, 1160, 115 S.W. 2d 529 (1938).

40. Van Hecke 1928, 540.

41. *Lion's Head Lake v. Brzezinski* 23 N.J. Misc. 290, *290; 43 A.2d 729 (1945).

42. Godsil 2006, 548.

43. Van Hecke 1928, 412.

44. Because petition restrictions were not drafted in the context of a sale or transfer of property, they were often recorded as "wild deeds" that were not indexed or attached to the core property records. See Brooks and Rose 2013, 80–81, 150–52.

45. Appellants' Abstract of the Record at 17–44, *Dolan v. Richardson*, 181 S.W.2d 997 (Mo. Ct. App. 1944) (No. 26502), Supreme Court Case Files, Record Group 600, Missouri State Archives, Jefferson City.

46. Testimony of William Gavigan, Appellant's Abstract of the Records, *Dolan v. Richardson*, St. Louis Court of Appeals (March 1944), 16–44, 5, Supreme Court Case Files, Record Group 600, Missouri State Archives, Jefferson City.

47. See Charles Houston, Potentialities of Change of Neighborhood Doctrine (July 9, 1945), and Spottiswoode Robinson, Analysis of Cases Where Person Selling to Negro Did Not Sign Covenant, in Chicago Conference on Restrictive Covenants, folder 131, Group II, Series B, Papers of the NAACP, Part 05: Campaign against Residential Segregation, 1914–1955 [microfilm].

48. Richardson 1945.

49. See George Vaughn (July 9, 1945), in Chicago Conference on Restrictive Covenants, folder 131, Group II, Series B, Papers of the NAACP, Part 05: Campaign against Residential Segregation, 1914–1955 [microfilm]; Vose 1959, 112.

50. See testimony of residents, *Shelley v. Kraemer*, Transcript of the Record before the St. Louis Court of Appeals (1946), Supreme Court Case Files, Record Group 600, Missouri State Archives, Jefferson City, 66–111; *St. Louis Argus* (April 4, 1941), 1; (June 6, 1941), 1; (July 11, 1941), 1.

51. Vose 1959, 117–18.

52. Plotkin 2001, 41–42.

53. Long and Johnson 1947, 19–20.

54. Richardson 1945.

55. *Pickle v. McCawley*, 329 Mo. 166; 44 SW 2d 857; 1931 LEXIS 693; *Mueninghaus v. James*, 324 Mo. 767; 24 SW 2d 1017; 1930 LEXIS 548.

56. "Home Sale to Negro Arouses Page Blvd" (July 18, 1937), St. Louis Public Library, Discrimination in Housing, Clippings Collection.

57. *Mueninghaus v. James*, 24 S.W.2d 1017 (Mo. 1930).

58. *Thornhill v. Herdt*, 130 S.W.2d 175 (Mo. Ct. App. 1939).

59. "Court Finds against Old Negro Restriction" (September 28, 1943), "Discrimination in Housing," St. Louis Public Library, Discrimination in Housing, Clippings Collection.

60. *Shelley v. Kraemer*, Transcript of the Record before the St. Louis Court of Appeals (1946), Supreme Court Case Files, Record Group 600, Missouri State Archives, Jefferson City, 218–19.

61. *Shelley v. Kraemer*, Transcript of the Record before the St. Louis Court of Appeals (1946), Supreme Court Case Files, Record Group 600, Missouri State Archives, Jefferson City.

62. Vose 1959, 112; Richardson 1945; Brooks and Rose 2013, 79–84.

63. "Housing-Cote Brilliante Ave" (June 1927), Series 1, Box 5, Urban League of St. Louis Records, Special Collections, Washington University, University City, Mo.; Brooks and Rose 2013, 80–81, 150–52; see also Appellant's Abstract of the Record, *Thornhill v. Herdt*, Supreme Court Case Files, Record Group 600, Missouri State Archives, Jefferson City, 6.

64. *Kraemer v. Shelley*, Transcript of the Record before the St. Louis Court of Appeals (1946), Supreme Court Case Files, Record Group 600, Missouri State Archives, Jefferson City, 15, 216; Brooks and Rose 2013.

65. *Sanborn v. McLean*, 206 N.W. 496 (Mich. 1925).

66. Monchow 1928, 31; Jaffee 2007.

67. *Northwest Civic Ass'n v. Sheldon*, 317 Mich. 416; *Schulte v. Starks* 238 Mich. 102; *Eveleth v. Best* 322 Mich. 637; *Ridgway v. Cockburn* 163 Mich. 511.

68. Hadley Park, City of St. Louis Recorder, Deed Book 2332-343 (1910); Bessie Place, City of St. Louis Recorder, Deed Book 5307-188 (1932).

69. Jarwala 2020.

70. Appellant's Abstract of the Record, Thornhill No 24939, St. Louis Court of Appeals (1938), Supreme Court Case Files, Record Group 600, Missouri State Archives, Jefferson City.

71. In *Thornhill*, the Court framed the goal of neighborhood restriction as a collective action problem:

> A neighborhood scheme of restrictions to be effective and enforceable must have certain characteristics. It must be universal; that is, the restrictions must apply to all lots of like character brought within the scheme. Unless it be universal it cannot be reciprocal. If it be not reciprocal, then it must as a neighborhood scheme fall, for the theory which sustains a scheme or plan of this character is that the restrictions are a benefit to all. The consideration to each lot owner for the imposition of the restriction upon his lot is that the same restrictions are imposed upon the lots of others similarly situated. If the restrictions upon all lots similarly located are not alike, or some lots are not subject to the restrictions while others are, then a burden would be carried by some owners without a corresponding benefit.

See Appellant's Abstract of the Record, *Thornhill v. Herdt* No 24939, St. Louis Court of Appeals (1938), Supreme Court Case Files, Record Group 600, Missouri State Archives, Jefferson City, 26.

72. Respondents' Statement, Points and Authorities, and Argument at 26, *Thornhill v. Herdt*, 130 S.W.2d 175 (No. 24939).

73. Hirsch 1983, 29–31.

74. Appellant's Abstract of the Record, *Thornhill v. Herdt*, No 24939, St. Louis Court of Appeals (1938), Supreme Court Case Files, Record Group 600, Missouri State Archives, Jefferson City, 26.

75. *St. Louis Argus* clippings, 1924, Branch Files, St. Louis 1924, Papers of the NAACP, Part 05: Campaign against Residential Segregation, 1914–1955 [microfilm].

76. Brooks and Rose 2013, 131–32; Monchow 1928, 24; *Pickel v. McCawley* 329 Mo. 166; 44 S.W. 2d 857; 1931 LEXIS 693.

77. "Refuses Injunction Restraining Negroes from Enright Area" (September 28, 1943); "Court Finds against Old Negro Restriction on Enright Blocks" (September 27, 1943), St. Louis Public Library, Discrimination in Housing, Clippings Collection.

78. *Koehler v. Rowland* 275 Mo. 573.

79. *Hundley v. Gorewitz*, 132 F.2d 23 (1942); see also *Thornhill v. Herdt*, 130 S.W.2d 175 (Mo. Ct. App. 1939); Jarwala 2020.

80. *Pickel v. McCawley*, 44 S.W.2d 857 (Mo. 1931).

81. Appellant's Abstract of the Record, *Pickel v. McCawley* 329 Mo. 166 (1931) (No. 29630), Supreme Court Case Files, Record Group 600, Missouri State Archives, Jefferson City.

82. Cayton and Drake 1945.

83. "Court Rules Negroes May Live at 3019-21 Vine Grove" (1938), St. Louis Public Library, Discrimination in Housing, Clippings Collection.

84. *University of Chicago Law Review* 1940, 713.

85. *Porter v. Johnson*, 232 Mo. App. 1150 (1938).

86. Appellant's Abstract of the Record, *Thornhill v. Herdt*, No. 24939, St. Louis Court of Appeals (1938), 26, Supreme Court Case Files, Record Group 600, Missouri State Archives, Jefferson City.

87. Appellant's Abstract of the Record, *Thornhill v. Herdt*, No. 24939, St. Louis Court of Appeals (1938), 173, Supreme Court Case Files, Record Group 600, Missouri State Archives, Jefferson City.

88. Gordon 2008.

89. Plotkin 1999, 171–81.

90. Farr 1939, 479.

91. Charles Houston, Potentialities of Change of Neighborhood Doctrine (July 9, 1945), Chicago Conference on Restrictive Covenants, folder 131, Group II, Series B, Papers of the NAACP, Part 05: Campaign against Residential Segregation, 1914–1955 [microfilm]; Vose 1959, 60–61; Brooks and Rose 2013, 130–31.

92. Pascoe 1996, 44–69.

93. On restrictions against Jews, see Fogelson 2005, 128–31; Glotzer 2020, 126–28, 132–34; Dawson 2019.

94. Ehrman-Solberg et al. 2020, Victory View Subdivision, Robbinsdale.

95. Plotkin 1999, 1–24, 29.

96. General Warranty Deed and Restrictions, South Richmond Heights, St. Louis County Recorder, Deed Book 343-158 (1914).

97. *Mrsa v. Reynolds*, 317 Mich. 632, *634; 27 N.W.2d 40 (1947).

98. Appellants' Abstract of the Record, at 84–85, *Dolan v. Richardson*, 181 S.W.2d 997 (Mo. Ct. App. 1944) (No. 26502), Supreme Court Case Files, Record Group 600, Missouri State Archives, Jefferson City.

99. *The Civil Rights Cases*, 109 U.S. 3 (1883).

100. *Plessy v. Ferguson*, 163 U.S. 537.

101. Robert Weaver, "Public Policy," in Chicago Conference on Restrictive Covenants, Group II, Series B, Papers of the NAACP, Part 05: Campaign against Residential Segregation, 1914–1955 [microfilm].

102. Vose 1959; Gonda 2015.

103. See Friedman 2012.

104. *Koehler v. Rowland*, 205 S.W. 217 (Mo. 1918).

105. Vose 1959, 64–68; Gonda 2005, 135–50.

106. Weaver 1948, 184, 190.

107. Appellants' Abstract of the Record at 9, *Dolan*, 181 S.W.2d. 997, Supreme Court Case Files, Record Group 600, Missouri State Archives, Jefferson City.

108. "Refuses Injunction Restraining Negroes from Enright Area" (September 28, 1943); "Court Finds against Old Negro Restriction on Enright Blocks" (September 27, 1943), St. Louis Public Library, Discrimination in Housing, Clippings Collection.

109. Monday, July 9, 1945, meeting notes, Chicago Conference on Restrictive Covenants, folder 131, Group II, Series B. Papers of the NAACP, Part 05: Campaign against Residential Segregation, 1914–1955 [microfilm].

110. This connection was made as early as 1892 in *Gandolfo v. Hartman*, a California case that struck down a restriction against "Chinamen" on the grounds that—as the trial judge reasoned—it made little sense to hold that state and local governments could not discriminate by race but that "a citizen of the state may lawfully do so by contract, which the courts may enforce." Brooks and Rose 2013, 51–53.

111. Appellants' Abstract of the Record, *Dolan v. Richardson*, 181 S.W.2d 997 (Mo. Ct. App. 1944) (No. 26502), 10, 43–45, Supreme Court Case Files, Record Group 600, Missouri State Archives, Jefferson City.

112. Richardson 1945, 53–57.

113. Avins 1966, 19.

114. *Dolan v. Richardson*, 181 S.W.2d 997.

115. Richardson 1945, 56.

116. Gonda 2015, 103–14, 120–34; Letter from Thurgood Marshall to St. Louis Real Estate Board (1947), Group II, Series B, Legal File, Restrictive Covenants, Restrictive Covenants in Missouri 1944–1950, Papers of the NAACP, Part 05: Campaign against Residential Segregation, 1914–1955 [microfilm].

117. Most notably in *Hansberry v. Lee*, 311 U.S. 32 (1940).

118. Brooks and Rose 2013, 51–56; *Kraemer v. Shelley*, Transcript of the Record before the St. Louis Court of Appeals (1946), Supreme Court Case Files, Record Group 600, Missouri State Archives, Jefferson City, 18. In *Gandolfo* (1892), the court held that

> it would be a very narrow construction of the constitutional amendment in question and of the decisions based upon it, and a very restricted application of the broad principles upon which both the amendment and the decisions proceed, to hold that, while state and municipal legislatures are forbidden to discriminate against the Chinese in their legislation, a citizen of the state may lawfully do so by contract, while the courts

may enforce. Such a view is, I think entirely inadmissible. Any result inhibited by the constitution can no more be accomplished by contract of individual citizens than by legislation, and the courts should no more enforce the one than the other. This would seem to be very clear.

Gandolfo v. Hartman, 49 F. 181 (9th Cir. 1892).

119. Transcript of Record, *Kraemer v. Shelley* (Mo. Ct. App. 1945).

120. Vose 1959, 201–2; Letter drafted by Marshall re St. Louis Real Estate Board, Group II, Series B, Legal File, Restrictive Covenants, Restrictive Covenants in Missouri 1944–1950, Papers of the NAACP, Part 05: Campaign against Residential Segregation, 1914–1955 [microfilm].

121. Rubenstein 1997, 1630; Brooks and Rose 2013, Gonda 2005, 156.

122. Vose 1959, 199–210.

123. May Acres, St. Louis County Recorder, Deed Book 2250-488, 1947.

124. See Helper 1969; Ross and Yinger 2002; Hirsch 1983; Sugrue 1995; Bell 2013.

125. *St. Louis Star-Times* clipping (October 2, 1948), Group II, Series B, Legal File, Restrictive Covenants, Restrictive Covenants in Missouri 1944–1950, Papers of the NAACP, Part 05: Campaign against Residential Segregation, 1914–1955 [microfilm].

126. Michney and Winling 2020; Rothstein 2017, 63–67; Gordon 2008, 88–111; Teaford 2000; Goetz 2013; Hirsch 2000a, 159.

127. McGraw and Nesbit 1953; Abrams 1955, 224–25; Stach 1988, 59; Dawson 2019; Landres Chilton to Roy Wilkins (May 12, 1948), Part 5, Reel 22: 0041, Papers of the NAACP, Part 05: Campaign against Residential Segregation, 1914–1955 [microfilm]. In Milwaukee, developers admitted in 1958 to using "plan approval" as "a kind of substitute for the recently outlawed racial covenants." See Consigny and Zile 1958, 625.

128. See Ehrman-Solberg et al. 2020, Chicago Avenue Highlands, Minneapolis; Seven Oaks, Minneapolis.

129. St. Louis County Recorder, Deed Book 2406-606, Yorkshire #3 (1948); see also (by the same developer), York Hills 790-455 (1929); Yorkshire 2105-544 (1945); Yorkshire #2 2252-576 (1947); and Yorkshire #4 Plat Book 45-42 (1949).

130. Funiak 1948.

131. Brooks and Rose 2013, 172–74; see also McGraw and Nesbit 1953.

132. *Correll v. Earley*, 1951 Okla. 317, 237 P.2d 1017, 205 Okla. 366; *Weiss v. Leaon*, 259 Mo. 1054, 225 S.W.2d 127 (1949).

133. *Barrows v. Jackson*, 346 U.S. 249 (1953); Vose 1959, 12.

134. Myrdal 1944, 624.

135. Anderson 2010, 11–16.

136. Brooks and Rose 2013, quote at 2; Jost 1984.

137. Bayer-Pacht 2010; Weisbord and Sterk 2021.

138. Chin 2004.

139. Fair Housing Act, 42 U.S.C. § 3604 (1968).

140. See *Mayers v. Ridley*, 465 F. 2d 630, D.C. Cir. 1972; Brooks and Rose 2013, 221–23; *Maryland Law Review* 1974; Quinn 1979, 4.

141. For most states, counties are the primary substate administrative division. Louisiana has parishes; Alaska has boroughs for developed areas and census areas for undeveloped areas. The cities of Baltimore, St. Louis, and Carson City (Nevada) all have the status (and perform the functions) of counties, as do forty-one independent cities in Virginia. See U.S. Census Bureau 1994, chapter 4.

142. Majumdar 2007.

143. See, for example, Colo. Rev. Stat. Ann. § 38-30-169.

144. Real Property: Discriminatory Restrictions, Cal. AB-1466 §12965.1 (2022).

145. See, for example, Kan. Stat. Ann. 44-1018 (2018).

146. See Minn. Stat. §507.18 (2012).

147. See Just Deeds, accessed May 3, 2023, https://justdeeds.org/; Hennepin County, "Real Estate Recording Information," accessed May 3, 2023, https://www.hennepin.us/residents/property/real-estate-recording-information.

148. See Mo. Stat. 442.403 (1993); 213.041 (2005); HB 1662 (2022).

149. Iowa Code § 523I.307 (2022).

150. *May v. Spokane County*, Supreme Court of Washington, No. 99598-2 (March 31, 2022); Weiss 2022.

151. Certification of Enrollment, Engrossed Second Substitute Bill 1335, Chapter 256, Laws of 2021, State of Washington, 67th Legislature (2021).

152. Second Substitute House Bill 1474, State of Washington, 68th Legislature (2023), https://app.leg.wa.gov/bi/tld/documentsearchresults?biennium=2023-24&name=1474.

153. As the legal scholar Gabriel Chin (2004, 124) notes:

> Every state should know whether, when and to what extent African Americans and members of other races were excluded from public and private housing, jobs, and education through the actions of the state, and other ways in which race discrimination shaped the laws and activities of the government. Every state should know what was done about that discrimination, through litigation, voluntary changes in policy, or otherwise. Every state should attempt to identify the laws and governmental structures shaped by racial discrimination. Finally, every state should estimate the present consequences of historical discrimination. Systematic and responsible generation of facts and information would allow discussion and legislation about race and justice in ways that are now impossible.

Chapter 6: Long Shadow: The Durable Inequalities of Private Restriction

1. Cutler, Glaeser, and Vigdor 1999; Logan and Stults 2021.

2. Massey and Denton 1993; Wilson 1987.

3. "Residential segregation in the basis of race simultaneously reduces the likelihood that affluent blacks benefit from the advantages of concentrated affluence while increasing the odds that poor blacks suffer disadvantages of concentrated poverty." Massey and Rugh 2021, 180.

4. Galster and Sharkey 2017; Sampson 2012; Widestrom 2015.

5. Bruch and Gordon 2019; Mallach 2020; Oliver and Shapiro 1995; Rugh and Massey 2010; Taylor 2019.

6. Chetty et al. 2014; Chetty et al. 2020; Sharkey 2013; Ellen, Steil, and De La Roca 2016; Massey 2020.

7. Tilly 1998. In the absence of disturbance or challenge, categorical inequality tends to grow and reproduce "like ivy on a brick wall" (99).

8. Morris 2000; Lamont, Beljean, and Clair et al. 2014.

9. Anderson 2010.

10. Lamont, Beljean, and Clair 2014.

11. Tilly 1998, 170–75.

12. Glotzer 2020; Gotham 2002.

13. Lamont, Beljean, and Clair 2014.

14. Young 1990.

15. Hayward 2010.

16. Faber 2021: Hayward 2010.

17. Tilly 1998, 190–91; Valentino and Vaisey 2022.

18. On St. Louis: Ervin 2017; Lang 2009; Lipsitz 1995. On Minneapolis: Montrie 2022. On Waterloo: Jones 1997. "Politically enforced categorical inequality," as Tilly 1998 (125) notes, "sustain widespread discrimination but, with changed political alignments, also offers significant opportunities for collective action on the part of underdogs."

19. Spear 1967.

20. Faber 2021; Crowder and Krysan 2017.

21. Alon 2009; Valentino and Vaisey 2022.

22. Derenoncourt 2022; Muhammad 2010.

23. Blakely and Snyder 1997; for second-hand suburbs, see Sugrue 2011.

24. Reardon and Bischoff 2011; Allard 2017; Alon 2009.

25. Saatciolgu and Skrtic 2019.

26. Oliver and Shapiro 1995; see also Hirsch 1983.

27. Lamont, Beljean, and Clair 2014.

28. Derenoncourt 2022.

29. Peñalver 2009, 831.

30. Schindler 2015.

31. Anderson 2010, 9–12.

32. Lamont, Beljean, and Clair 2014; Valentino and Vaisey 2022; Massey 2007.

33. On this point, see Hayward 2013, 63; and Taylor 2019 (noting the "sleight of hand" that stripped neighborhoods and their residents of wealth, and then blamed them for the damage left behind), 223.

34. Quillian 2014; Quillian and Pager 2010.

35. Valentino and Vaisey 2022.

36. Schneider and Ingram 1993.

37. Massey and Rugh 2021; Charles 2006, chapter 4; DiTomaso 2013, 6; Massey 2020, Bonilla-Silva and Embrick 2007; Hayward 2013; Mills 2017.

38. Charles 2003; Crowder and Krysan 2017; Hayward 2013; Korver-Glenn 2018.
39. Quoted in Ellis 2020.
40. Michael Katz warns of the need to pay attention to private actors, and to beware the view of "naturalized public failure as the master narrative of urban history." Katz 2012, 157.
41. Gotham 2002, chapter 2; Helper 1969.
42. Weiss 1987; Glotzer 2020; Michney and Winling 2021; Kahrl 2018; Molotch 1976.
43. Abrams 1955, 150.
44. James Bush to Charles Gorman (December 29, 1943), Box 1, folder 2, James T. Bush Real Estate Records, State Historical Society of Missouri-St. Louis.
45. Helper 1969; Ross and Yinger 2002; Korver-Glenn 2018; Davis 1965.
46. *St. Louis Star-Times* (October 2, 1948), clipping in Group II, Series B, Legal File, Restrictive Covenants, *Shelley v. Kraemer*. St. Louis, Missouri [Restrictive Covenants], 1946–1948, Papers of the NAACP, Part 05: Campaign against Residential Segregation, 1914–1955 [microfilm].
47. Gordon 2008.
48. Davis 1965; see also Slingsby 1980, 88–98.
49. Hartley and Rose 2023.
50. See Kucheva and Sander 2014.
51. Jarwala 2020.
52. Weaver 1948, 234–38.
53. Monchow 1928, 5.
54. Hayward 2013, 63; see also Helper 1969.
55. Albert Wenzlick Real Estate Co. (1910–1960) Records, 1924–1960, S0190, State Historical Society of Missouri-St. Louis.
56. Rovner 2021; Michney and Winling 2021; Gotham 2000c, 621.
57. Korver-Glenn 2021; Light 2011.
58. Babcock 1924, 21, 208–11.
59. Abrams 1955, 166.
60. Korver-Glenn 2021, 116–25.
61. Brown 2010.
62. Glotzer 2020, 185.
63. Howell and Korver-Glenn 2022.
64. Ross and Yinger 2002; Howell 2006; Rusk 2001; Rugh and Massey 2010; Squires 2003.
65. Muhammad 2010, chapter 2; Fergus 2013; Squires 2003.
66. Pager and Shepherd 2008; Squires 2005.
67. Weiss 1987, 4, 10–11, 68–72; Brooks and Rose 2013, 37–42; Consigny and Zile 1958.
68. Flint 1977, 15, 93–95; Brady 2021.
69. Troesken and Walsh 2019; Pollard 1931.
70. Bae and Freeman 2021; Troesken and Walsh 2019.
71. Nelson 1996; Silver 1991; Rice 1968.
72. Flint 1977, 102; Whittemore 2018; Shertzer, Twinam, and Walsh 2016.

73. Silver 1991; Rice 1968; Nelson 1996; Flint 1977; Slingsby 1980, 55–56.
74. Freund 2007, 81–83: Pendall 2000; Nelson 1996; Whittemore 2018.
75. Quoted in Nightingale 2012, 323.
76. Quoted in Flint 1977, 103. See also Barone 2018.
77. Whittemore 2021; Trounstine 2018; Brooks and Rose 2013, 38.
78. Whittemore 2018, 2021; Shertzer, Twinam, and Walsh 2016; Nelson 1996.
79. Rabin 1989. Shertzer, Twinam, and Walsh 2016, 2022; Flint 1977, 46–50.
80. Committee on Subdivision Layout 1931, 15.
81. Committee on City Planning and Zoning 1931, 15; Monchow 1928, 70.
82. Bassett 1922a, 317; 1922b, 26–27; Brooks and Rose 2013, 36–37; Stach 1988, 44–45; Weiss 1987, 71–72; Brady 2021.
83. Van Hecke 1928, 420.
84. Nightingale 2012, 318–21.
85. Rice 1968, 184; Weiss 1987, 79-82; Flint 1977.
86. Brady 2021, 1674.
87. Bartholomew 1918, 26, 34; Gordon 2008, 122–24; Flint 1977, 304–06.
88. See online appendix map 4A.1.
89. Gordon 2008, 112–52; Flint 1977, 148–63.
90. Tentative Zoning Ordinance for the City of Minneapolis (1923), Harland Bartholomew and Associates Collection, Series 2, Bound City Planning Reports, 1919–1958, volume 38, part 5, section 5, Minneapolis, Washington University Special Collections, St. Louis; Minneapolis Chamber of Commerce 1947. Minnesota enabled municipal zoning in 1913 and Iowa in 1922; Waterloo passed its first ordinance in 1924. See Baker 1925.
91. HBA Historical Sketch (n.d.), Box 4, folder 3, Charles Vatterott Research Collection, S1004, State Historical Society of Missouri, St. Louis.
92. Quoted in Weiss 1987, 68.
93. Van Hecke 1928, 419–20; see also Weiss 1987, 68–72.
94. Nelson 1996; Whittemore 2021.
95. Hayward 2013; Danielson 1976; Freund 2007, 92–98.
96. Minneapolis Chamber of Commerce 1947, 8–18.
97. See Gordon 2008, 112–52.
98. St. Louis County Recorder, Deed Book 2214-526 (Fourland Place, 19460; see also 2381-488, White Cliffe Terrace, 1948).
99. St. Louis County Recorder, Deed Book 2527 (Bayless Court, 1948).
100. St. Louis County Recorder, Plat Book 44-55 (Regina Gardens, 1949).
101. Brady 2021.
102. Furth and Webster 2023.
103. Haar 1953.
104. 1950 from FHA, "Summary of FHA Insuring Operations," Insured Mortgage Portfolio 15:1 (1950), 29; 2022 from U.S. Census Quarterly Starts and Completions by Purpose and Design, Table Q1, accessed May 7, 2023, https://www.census.gov/construction/nrc/pdf/quarterly_starts_completions.pdf.

105. Haar 1953, 1056.
106. Frug 1998; Ham 1997; Gordon 2008; Orfield 2006.
107. Cui 2023; Sahn 2022.
108. Cui 2023, figure 1.
109. Freund 2007; Hirsch 1983, 252–54; Hirsch 2000b; Gotham 2000a.
110. Faber 2020.
111. Michney and Winling 2020; Radford 1996.
112. Molotch 1976; Michney and Winling 2021; Weiss 1987; Gotham 2000c; Abrams 1955.
113. See Esping Anderson 1990; Noble 1997; Somers 2008, 73–82.
114. Mettler 2011.
115. Goetz 2013.
116. Michney 2022; Greer 2013; Michney and Winling 2020; Hillier 2005.
117. Quoted in Michney 2022, 324.
118. Michney 2022; Woods 2018; Santucci 2020; Greer 2013; Perzynski et al. 2022.
119. See, for example, Greer 2013 and Fishback et al. 2020, noting the prevalence of "nonracial" criteria.
120. See Area Descriptions in FHLBB, Division of Research and Statistics 1940.
121. Michney 2022.
122. Woods 2018.
123. Greer 2013.
124. Area Descriptions in FHLBB, Division of Research and Statistics 1940.
125. See online appendix maps 6A.1 and 6A.2.
126. Area Description B-44, FHLBB, Division of Research and Statistics 1940.
127. Area Descriptions C-2, C-6, C-48; D-1, D2, and D-4, D-9, FHLBB, Division of Research and Statistics 1940.
128. Area Description D-20, FHLBB, Division of Research and Statistics 1940. See also D-19 (in Mill Creek): "Practically this entire district is occupied by Negroes. . . . The entire area presents a run-down and unsightly appearance and can safely be described as being 'practically hopeless' from a residential standpoint."
129. Area Description D-15, FHLBB, Division of Research and Statistics 1940.
130. Area Description C-63, FHLBB, Division of Research and Statistics 1940.
131. See online appendix map 6A.3.
132. Waterloo area descriptions (1937) from Mapping Inequality (Nelson et al., n.d.).
133. See online appendix map 6A.4.
134. Minneapolis area descriptions (1937) from Mapping Inequality (Nelson et al., n.d.).
135. Fishback et al. 2022.
136. Michney 2022; Michney and Winling 2020; Hillier 2005.
137. Hillier 2003b; Michney and Winling 2020; Crossney and Bartelt 2005b; Fishback et al. 2022.
138. Greer 2013; Crossney and Bartelt 2005a; Michney 2022.
139. See Crossney and Bartelt 2005a, who note "HOLC ratings that occurred at one point in time and racial segregation that is found later may or may not be causally linked,

and implying such a relationship almost certainly oversimplifies both the mortgage market and segregation in the cities" (559).

140. HOLC descriptions, as Jacob Faber suggests, may mark the "rigidity of the economic organization of neighborhoods over time" (2021, 1069).

141. Gioielli 2022.

142. See Aronson et al. 2021; Namin et al. 2022; Faber 2020; Faber 2020.

143. Michney and Winling 2020; Hillier 2003a.

144. Faber 2020.

145. Hillier 2003b.

146. Faber 2020.

147. Faber 2020.

148. See FHA 1935–1950.

149. Weiss 1987, 142.

150. Greer 2014.

151. Checkoway 1980; Gotham 2000a.

152. Weaver 1948, 72.

153. FHA 1935, 41; Fishback et al. 2022.

154. FHLBB 1936, 61.

155. Michney 2022.

156. Greer 2014.

157. FHA 1936, section 228–29; Freund 2007, 118–35; Nightingale 2012, 341–56.

158. FHA 1938, section 980(3)-g.

159. Quoted in Hirsch 2000b, 159.

160. Gotham 2000a, 310; Checkoway 1980; Weiss 1987.

161. FHA 1935, 16; Weiss 1987, 145–48; Jackson 1980, 205; Dean 1947; Rothstein 2017; Gotham 2000a.

162. Xu 2022; Greer 2014; Fishback et al. 2022.

163. Cebul 2020.

164. Teaford 2000; Checkoway 1980. On St. Louis, see Gordon 2008, chapters 4 and 5; on Minneapolis, see Vargo 2013.

165. Hirsch 2000a.

166. Myrdal 1944, 626.

167. Hirsch 1983, 2000a, 2000b; Freund 2007, 99–133, quote at 133.

168. Calculated from FHA 1942, 150.

169. Hayward 2010.

170. Hacker 2005.

171. Taylor 2019; Goetz 2013; Gotham 2000b.

172. Gordon 2019a; Rios 2020; Sharkey 2020.

173. Soss and Weaver 2017; Balto 2019; Capers 2009. On St. Louis, see Boyles 2015; Rios 2020; Gordon 2019a.

174. Massey 2020.

175. Anderson 2010, 2; see also Mills 2019, identifying housing inequality as the central node in a "multiple interacting set" of exploitation and disadvantage.

176. Robertson, Parker, and Tach 2023; Xu 2022.
177. Orfield 2006.
178. Goetz 2002.
179. Sood, Speagle, and Ehrman-Solberg 2019.
180. Quoted in U.S. Commission on Civil Rights 1977, 1.
181. Seiple et al. 2017.
182. U.S. Commission on Civil Rights 1977.
183. Stebbins and Comen 2018.
184. See Bruch and Gordon 2019.
185. Gordon 2008, 2019a.
186. Prener 2021.
187. Bruch and Gordon 2019.
188. Taylor 2019; Yinger 1995; Kahrl 2018; Flippen 2004; Howell and Korver-Glenn 2018.
189. Gordon 2019a.
190. Kucheva and Sander 2014; Nourse and Phares 1975.
191. Hayward 2013, 52–53.
192. On wealth, see Oliver and Shapiro 1995; Shapiro 2017; Percheski and Gibson-Davis 2020.
193. Erickson 2016; Erickson and Highsmith 2018; Garcia and Yosso 2013; Jargowsky 2014; Lareau 2014; Owens 2017.
194. Trounstine 2018; Anderson 2009, 940.
195. Mills 1997, 50.
196. Fergus 2013; Walker, Keane, and Burke 2010.
197. Eichenlaub, Tolnay, and Alexander 2010; Derenoncourt 2022; Tolnay 2003.

Appendix: Note on Methods

1. Scholars have noted the importance of the FHA, but documentation has been slowed by the fact that the agency destroyed its run of local maps and assessments. See Freund 2007; Greer 2014; Fishback et al. 2022.
2. Glotzer 2020; Fogelson 2005; Gotham 2000a.
3. Long and Johnson 1947, 12.
4. Gotham 2000c, 618.
5. Many ongoing projects are represented under the auspices of the National Covenants Research Coalition; see https://www.nationalcovenantsresearchcoalition.com/ (accessed May 12, 2023).
6. Witgen 2019.
7. The only exception to this practice is the Torrens system, which grants title by registration, rather than by documenting the full chain of title. Twenty states make limited use of the Torrens system. See Patton 1934; Monchow 1928.
8. Monchow 1928, 20.
9. Weisbord and Sterk 2021.

10. On "metes and bounds," see Brady 2019. An 1890 legal description in St. Louis County, for example, reads in part: "Beginning at a point in the south line of the right of way of the St. Louis and San Francisco Railroad, two chains thirty six links from a stone in the center of the Quinette Road, which stone is twenty chains and twenty seven links east of the center of said Section number Ten, and then south thirty eight chains twenty six links to a stone (mark on Natural Rock) from which a black oak twelve inches in diameter bears north two and half degrees east nineteen links, a black oak thirteen inches in diameter" (St. Louis County Recorder, Deed Book 49-63). The description of a restricted parcel (Miscellaneous Records 59-257 [1949]) in Black Hawk County, Iowa, for example, reads: "south one half of the east ten acres of the southeast quarter of the southwest quarter of section 18 in Township 89 North, Range 12 west of the 5th Principal Meridian."

11. Bayer-Pacht 2010.

12. Weisbord and Sterk 2021.

13. Weisbord and Sterk 2021; Bayer-Pacht 2010.

14. Santucci 2020.

15. See, for example, Johnson County Recorder, Deed Book 159-56.

16. Gordon 2023a.

17. Glotzer 2020; Gotham 2000c; Fogelson 2005.

18. Email communication with James Gregory, Segregated Seattle (September 2021).

19. Long and Johnson 1947; Gordon 2023a.

20. Ehrman-Solberg et al. 2020; see also Bakelmun and Shoenfeld 2020.

21. Santucci 2020.

22. In Philadelphia, for example, Santucci (2020) utilized digitized records for 1920 to 1938, because earlier ones (though digitized) were handwritten.

23. Monchow 1928, 27.

24. See Dean 1947 (Queens, Nassau, and Southern Westchester Counties, New York); Hart 1991; and Smith 2018 (Portland, Oregon). See also Quinn 1979; Consigny and Zile 1958; and Zile 1959 (all Milwaukee).

25. See Stach 1988 (Columbus, Ohio); Dawson 2019 (Shaker Heights, Ohio); Glotzer 2020 (Baltimore); Gotham 2000c (Kansas City, Missouri); Chase 1995 (Wilmington, Delaware); Fogelson 2005 (Los Angeles); Jaffee 2007 (Beaver Hills, Connecticut).

26. Santucci 2020.

27. This stage was completed in collaboration with student interns and community members organized by the Metropolitan St. Louis Equal Housing and Opportunity Center and Legal Services of Eastern Missouri. Funding for this research was provided by the Commonwealth Project (Harvard University), the St. Louis Association of Realtors, and an Arts and Humanities Initiative Grant from the University of Iowa. I am indebted to Peter Hoffman of Legal Services of Eastern Missouri for unearthing the catalog of restrictions.

28. Email communication with Sarah Shoenfeld, Mapping Segregation DC (September 2021).

29. In Milwaukee suburbs (Waukesha County) 85 percent of restrictions are recorded in "master agreements" such as subdivision indentures. See Conisgny and Zile 1958; Zile 1959.
30. Email communication with James Gregory, Segregated Seattle (September 2021).
31. Email communication with LaDale Winling, Chicago Covenants Project (October 2021).
32. For most states, counties are the primary substate administrative division. Louisiana has parishes; Alaska has boroughs for developed areas and census areas for undeveloped land. The cities of Baltimore, St. Louis, and Carson City (Nevada) all have the status (and perform the functions of) counties, as do forty-one independent cities in Virginia. See U.S. Census Bureau 1994, chapter 4.
33. See U.S. Census Bureau 1994, chapter 4; 2023.
34. U.S. Department of Interior 1983; Libecap and Lueck 2011; Brady 2019.
35. Conzen 2001.
36. Conzen 2001.
37. Adams 1970; Hoyt 1933; Fellman 1957.
38. Santucci 2020.
39. Consistency over time in city block numbering also facilitated the mapping of covenants in Washington, D.C. Bakelmun and Shoenfeld 2020, 66–67.
40. Hanchett 1996.
41. Ehrman-Solberg et al. 2020.

REFERENCES

Abrams, Charles. 1955. *Forbidden Neighbors: A Study of Prejudice in Housing.* New York: Harper.

Adams, John. 1970. Residential Structure of Midwestern Cities. *Annals of the Association of American Geographers* 60(1): 37–62.

Akbar, Prottoy, Sijie Li, Allison Shertzer, and Randall P. Walsh. 2020. "Racial Segregation in Housing Markets and the Erosion of Black Wealth." NBER Working Paper No. 25805.

Allard, Scott W. 2017. *Places in Need: The Changing Geography of Poverty.* New York: Russell Sage Foundation.

Alon, Sigal. 2009. "The Evolution of Class Inequality in Higher Education: Competition, Exclusion, and Adaptation." *American Sociological Review* 74: 731–55.

American Institute of Real Estate Appraisers. 1951. *The Appraisal of Real Estate.* Chicago: The Institute.

Ananat, Elizabeth Oltmans. 2011. "The Wrong Side(s) of the Tracks: The Causal Effects of Racial Segregation on Urban Poverty and Inequality." *American Economic Journal: Applied Economics* 3(2): 34–66.

Anderson, Elizabeth. 2010. *The Imperative of Integration.* Princeton: Princeton University Press.

Anderson, Michele Wilde. 2009. "Mapped Out of Local Democracy." *Stanford Law Review* 62(4): 931–1003.

Aronson, Daniel, Jacob Faber, Daniel Hartley, Bhashkar Mazumder and Patrick Sharkey. 2021. "The Long-Run Effects of the 1930s HOLC 'Redlining' Maps on Place-Based Measures of Economic Opportunity and Socioeconomic Success." *Regional Science and Urban Economics* 86: 1–15.

Avins, Alfred. 1966. "The Civil Rights Act of 1875 and the Civil Rights Cases Revisited: State Action, the Fourteenth Amendment, and Housing." *UCLA Law Review* 14(1): 5–25.

Ayers, Oliver. 2021. "Fred Trump, the Ku Klux Klan and Grassroots Redlining in Interwar America." *Journal of Urban History* 47(1): 3–28.

Babcock, Frederick. 1924. *The Appraisal of Real Estate.* New York: MacMillan.

Bae, Hyun Hye, and Lance Freeman. 2021. "Residential Segregation at the Dawn of the Great Migration: Evidence from the 1910 and 1920 Census." *Social Science History* 45(1): 27–53.

Bakelmun, Ashley, and Sarah Jane Shoenfeld. 2020. "Open Data and Racial Segregation: Mapping the Historic Imprint of Racial Covenants and Redlining on American Cities." In *Open Cities | Open Data*, edited by Scott Hawken, Hoon Han, and Chris Pettit. Singapore: Palgrave Macmillan.

Baker, Dwayne Marshall. 2020. "Inclusion and Exclusion in Establishing the Delmar Loop Transit-Oriented Development Site." *Journal of Planning Education and Research* (online June 2020). DOI: https://doi.org/10.1177/0739456X20929760.

Baker, Newman F. 1925. "Constitutionality of Zoning Laws." *Illinois Law Review* 20(3): 213–48.

Balto, Simon. 2019. *Occupied Territory: Policing Black Chicago from Red Summer to Black Power.* Chapel Hill: University of North Carolina Press.

Barone, Ana Cláudia Castilho. 2018. "Harland Bartholomew and Racially Informed Zoning: The Case of St. Louis." *Revista Brasileira De Estudos Urbanos E Regionais* 20(3): 437–56.

Bartholomew, Harland. 1917. *A Major Street Plan for St. Louis.* St. Louis: City Plan Commission.

———. 1918. *The Zone Plan.* St. Louis: City Plan Commission.

Bassett, Edward M. 1922a. *Zoning. Technical Pamphlet No. 5.* New York: National Municipal League.

———. 1922b. "Zoning vs. Private Restrictions." *National Real Estate Journal,* January 2, 1922, 26–27.

Bateman, David A., Ira Katznelson, and John S. Lapinski. 2018. *Southern Nation: Congress and White Supremacy after Reconstruction.* New York: Russell Sage Foundation; Princeton: Princeton University Press.

Bayer-Pacht, Emily. 2010. "The Computerization of Land Records: How Advances in Recording Systems Affect the Rationale behind Some Existing Chain of Title Doctrine." *Cardozo Law Review* 32(1): 337–72.

Beito, David, and Bruce Smith. 1990. "The Formation of Urban Infrastructure through Nongovernmental Planning: The Private Places of St. Louis, 1869–1920." *Journal of Urban History* 16(3): 263–303.

Bell, Jeannine. 2013. *Hate Thy Neighbor: Move-in Violence and the Persistence of Racial Segregation in American Housing.* New York: New York University Press.

Bell, Wendell. 1954. "A Probability Model for the Measurement of Ecological Segregation," *Social Forces* 32(4): 357–64.

Bell, Wendell, and Ernest M. Willis. 1957. "The Segregation of Negroes in American Cities: A Comparative Analysis." *Social and Economic Studies* 6(1): 59–75.

Bischoff, Kendra. 2008. "School District Fragmentation and Racial Residential Segregation." *Urban Affairs Review* 44(2): 182–217.

Blakely, Edward James, and Mary Gail Snyder. 1997. *Fortress America: Gated Communities in the United States*. Washington, D.C.: Brookings Institute.

Block, Sharon. 2018. *Colonial Complexions: Race and Bodies in Eighteenth-Century America*. Philadelphia: University of Pennsylvania Press.

Boger, Gretchen. 2009. "The Meaning of Neighborhood in the Modern City." *Journal of Urban History* 35(2): 236–58.

Bonilla-Silva, Eduardo, and David G. Embrick. 2007. "'Every Place Has a Ghetto . . .': The Significance of Whites' Social and Residential Segregation." *Symbolic Interaction* 30(3): 323–45.

Boone, Christopher D. A., and Laurence Wilse-Samson. 2021. "Structural Change and Internal Labor Migration: Evidence from the Great Depression." *Review of Economics and Statistics* (2021): 1–54.

Boustan, Leah Platt. 2017. *Competition in the Promised Land: Black Migrants in Northern Cities and Labor Markets*. Princeton: Princeton University Press.

Boustan, Leah P., and Robert A. Margo. 2013. "A Silver Lining to White Flight? White Suburbanization and African-American Homeownership, 1940–1980." *Journal of Urban Economics* 78: 71–80.

Boyle, Kevin. 2005. *Arc of Justice: A Saga of Race, Civil Rights, and Murder in the Jazz Age*. New York: Henry Holt.

Boyles, Andrea S. 2015. *Race, Place, and Suburban Policing*. Berkeley: University of California Press.

Brady, David, and Michael Wallace. 2001. "Deindustrialization and Poverty: Manufacturing Decline and AFDC Recipiency in Lake County, Indiana 1964–93." *Sociological Forum* 16(2): 321–58.

Brady, Maureen E. 2019. "The Forgotten History of Metes and Bounds." *Yale Law Journal* 128(4): 872–953.

———. 2021. "Turning Neighbors into Nuisances." *Harvard Law Review* 134(5): 1609–82.

Breaux, Richard M. 2002. "'Maintaining a Home for Girls': The Iowa Federation of Colored Women's Clubs at the University of Iowa, 1919–1950." *Journal of African American History* 87(2): 236–55.

Brooks, Richard. 2011. "Covenants Without Courts: Enforcing Residential Segregation with Legally Unenforceable Agreements." *American Economic Review* 101(3): 360–65.

Brooks, Richard, and Carol M. Rose. 2013. *Saving the Neighborhood: Racially Restrictive Covenants, Law, and Social Norms*. Cambridge, Mass.: Harvard University Press.

Brown, Dorothy Andrea. 2010. "Shades of the American Dream." *Washington University Law Review* 87: 329–78.

Brubaker, Rogers. 2015. *Grounds for Difference*. Cambridge, Mass.: Harvard University Press.

Bruce, Andrew, 1927. "Racial Zoning by Private Contract in the Light of the Constitution's Rule against Restraints on Alienation." *Illinois Law Review* 21: 704–17.

Bruch, Sarah K., and Colin Gordon. 2019. "Home Inequity: Race, Wealth, and Housing in St. Louis, 1940–2016." *Housing Studies* 35(9): 1285–308.

Bruch, Sarah K., Aaron J. Rosenthal, and Joe Soss. 2019. "Unequal Positions: A Relational Approach to Racial Inequality Trends in the US States, 1940–2010." *Social Science History* 43(1): 159–84.

Capers, Benjamin. 2009. "Policing, Race, and Place." *Harvard Civil Rights–Civil Liberties Law Review* 44: 44–78.

Carriere, Michael. 2011. "Fighting the War against Blight: Columbia University, Morningside Heights, Inc., and Counterinsurgent Urban Renewal." *Journal of Planning History* 10(1): 5–29.

Cayton, Horace R. 1940. "Negro Housing in Chicago." *Social Action*, April 15, 1940, 4–36.

Cayton, Horace R., and St. Clair Drake. 1945. *Black Metropolis; a Study of Negro Life in a Northern City.* New York: Harper & Row.

Cebul, Brent. 2020. "Tearing Down Black America." *Boston Review*, July 22, 2020. https://www.bostonreview.net/articles/brent-cebul-tearing-down-black-america/.

Charles, Camille Zubrinsky. 2003. "The Dynamics of Racial Residential Segregation." *Annual Review of Sociology* 29: 167–207.

———. 2006. *Won't You Be My Neighbor? Race, Class, and Residence in Los Angeles.* New York: Russell Sage Foundation.

Chase, Susan Mulcahy. 1995. The Process of Suburbanization and the Use of Race Restrictive Deed Covenants as Private Zoning, Wilmington, Delaware, 1900–1941." Ph.D. diss., University of Delaware.

Checkoway, Barry. 1980. "Large Builders, Federal Housing Programmes, and Postwar Suburbanization." *International Journal of Urban and Regional Research* 4(1): 21–45.

Chetty, Raj, Nathaniel Hendren, Maggie R. Jones, and Sonya R. Porter. 2020. "Race and Economic Opportunity in the United States: An Intergenerational Perspective." *Quarterly Journal of Economics* 135(2): 711–83.

Chetty, Raj, Nathaniel Hendren, Patrick Kline, and Emmanuel Saez. 2014. "Where Is the Land of Opportunity? The Geography of Intergenerational Mobility in the United States." *Quarterly Journal of Economics* 129(4): 1553–623.

Chin, Gabriel J. 2004. "Jim Crow's Long Goodbye." *Constitutional Commentary* 21(1): 107–32.

Cohen, Alfred E. 1921. "Racial Restrictions in Covenants in Deeds." *Virginia Law Register* 6(10): 737–43.

Committee on City Planning and Zoning. 1931. *Tentative Report of the Committee on City Planning and Zoning.* Washington, D.C.: President's Conference on Homebuilding and Homeownership.

Committee on Negro Housing. 1931. *Tentative Report of the Committee on Negro Housing.* Washington, D.C.: President's Conference on Homebuilding and Homeownership.

Committee on Subdivision Layout. 1931. *Tentative Report of the Committee on Subdivision Layout.* Washington, D.C.: President's Conference on Homebuilding and Homeownership.

Connolly, Nathan. 2014. *A World More Concrete.* Chicago: University of Chicago Press.

Consigny, Robert H., and Zigurds L. Zile. 1958. "Use of Restrictive Covenants in a Rapidly Urbanizing Area—Part I." *Wisconsin Law Review* 1958(4): 610–40.

Conzen, Michael P. 2001. "The Study of Urban Form in the United States." *Urban Morphology* 5(1): 3–14.

Cooper-McCann, Patrick. 2016. "The Trap of Triage: Lessons from the Team Four Plan." *Journal of Planning History* 15(2): 149–69.

Crossney, Kristen B., and David W. Bartelt. 2005a. "The Legacy of the Home Owners' Loan Corporation." *Housing Policy Debate* 16(3–4): 547–74.

———. 2005b. "Residential Security, Risk, and Race: The Home Owners' Loan Corporation and Mortgage Access in Two Cities." *Urban Geography* 26(8): 707–36.

Crowder, Kyle, and Maria Krysan. 2017. *Cycle of Segregation: Social Processes and Residential Stratification*. New York: Russell Sage Foundation.

Cui, Tianfang. 2023. "The Emergence of Exclusionary Zoning Across American Cities." Wharton School, University of Pennsylvania. Unpublished manuscript. https://tom -cui.com/assets/pdfs/LotsEZ_Latest.pdf.

Cutler, David M., and Edward L. Glaeser. 1997. "Are Ghettos Good or Bad?" *Quarterly Journal of Economics* 112(3): 827–72.

Cutler, David M., Edward L. Glaeser, and Jacob L. Vigdor. 1999. "The Rise and Decline of the American Ghetto." *Journal of Political Economy* 107(3): 455–506.

Danielson, Michael N. 1976. "The Politics of Exclusionary Zoning in Suburbia." *Political Science Quarterly* 91(1): 1–18.

Davis, F. James. 1965. "The Effects of a Freeway Displacement on Racial Housing Segregation in a Northern City." *Phylon* 26(3): 209–15.

Davis, Mike. 2006. *City of Quartz: Excavating the Future in Los Angeles*. London: Verso.

Dawson, Virginia P. 2019. "Protection from Undesirable Neighbors: The Use of Deed Restrictions in Shaker Heights, Ohio." *Journal of Planning History* 18(2): 116–36.

Dean, John P. 1947. "Only Caucasian: A Study of Race Covenants." *Journal of Land & Public Utility Economics* 23(4): 428–32.

Delegard, Kristen. 2016. "Mapping Prejudice: Visualizing the Hidden Histories of Race and Privilege in Minneapolis." Accessed April 15, 2023. https://www.mappingprejudice.org.

———. 2019. "Emanual Cohen and the Battle Against Anti-Semitism in Minneapolis." Twin Cities PBS (TPT Originals). March 5, 2019. https://www.tptoriginals.org/emanuel -cohen-and-the-battle-against-anti-semitism-in-minneapolis.

Derenoncourt, Ellora. 2022. "Can You Move to Opportunity? Evidence from the Great Migration." *American Economic Review* 112(2): 369–408.

DeSena, Judith N. 1994. "Local Gatekeeping Practices and Residential Segregation." *Sociological Inquiry* 64(3): 307–21.

Desnoyer, Brad, and Anne Alexander. 2017. "Race, Rhetoric, and Judicial Opinions: Missouri as a Case Study." *Maryland Law Review* 76(3): 696–726.

Dillingham, William Paul. 1911. *Dictionary of Races or Peoples*. Reports of the Immigration Commission. Washington: Government Printing Office.

DiTomaso, Nancy. 2013. *The American Non-Dilemma: Racial Inequality Without Racism*. New York: Russell Sage Foundation.

Dorr, Jeffrey R. 2015. "Race in St. Louis's Catholic Church: Discourse, Structures, and Segregation, 1873–1941." Ph.D. diss., Saint Louis University.

Du Bois, W. E. B. 1899. *The Philadelphia Negro a Social Study.* Philadelphia: University of Pennsylvania Press.

———. 1923. "The Superior Race (An Essay)." *Smart Set: A Magazine of Cleverness* 70(4): 55–60.

———. 1925. "The Challenge of Detroit." *Crisis* 31(November): 7–10.

Dusen, Gerald Van. 2019. *Detroit's Birwood Wall: Hatred and Healing in the West Eight Mile Community.* Cheltenham, UK: Arcadia Publishing Incorporated.

Ehrman-Solberg, Kevin, Penny Petersen, Marguerite Mills, Kirsten Delegard, and Ryan Matke. 2020. Racial Covenants in Hennepin County [dataset]. University of Minnesota. November 25, 2020. https://conservancy.umn.edu/handle/11299/217209.

Eichenlaub, Suzanne C., Stewart E. Tolnay, and J. Trent Alexander. 2010. "Moving Out but Not Up: Economic Outcomes in the Great Migration." *American Sociological Review* 75(1): 101–25.

Ellen, Ingrid Gould, Justin P. Steil, and Jorge De La Roca. 2016. "The Significance of Segregation in the 21st Century." *City & Community* 15(1): 8–13.

Ellis, Justin. 2020. "Minneapolis Had This Coming." *Atlantic,* June 9, 2020. https://www.theatlantic.com/ideas/archive/2020/06/minneapolis-long-overdue-crisis/612826.

Ely, James W. 1998. "Reflections on Buchanan v. Warley: Property Rights, and Race." *Vanderbilt Law Review* 51(4): 953–73.

Endersby, James W., and William T. Horner. 2016. *Lloyd Gaines and the Fight to End Segregation.* Columbia: University of Missouri Press.

Erickson, Ansley T. 2016. *Making the Unequal Metropolis: School Desegregation and Its Limits.* Chicago: University of Chicago Press.

Erickson, Ansley T., and Andrew R. Highsmith. 2018. "The Neighborhood Unit: Schools, Segregation, and the Shaping of the Modern Metropolitan Landscape." *Teachers College Record* 120(3): 1–36.

Ervin, Keona K. 2017. *Gateway to Equality: Black Women and the Struggle for Economic Justice in St. Louis.* Lexington: University of Kentucky Press.

Esping Anderson, Gosta. 1990. *The Three Worlds of Welfare Capitalism.* Cambridge: Polity.

Executive Council of the State of Iowa. 1905. *Census of Iowa for the Year 1905.* Des Moines.

———. 1915. *Census of Iowa for the Year 1915.* Des Moines.

———. 1925. *Census of Iowa for the Year 1925.* Des Moines.

Faber, Jacob W. 2020. "We Built This: Consequences of New Deal Era Intervention in America's Racial Geography." *American Sociological Review* 85(5): 739–75.

———. 2021. "Contemporary Echoes of Segregationist Policy: Spatial Marking and the Persistence of Inequality." *Urban Studies* 58(5): 1067–86.

Farr, Newton C. 1939. "The Validity of Race-Restriction Agreements." *Journal of Land & Public Utility Economics* 15(4): 477–79.

Federal Home Loan Bank Board (FHLBB). 1936. *Third Annual Report of the Federal Home Loan Bank Board.* Washington: Government Printing Office.

———. 1938. *Fifth Annual Report of the Federal Home Loan Bank Board.* Washington: Government Printing Office.

Federal Housing Administration (FHA). 1935–1950. Annual Report of the Federal Housing Administration. Washington: Government Printing Office.

————. 1936. *Underwriting Manual.* Washington: Government Printing Office.

————. 1938. *Underwriting Manual,* revised edition. Washington: Government Printing Office.

————. 1942. "FHA Homes in Metropolitan Districts: Characteristics of Mortgages, Homes, Borrowers under the FHA Plan, 1934–1940." Washington: Government Printing Office.

Fellman, Jerome D. 1957. "Pre-Building Growth Patterns of Chicago." *Annals of the Association of American Geographers* 47(1): 59–82.

Fergus, Devin. 2013. "The Ghetto Tax: Auto Insurance, Postal Code Profiling, and the Hidden History of Wealth Transfer." In *Beyond Discrimination: Racial Inequality in a Post-racist Era,* edited by Fredrick C. Harris and Robert C. Lieberman. New York: Russell Sage Foundation.

FHLBB, Division of Research and Statistics. 1940. "Security Area Map Folder of Metropolitan St. Louis in Missouri." October 15, 1940. Series 195.3. Records of the Home Owners' Loan Corporation, 1933–1951. Record Group 195. FHLBB. College Park, Md.: National Archives and Records Administration.

Fiel, Jeremy. 2022. "Relational Segregation: A Structural View of Categorical Relations," *Sociological Theory* 39(3): 153–79.

Fields, Barbara J. 1990. "Slavery, Race and Ideology in the United States of America." *New Left Review* 1(181): 95–118.

————. 2001. "Whiteness, Racism, and Identity." *International Labor and Working-Class History* 60(60): 48–56.

Fishback, Price V., Jessica LaVoice, Allison Shertzer, and Randall Walsh. 2020. "The HOLC Maps: How Race and Poverty Influenced Real Estate Professionals' Evaluation of Lending Risk in the 1930s." NBER Working Paper 28146.

Fishback, Price, Jonathan Rose, Kenneth A. Snowden, and Thomas Storrs. 2022. "New Evidence on Redlining by Federal Housing Programs in the 1930s." *Journal of Urban Economics* (online May 2022). DOI: https://doi-org.proxy.lib.uiowa.edu/10.1016/j.jue.2022.103462.

Fisher, Damany Morris. 2008. "Far from Utopia: Race, Housing, and the Fight to End Residential Segregation in Sacramento, 1900–1980." Ph.D. diss., University of California at Berkeley.

Fisher, Robert. 1990. "Protecting Community and Property Values: Civic Clubs in Houston, 1909–70," In *Urban Texas: Politics and Development,* edited by Char Miller. College Station: Texas A&M University Press.

Fishman, Robert. 1987. *Bourgeois Utopias: The Rise and Fall of Suburbia.* New York: Basic Books.

Flint, Barbara. 1977. "Zoning and Residential Segregation: A Social and Physical History, 1910–1940." Ph.D. diss., University of Chicago.

Flippen, Chenoa. 2004. "Unequal Returns to Housing Investments? A Study of Real Housing Appreciation among Black, White, and Hispanic Households." *Social Forces* 82(4): 1523–51.

Fogelson, Robert. 2005. *Bourgeois Nightmares: Suburbia, 1870–1930*. New Haven: Yale University Press.

Fox, Cybelle, and Thomas A. Guglielmo. 2012. "Defining America's Racial Boundaries: Blacks, Mexicans, and European Immigrants, 1890–1945." *American Journal of Sociology* 118(2): 327–79.

Freund, David. 2007. *Colored Property: State Policy and White Racial Politics in Suburban America*. Chicago: University of Chicago Press.

Friedman, David A. 2012. "Bringing Order to Contracts against Public Policy." *Florida State University Law Review* 39(3): 563–622.

Frug, Gerald E. 1998. "City Services." *New York University Law Review* 73(1): 23–96.

Funiak, William Q. de. 1948. "Contracts Enforceable in Equity." *Virginia Law Review* 34(6): 637–61.

Furth, Salim, and MaryJo Webster. 2023. "Single-Family Zoning and Race: Evidence from the Twin Cities." *Housing Policy Debate* (online March 2023). DOI: https://doi.org/10.1080/10511482.2023.2186750.

Galster, George, and Patrick Sharkey. 2017. "Spatial Foundations of Inequality: A Conceptual Model and Empirical Overview." *RSF: The Russell Sage Foundation Journal of the Social Sciences* 3(2): 1–33. DOI: https://doi.org/10.7758/RSF.2017.3.2.01.

Garb, Margaret. 2005. *City of American Dreams: A History of Home Ownership and Housing Reform in Chicago, 1871–1919*. Chicago: University of Chicago Press.

———. 2006. "Drawing the 'Color Line': Race and Real Estate in Early Twentieth-Century Chicago." *Journal of Urban History* 32(5): 773–87.

Garcia, David. 2018. *Strategies of Segregation: Race, Residence, and the Struggle for Educational Equality*. Berkeley: University of California Press.

Garcia, David G., and Tara J. Yosso. 2013. "'Strictly in the Capacity of Servant': The Interconnection between Residential and School Segregation in Oxnard, California, 1934–1954." *History of Education Quarterly* 53(1): 64–89.

Gibson, Campbell, and Kay Jung. 2005. "Historical Census Statistics on Population Totals By Race, 1790 to 1990, and by Hispanic Origin, 1970 to 1990, for Large Cities and Other Urban Places in the United States." Population Division, Working Paper 76. Washington: U.S. Census Bureau.

———. 2006. "Historical Census Statistics on the Foreign Born-Population of the United States: 1850–2000." Population Division, Working Paper 81. Washington: U.S. Census Bureau.

Gioielli, Robert. 2022. "The Tyranny of the Map: Rethinking Redlining." *The Metropole Blog*. Urban History Association. November 3, 2022. https://themetropole.blog/2022/11/03/the-tyranny-of-the-map-rethinking-redlining/.

Glotzer, Paige. 2020. *How the Suburbs Were Segregated: Developers and the Business of Exclusionary Housing, 1890–1960*. New York: Columbia University Press.

Godsil, Rachel D. 2006. "Race Nuisance: The Politics of Law in the Jim Crow Era." *Michigan Law Review* 105(3): 505–57.

Goetz, Edward. 2002. *Hollman v. Cisneros: Deconcentrating Poverty in Minneapolis. Report 2: Planning for Northside Redevelopment*. Minneapolis: Center for Urban and Regional Affairs, University of Minnesota.

————. 2013. *New Deal Ruins: Race, Economic Justice, and Public Housing Policy.* Ithaca: Cornell University Press.

Gonda, Jeffrey. 2015. *Unjust Deeds: The Restrictive Covenants Cases and the Making of the Civil Rights Movement.* Chapel Hill: University of North Carolina Press.

Gordon, Colin. 2008. *Mapping Decline: St. Louis and the Fate of the American City.* Philadelphia: University of Pennsylvania Press.

————. 2014. "Declining Cities, Declining Unions: Urban Sprawl and U.S. Inequality." *Dissent,* December 10, 2014. https://www.dissentmagazine.org/online_articles/urban -sprawl-union-decline-cities-labor-inequality-united-states.

————. 2019a. *Citizen Brown: Race, Democracy and Inequality in the St. Louis Suburbs.* Chicago: University of Chicago Press.

————. 2019b. *Race in the Heartland: Equity, Opportunity, and Public Policy in the Midwest.* Washington, D.C.: Economic Policy Institute.

————. 2019c. "The New Deal State and Segregation." *Jacobin,* August 12, 2019. https:// jacobin.com/2019/08/new-deal-segregation-richard-rothstein-walker-color-of-law.

————. 2023a. "Dividing the City: Race-Restrictive Covenants and the Architecture of Segregation in St. Louis." *Journal of Urban History* 49(1): 160–82.

————. 2023b. Racial Restrictions in the City of St. Louis, Missouri [dataset]. University of Iowa and Russell Sage Foundation, June. https://www.russellsage.org/publications /patchwork-apartheid.

————. 2023c. Racial Restrictions in Black Hawk County, Iowa [dataset]. University of Iowa and Russell Sage Foundation, June. https://www.russellsage.org/publications /patchwork-apartheid.

————. 2023d. Racial Restrictions in Johnson County, Iowa [dataset]. University of Iowa and Russell Sage Foundation, June. https://www.russellsage.org/publications/patchwork -apartheid.

————. 2023e. Racial Restrictions in St. Louis County, Missouri [dataset]. University of Iowa and Russell Sage Foundation, June. https://www.russellsage.org/publications/patchwork -apartheid.

Gossett, Thomas F. 1963. *Race: The History of an Idea in America.* Dallas: Southern Methodist University Press.

Gotham, Kevin Fox. 2000a. "Racialization and the State: The Housing Act of 1934 and the Creation of the Federal Housing Administration." *Sociological Perspectives* 43(2): 291–317. DOI: https://doi.org/10.2307/1389798.

————. 2000b. "Separate and Unequal: The Housing Act of 1968 and the Section 235 Program." *Sociological Forum* 15(1): 13–37.

————. 2000c. "Urban Space, Restrictive Covenants and the Origins of Racial Residential Segregation in a US City, 1900–50." *International Journal of Urban and Regional Research* 24(3): 616–33.

————. 2002. *Race, Real Estate, and Uneven Development: The Kansas City Experience, 1900–2000.* Albany: SUNY Press.

Gottlieb, Peter. 1987. *Making Their Own Way: Southern Blacks' Migration to Pittsburgh, 1916-30.* Urbana: University of Illinois Press.

Governor's Interracial Commission. 1947. *The Negro and His Home in Minnesota.* Minneapolis: Governor's Interracial Commission.

Grannis, Rick. 2005. "T-Communities: Pedestrian Street Networks and Residential Segregation in Chicago, Los Angeles, and New York." *City & Community* 4(3): 295–321.

Greer, James. 2013. "The Home Owners' Loan Corporation and the Development of the Residential Security Maps." *Journal of Urban History* 39(2): 275–96.

———. 2014. "Historic Home Mortgage Redlining in Chicago." *Journal of the Illinois State Historical Society* 107(2): 204–33.

Gregory, James. 2005. *The Southern Diaspora: How the Great Migrations of Black and White Southerners Transformed America.* Chapel Hill: University of North Carolina Press.

Gregory, James, et al. 2016. "Segregated Seattle." Seattle Civil Rights and Labor History Project. Accessed April 15, 2023. https://depts.washington.edu/civilr/segregated.htm.

Grossman, James R. 1989. *Land of Hope: Chicago, Black Southerners, and the Great Migration.* Chicago: University of Chicago Press.

Haar, Charles M. 1953. "Zoning for Minimum Standards: The Wayne Township Case." *Harvard Law Review* 66(6): 1051–63.

Hacker, Jacob S. 2005. "Policy Drift: The Hidden Politics of U.S. Welfare State Retrenchment." In *Beyond Continuity: Institutional Change in Advanced Political Economies*, edited by Wolfgang Streeck and Kathleen Thelen. Oxford: Oxford University Press.

Hacking, Ian. 2005. "Why Race Still Matters." *Daedalus* 134(1): 102–16.

Ham, Bernard K. 1997. "Exclusionary Zoning and Racial Segregation: A Reconsideration of the Mount Laurel Doctrine." *Constitutional Law Journal* 7(2): 577–93.

Hanchett, Thomas W. 1996. "U.S. Tax Policy and the Shopping-Center Boom of the 1950s and 1960s." *American Historical Review* 101(4): 1082–110.

Haney López, Ian F. 2006. *White by Law: The Legal Construction of Race.* New York: New York University Press.

Harlan, Chico. 2014. "In St. Louis, Delmar Boulevard Is the Line That Divides a City by Race and Perspective." *Washington Post*, August 22, 2014. https://www.washingtonpost.com/national/in-st-louis-delmar-boulevard-is-the-line-that-divides-a-city-by-race-and-perspective/2014/08/22/de692962-a2ba-4f53-8bc3-54f88f848fdb_story.html.

Hart, Eric. 1991. "The Process of Neighborhood Development: The Role of Restrictive Covenants in the Development of Residential Subdivisions." MA thesis, Portland State University.

Hartley, Daniel A., and Jonathon Rose. 2023. "Blockbusting and the Challenges Faced by Black Families in Building Wealth through Housing in the Postwar United States." FRB of Chicago Working Paper No. 2023-02.

Hayden, Dolores. 2003. *Building Suburbia: Green Fields and Urban Growth, 1820–2000.* New York: Pantheon.

Haynes, Kinglsey E., and Zachary Machunda. 1987. "Spatial Restructuring of Manufacturing and Employment Growth in the Rural Midwest: An Analysis for Indiana." *Economic Geography* 63(4): 319–33.

Hayward, Clarissa Rile. 2010. "Bad Stories: Narrative, Identity, and the State's Materialist Pedagogy." *Citizenship Studies* 14(6): 651–66.

———. 2013. *How Americans Make Race: Stories, Institutions, Spaces.* New York: Cambridge University Press.

Helper, Rose. 1969. *Racial Policies and Practices of Real Estate Brokers*. Minneapolis: University of Minnesota Press.

Hennepin County Library. n.d. Digital Map Collection. Minnetonka, Minn. https://digitalcollections.hclib.org/digital/collection/p17208coll17.

Hillier, Amy E. 2003a. "Who Received Loans? Home Owners' Loan Corporation Lending and Discrimination in Philadelphia in the 1930s." *Journal of Planning History* 2(1): 3–24.

———. 2003b. "Redlining and the Homeowners' Loan Corporation." *Journal of Urban History* 29(4): 394–420.

———. 2005. "Residential Security Maps and Neighborhood Appraisals: The Home Owners' Loan Corporation and the Case of Philadelphia." *Social Science History* 29(2): 207–33.

Hirsch, Arnold R. 1983. *Making the Second Ghetto: Race and Housing in Chicago, 1940–1960*. New York: Cambridge University Press.

———. 2000a. "Choosing Segregation: Federal Housing Policy between Shelley and Brown." In *From Tenements to the Taylor Homes: In Search of an Urban Housing Policy in Twentieth-Century America*, edited by John F. Bauman, Roger Biles, and Kristin M. Szylvian. University Park: Pennsylvania State University Press.

———. 2000b. "Containment on the Home Front." *Journal of Urban History* 26(2): 158–89.

Hochschild, Jennifer, and Vesla Weaver. 2007. "Policies of Racial Classification and the Politics of Racial Inequality." In *Remaking America: Democracy and Public Policy in an Age of Inequality*, edited by Joe Soss, Jacob S. Hacker, and Suzanne Mettler. New York: Russell Sage Foundation.

Holt, Thomas C. 1995. "Marking: Race, Race-making, and the Writing of History." *American Historical Review* 100(100)1: 1–20.

Horiuchi, Lynne. 2007. "Object Lessons in Home Building: Racialized Real Estate Marketing in San Francisco." *Landscape Journal* 26(1): 61–82.

Howell, Benjamin. 2006. "Exploiting Race and Space: Concentrated Subprime Lending as Housing Discrimination." *California Law Review* 94(1): 101–47.

Howell, Junia, and Elizabeth Korver-Glenn. 2018. "Neighborhoods, Race, and the Twenty-First-Century Housing Appraisal Industry." *Sociology of Race and Ethnicity* 4(4): 473–90.

———. 2022. *Appraised: The Persistent Evaluation of White Neighborhoods as More Valuable than Communities of Color*. University City: Weidenbaum Center on the Economy, Government, and Public Policy, Washington University.

Hoyt, Homer. 1933. *One Hundred Years of Land Values in Chicago*. Chicago: University of Chicago Press.

Hunter, Julius. 1988. *Westmoreland and Portland Places: The History and Architecture of America's Premier Private Streets*. Columbia: University of Missouri Press.

Hurley, Andrew, and E. Murray. 2022. "Visions, Plans, and Schemes: Reconstructing African American St. Louis after the 1927 Tornado." *Journal of Planning History* 21(4): 295–315.

Iowa Digital Library. n.d. Map Collection. University of Iowa Libraries. Iowa City, Iowa.

Jackson, Kenneth. 1967. *The Ku Klux Klan in the City, 1915–1930*. Chicago: University of Chicago Press.

———. 1980. "Race, Ethnicity, and Real Estate Appraisal: The Home Owners Loan Corporation and the Federal Housing Administration." *Journal of Urban History* 6(4): 419–52.

———. 1985. *Crabgrass Frontier: The Suburbanization of the United States*. New York: Oxford University Press.

Jacobson, Matthew Frye. 1999. *Whiteness of a Different Color: European Immigrants and the Alchemy of Race*. Cambridge, Mass.: Harvard University Press.

Jaffee, Valerie. 2007. "Private Law or Social Norms? The Use of Restrictive Covenants in Beaver Hills." *Yale Law Journal* 116(6): 1302–42.

Jargowsky, Paul A. 2014. "Segregation, Neighborhoods, and Schools." In *Choosing Homes, Choosing Schools*, edited by Annette Lareau and Kimberly Goyette. New York: Russell Sage Foundation.

Jarwala, Alisha. 2020. "The More Things Change: Hundley v. Gorewitz and 'Change of Neighborhood' in the NAACP's Restrictive Covenant Cases." *Harvard Civil Rights-Civil Liberties Law Review* 55(2): 707–31.

John R. Borchert Map Library. n.d. University of Minnesota. Minneapolis, Minn. https://www.lib.umn.edu/collections/borchert.

Jones, Herbert Plummer. 1997. "The Shaping of Freedom: Industrial Urbanism and the Modern Civil Rights Movement in Waterloo, Iowa, 1910–1970." Ph.D. diss., University of Iowa.

Jones-Correa, Michael. 1999. "American Riots: Structures, Institutions and History." Russell Sage Foundation Working Paper No. 148.

———. 2000. "The Origins and Diffusion of Racial Restrictive Covenants." *Political Science Quarterly* 15(4): 541–68.

Jost, Timothy Stoltzfus. 1984. "The Defeasible Fee and the Birth of the Modern Residential Subdivision." *Missouri Law Review* 49(4): 695–740.

Jubara, Amalea, and Yaxuan Zhang. 2021. "Mapping Block-Level Segregation: The Twin Cities' Black Population, 1980–2010." Minnesota Population Center. February 10, 2021. https://blog.popdata.org/mapping-segregation.

Kahen, Harold I. 1945. "Validity of Anti-Negro Restrictive Covenants: A Reconsideration of the Problem." *University of Chicago Law Review* 12(2): 198–213.

Kahrl, Andrew. 2018. "The Short End of Both Sticks: Property Assessments and Black Taxpayer Disadvantage in Urban America." In *Shaped by the State: Toward a New Political History of the Twentieth Century*, edited by Brent Cebul, Lily Giesmer, and Mason Williams. Chicago: University of Chicago Press.

Kain, John. 1968. "Housing Segregation, Negro Unemployment, and Metropolitan Decentralization." *Quarterly Journal of Economics* 82(2): 175–97.

Kasarda, John D. 1989. "Urban Industrial Transition and the Underclass." *Annals of the American Academy of Political and Social Science* 501(1): 26–47.

Katz, Michael B. 2012. *Why Don't American Cities Burn?* Philadelphia: University of Pennsylvania Press.

Katznelson, Ira, Kim Geiger, and Daniel Kryder. 1993. "Limiting Liberalism: The Southern Veto in Congress, 1933–1950." *Political Science Quarterly* 108(2): 283–306.

Kelleher, Daniel T. 1969. "The History of the St. Louis NAACP, 1914-1955." MA thesis, University of Southern Illinois at Edwardsville.

Klarman, Michael J. 1998. "Race and the Court in the Progressive Era." *Vanderbilt Law Review* 51(4): 881–952.

Kniskern, P. Wheeler. 1933. *Real Estate Appraisal and Valuation*. New York: The Ronald Press.

Knudsen, Daniel. 1989. "Deindustrialization of the U.S. Midwest, 1965–1985." Regional Economic Development Institute, School of Public and Environmental Affairs, Indiana University, Bloomington.

Koeth, Stephen M. 2019. "Crabgrass Catholicism: U.S. Catholics and the Historiography of Postwar Suburbia." *U.S. Catholic Historian* 37(4): 1–27.

Korngold, Gerald. 2001. "The Emergence of Private Land Use Controls in Large-Scale Subdivisions: The Companion Story to Village of Euclid v. Ambler Realty Co." *Case Western Reserve Law Review* 51(4): 617–43.

Korver-Glenn, Elizabeth. 2018. "Compounding Inequalities: How Racial Stereotypes and Discrimination Accumulate Across the Stages of Housing Exchange." *American Sociological Review* 83(4): 627–56.

———. 2021. *Race Brokers: Housing Markets and Segregation in 21st Century Urban America*. New York: Oxford University Press.

Kramer, Rory. 2017. "Defensible Spaces in Philadelphia: Exploring Neighborhood Boundaries through Spatial Analysis." *RSF: The Russell Sage Foundation Journal of the Social Sciences* 3(2): 81–101. DOI: https://doi.org/10.7758/RSF.2017.3.2.04.

Kucheva, Yana, and Richard Sander. 2014. "The Misunderstood Consequences of Shelley v. Kraemer." *Social Science Research* 48: 212–33.

Kusmer, Kenneth L. 1976. *A Ghetto Takes Shape: Black Cleveland, 1870–1930*. Urbana: University of Illinois.

Lamont, Michele, Stefan Beljean, and Matthew Clair. 2014. "What Is Missing? Cultural Processes and Causal Pathways to Inequality." *Socio-Economic Review* 12: 573–608.

Lang, Clarence. 2009. *Grassroots at the Gateway: Class Politics and Black Freedom Struggle in St. Louis, 1936–75*. Ann Arbor: University of Michigan Press.

Lareau, Annette. 2014. "Schools, Housing, and the Reproduction of Inequality." In *Choosing Homes, Choosing Schools*, edited by Annette Lareau and Kimberly Goyette. New York: Russell Sage Foundation.

Lee, Barrett A., Glenn Firebaugh, Stephen A. Matthews, Sean F. Reardon, Chad R. Farrell, and David O'Sullivan. 2008. "Beyond the Census Tract: Patterns and Determinants of Racial Segregation at Multiple Geographic Scales." *American Sociological Review* 73(5): 766–91.

Libecap, Gary D., and Dean Lueck. 2011. "The Demarcation of Land and the Role of Coordinating Property Institutions." *Journal of Political Economy* 119(3): 426–67.

Lichter, Daniel T., Domenico Parisi, and Michael C. Taquino. 2015. "Toward a New Macro-Segregation? Decomposing Segregation within and between Metropolitan Cities and Suburbs." *American Sociological Review* 80(4): 843–73.

Lieb, Emily. 2019. "The 'Baltimore Idea' and the Cities It Built." *Southern Cultures* 25(2): 104–19.

Lieberson, Stanley. 1963. *Ethnic Patterns in American Cities.* New York: Free Press of Glencoe.

———. 1980. *A Piece of the Pie: Blacks and White Immigrants since 1890.* Berkeley: University of California Press.

Light, Jennifer. 2011. "Discriminating Appraisals: Cartography, Computation, and Access to Federal Mortgage Insurance in the 1930s." *Technology and Culture* 52(3): 485–522.

Lipsitz, George. 1995. *A Life in the Struggle: Ivory Perry and the Culture of Opposition.* Philadelphia: Temple University Press.

Lloyd, Ernest Lee. 2013. "How Routing an Interstate Highway through South Minneapolis Disrupted an African-American Neighborhood." Ph.D. diss., Hamline University.

Logan, John R., Samuel Kye, H. Jacob Carlson, Elisabeta Minca, and Daniel Schleith. 2023. "The Role of Suburbanization in Metropolitan Segregation after 1940." *Demography* 60(1): 281–301.

Logan, John R., and Brian Stults. 2021. "The Persistence of Segregation in the Metropolis: New Findings from the 2020 Census." Diversity and Disparities Project, Brown University. Accessed May 4, 2023. https://s4.ad.brown.edu/Projects/Diversity.

Logan, John R., Weiwei Zhang, Richard Turner, and Allison Shertzer. 2015. "Creating the Black Ghetto: Black Residential Patterns before and during the Great Migration." *Annals of the American Academy of Political and Social Science* 660(1): 18–35.

Logan, Trevon D., and John M. Parman. 2017. "The National Rise in Residential Segregation." *Journal of Economic History* 77(1): 127–70.

———. 2022. "Racial Residential Segregation in the United States." Unpublished manuscript.

Long, Herman H., and Charles S. Johnson. 1947. *People vs. Property: Race Restrictive Covenants in Housing.* Nashville: Fisk University Press.

Longa, Ernesto A. 2007. "A History of America's First Jim Crow Law School Library and Staff." *Connecticut Public Interest Law Journal* 77(7): 96–112.

Lumpkins, Charles. 2008. *American Pogrom: The East St. Louis Race Riot and Black Politics.* Columbus: University of Ohio Press.

Majumdar, Rejeev D. 2007. "Racially Restrictive Covenants in the State of Washington: The Primer for Practitioners." *Seattle University Law Review* 30(4): 1095–117.

Mallach, Alan. 2020. "Over the Edge: Trajectories of African-American Middle Neighborhoods in St. Louis since 2000." *Journal of Urban Affairs* 42(7): 1063–85.

Manson, Steven, Jonathan Schroeder, David Van Riper, Tracy Kugler, and Steven Ruggles. 2022. IPUMS National Historical Geographic Information System: Version 17.0 [dataset]. Minneapolis, MN: IPUMS.

Marshall, T. H. 1950. *Citizenship and Social Class: And Other Essays.* Cambridge: Cambridge University Press.

Maryland Law Review. 1974. "Injunction Against the Recording of Deeds containing Racial Covenants: The Last of the Racial Covenant Cases? - Mayers v. Ridley." *Maryland Law Review* 34(3): 403–20.

Massey, Douglas S. 2007. *Categorically Unequal: The American Stratification System.* New York: Russell Sage Foundation.

———. 2020. "Still the Linchpin: Segregation and Stratification in the USA." *Race and Social Problems* 12(1): 1–12.

Massey, Douglas S., and Nancy Denton. 1988. "The Dimensions of Residential Segregation." *Social Forces* 67(2): 281–315.

———. 1993. *American Apartheid: Segregation and the Making of the Underclass.* Cambridge, Mass.: Harvard University Press.

Massey, Douglas S., and Jacob S. Rugh. 2021. "America's Unequal Metropolitan Geography: Segregation and the Spatial Concentration of Affluence and Poverty." In *Who Gets What? The New Politics of Insecurity,* edited by Frances M. Rosenbluth and Margaret Weir. New York: Cambridge University Press.

Massey, Douglas S., and Jonathan Tannen. 2018. "Suburbanization and Segregation in the United States, 1970–2010." *Ethnic and Racial Studies* 41(9): 1594–1611.

McGraw, B. T., and George B. Nesbitt. 1953. "Aftermath of Shelley versus Kraemer on Residential Restriction by Race." *Land Economics* 29(3): 280–87.

McGreevy, John T. 1996. *Parish Boundaries: The Catholic Encounter with Race in the Twentieth-Century Urban North.* Chicago: University of Chicago.

McGruder, Kevin. 2015. *Race and Real Estate: Conflict and Cooperation in Harlem, 1890–1920.* New York: Columbia University Press.

McWilliams, Carey. 1946. "Minneapolis: The Curious Twin." *Common Ground* (Autumn): 61–65.

Mettler, Suzanne. 2011. *The Submerged State: How Invisible Government Policies Undermine American Democracy.* Chicago: University of Chicago Press.

Meyer, Stephen Grant. 2000. *As Long as They Don't Move Next Door: Segregation and Racial Conflict in American Neighborhoods.* Lanham, Md.: Rowman & Littlefield.

Michney, Todd. M. 2022. "How the City Survey's Redlining Maps Were Made: A Closer Look at HOLC's Mortgagee Rehabilitation Division." *Journal of Planning History* 21(4): 316–44.

Michney, Todd M., and LaDale Winling. 2020. "New Perspectives on New Deal Housing Policy: Explicating and Mapping HOLC Loans to African Americans." *Journal of Urban History* 46(1): 150–80.

———. 2021. "The Roots of Redlining: Academic, Governmental, and Professional Networks in the Making of the New Deal Lending Regime." *Journal of American History* 108(1): 42–69.

Mills, Charles W. 1997. *The Racial Contract.* Ithaca: Cornell University Press.

———. 2017. *Black Rights/White Wrongs: The Critique of Racial Liberalism.* New York: Oxford University Press.

———. 2019. "Ideology." In *The Routledge Handbook of Epistemic Injustice,* edited by James Kidd, Jose Medina, and Gale Pohlhaus. London: Routledge.

Minneapolis Chamber of Commerce. 1947. *Report of the Rezoning Committee: Studies and Recommendations in Relation to the Zoning Ordinance of Minneapolis.* Minneapolis: Chamber of Commerce.

Mohl, Raymond. 2004. "Stop the Road: Freeway Revolts in American Cities." *Journal of Urban History* 30(5): 674–706.

Molotch, Harvey. 1976. "The City as a Growth Machine: Toward a Political Economy of Place." *American Journal of Sociology* 82(2): 309–32.

Monchow, Helen Corbin. 1928. *The Use of Deed Restrictions in Subdivision Development.* Chicago: Institute for Research in Land Economics and Public Utilities.

Montrie, Chad. 2019. "'A Bigoted, Prejudiced, Hateful Little Area': The Making of an All-White Suburb in the Deep North." *Journal of Urban History* 45(2): 300–320.

———. 2022. *Whiteness in Plain View: A History of Racial Exclusion in Minnesota.* Minneapolis: Minnesota Historical Society Press.

Morris, Aldon. 2000. "Building Blocks of Social Inequality: A Critique of Durable Inequality." *Comparative Studies in Society and History* 42(2): 482–86.

Mott, Seward H., and Max S. Wehrly. 1947. *Subdivision Regulations and Protective Covenants: Their Application to Land Development.* Washington, D.C.: Urban Land Institute.

Muhammad, Khalil Gibran. 2010. *The Condemnation of Blackness: Race, Crime, and the Making of Modern Urban America.* Cambridge, Mass.: Harvard University Press.

Myrdal, Gunnar. 1944. *An American Dilemma: The Negro Problem and Modern Democracy.* New York: Harper & Brothers.

Namin, Sima, Yuhong Zhou, Wei Xu, Emily McGinley, Courtney Jankowski, Purushottam Laud, and Kirsten Beyer. 2022. "Persistence of Mortgage Lending Bias in the United States: 80 Years after the Home Owners' Loan Corporation Security Maps." *Journal of Race, Ethnicity, and the City* 3(1): 70–94.

National Association for the Advancement of Colored People (NAACP). Papers of the NAACP, Part 05: Campaign against Residential Segregation, 1914–1955 (microfilm).

National Association of Real Estate Boards. 1924. *Code of Ethics* (NAREB). https://www.nar.realtor/about-nar/governing-documents/code-of-ethics/previous-editions-of-the-code-of-ethics.

———. 1950. *Code of Ethics* (NAREB). https://www.nar.realtor/about-nar/governing-documents/code-of-ethics/previous-editions-of-the-code-of-ethics.

Nelson, Janai S. 1996. "Residential Zoning Regulations and the Perpetuation of Apartheid." *UCLA Law Review* 43(5): 1689–731.

Nelson, Robert K., LaDale Winling, Richard Marciano, Nathan Connolly, et al. n.d. "Mapping Inequality: Redlining in New Deal America." American Panorama, edited by Robert K. Nelson and Edward L. Ayers. Accessed December 2, 2022. https://dsl.richmond.edu/panorama/redlining/.

Neymeyer, Robert. 1980. "May Harmony Prevail: The Early History of Black Waterloo." *Palimpsest* 61(3): 80–91.

Nightingale, Carl H. 2012. *Segregation: A Global History of Divided Cities.* Chicago: University of Chicago Press.

Noble, David. 1997. *Welfare as We Knew It.* New York: Oxford University Press.

Nolan, Carolyn. 2018. Annexation Files [shapefile of municipal incorporations and annexations]. St. Louis County Department of Planning.

Nourse, Hugh, and Donald Phares. 1975. "The Impact of FHA Insurance Practices on Urban Housing Markets in Transition: The St. Louis Case." *Urban Law Annual* 9: 111–28.

Oliver, Melvin, and Thomas Shapiro. 1995. *Black Wealth/White Wealth: A New Perspective on Racial Inequality.* New York: Routledge.

One Economy. 2017. *The State of Black Polk County*. April 2017. http://docs.wixstatic.com /ugd/15357c_96176cb20ad0416fa5f2df5d78c9ea6b.pdf.

Orfield, Myron. 2006. "Choice, Equal Protection, and Metropolitan Integration: The Hope of the Minneapolis Desegregation Settlement." *Law and Inequality* 24(2): 269–352.

Owens, Ann. 2017. "Racial Residential Segregation of School-Age Children and Adults: The Role of Schooling as a Segregating Force." *RSF: The Russell Sage Foundation Journal of the Social Sciences* 3(2): 63–80. DOI: https://doi.org/10.7758/RSF.2017.3.2.03.

Pacyga, Dominic. 1997. "Chicago's 1919 Race Riot: Ethnicity, Class and Urban Violence." In *The Making of Urban America*, edited by Raymond Mohl. Wilmington, Del.: Scholarly Resources.

Pager, Devah, and Hana Shepherd. 2008. "The Sociology of Discrimination: Racial Discrimination in Employment, Housing, Credit, and Consumer Markets." *Annual Review of Sociology* 34: 181–209.

Pascoe, Peggy. 1996. "Miscegenation Law, Court Cases, and Ideologies of 'Race' in Twentieth-Century America." *Journal of American History* 83(1): 44–69.

Patton, Rufford Guy. 1934. "The Torrens System of Land Title Registration." *Minnesota Law Review* 19: 519–35.

Peñalver, Eduardo. 2009. "Land Virtues." *Cornell Law Review* 94(4): 821–88.

Pendall, Rolf, 2000. "Local Land Use Regulation and the Chain of Exclusion." *Journal of the American Planning Association* 66(2): 125–42.

Percheski, Christine, and Christina M. Gibson-Davis. 2020. "A Penny on the Dollar: Racial Inequalities in Wealth among Households with Children." *Socius* 6. DOI: https://doi.org/10.1177/2378023120916616.

Perzynski, Adam, Kristen A. Berg, Charles Thomas, Anupama Cemballi, Tristan Smith, Sarah Shick, Douglas Gunzler, and Ashwini R. Sehgal. 2022. "Racial Discrimination and Economic Factors in Redlining of Ohio Neighborhoods." *Du Bois Review: Social Science Research on Race* (online December 2022), 1–17. DOI: https://doi.org/10.1017 /S1742058X22000236.

Phillips, Kimberly. 1999. *AlabamaNorth: African-American Migrants, Community, and Working Class Activism in Cleveland, 1915–1945*. Urbana: University of Illinois Press.

Philpott, Thomas. 1978. *The Slum and the Ghetto: Neighborhood Deterioration and Middle-Class Reform, Chicago 1818–1930*. New York: Oxford University Press.

Plotkin, Wendy. 1999. "Deeds of Mistrust: Race, Housing, and Restrictive Covenants in Chicago, 1900–1953," Ph.D. diss., University of Illinois at Chicago.

———. 2001. "'Hemmed In': The Struggle against Racial Restrictive Covenants and Deed Restrictions in Post-WWII Chicago." *Journal of the Illinois State Historical Society* 94(1): 39–69.

Pollard, W.L. 1931. "Outline of the Law of Zoning in the United States." *Annals of the American Academy of Political and Social Science* 155(2): 15–33.

Prener, Christopher G. 2021. "Demographic Change, Segregation, and the Emergence of Peripheral Spaces in St. Louis, Missouri." *Applied Geography* 133 (online June 2021). DOI: https://doi.org/10.1016/j.apgeog.2021.102472.

Prener, Christopher G., Taylor Braswell, Kyle Miller, and Joel Jennings. 2019. "Closing the Gateway: Street Closures, Bisected Geography, and Crime in St. Louis, MO." SocArXiv Papers. February 22, 2021. DOI: doi.org/10.31235/osf.io/2wext.

Quillian, Lincoln. 2014. "Social Psychological Processes in Studies of Neighborhoods and Inequality." In *Handbook of the Social Psychology of Inequality*, edited by Jane McLeod, Edward Lawler, and Michael Schwalbe. New York: Springer.

Quillian, Lincoln, and Devah Pager. 2010. "Estimating Risk: Stereotype Amplification and the Perceived Risk of Criminal Victimization." *Social Psychology Quarterly* 73(1): 79–104.

Quinn, Lois M. 1979. *Racially Restrictive Covenants: The Making of All-White Suburbs in Milwaukee County*. Milwaukee: ETI Publications.

Rabin, Yale. 1980. "Federal Urban Transportation Policy and the Highway Planning Process in Metropolitan Areas." *Annals of the American Academy of Political and Social Science* 451(1): 21–35.

———. 1989. "Expulsive Zoning: The Inequitable Legacy of Euclid." In *Zoning and the American Dream: Promises Still to Keep*, edited by Charles M. Haar and Jerold S. Kayden. Washington, D.C.: American Planning Association Press.

Radford, Gail. 1996. *Modern Housing for America: Policy Struggles in the New Deal Era*. Chicago: University of Chicago Press.

Radin, Margaret J. 1982. "Property and Personhood." *Stanford Law Review* 34(5): 957–1015.

Reardon, Sean F., and Kendra Bischoff. 2011. "Income Inequality and Income Segregation." *American Journal of Sociology* 116(4):1092–153.

Redford, Laura. 2017. "The Intertwined History of Class and Race Segregation in Los Angeles." *Journal of Planning History* 16(4): 305–22.

Revell, Keith. 1999. "The Road to Euclid v. Ambler: City Planning, State-Building, and the Changing Scope of the Police Power." *Studies in American Political Development* 13(1): 50–145.

Rice, Roger L. 1968. "Residential Segregation by Law, 1910–1917." *Journal of Southern History* 34(2): 179–99.

Richardson, Scovel. 1945. "Some of the Defenses Available in Restrictive Covenant Suits against Colored American Citizens in St. Louis." *National Bar Journal* 3(1): 50–56.

Rios, Jodi. 2020. *Black Lives and Spatial Matters: Policing Blackness and Practicing Freedom in Suburban St. Louis*. Ithaca: Cornell University Press.

Roberto, Elizabeth. 2018. "The Spatial Proximity and Connectivity Method for Measuring and Analyzing Residential Segregation." *Sociological Methodology* 48(1):182–224.

Roberto, Elizabeth, and Jackelyn Hwang. 2017. "Barriers to Integration: Physical Boundaries and the Spatial Structure of Residential Segregation." Paper presented at the Population Association of America, Chicago.

Robertson, Cassandra, Emily Parker, and Laura Tach. 2023. "Historical Redlining and Contemporary Federal Place-Based Policy: A Case of Compensatory or Compounding Neighborhood Inequality?" *Housing Policy Debate* 33(2): 429–52.

Roediger, David R. 2005. *Working toward Whiteness: How America's Immigrants Became White*. New York: Basic Books.

Roithmayr, Daria. 2010. "Racial Cartels." *Michigan Journal of Race & Law* 16(1): 45–79.

Rose, Carol M. 2022. "Property Law and Inequality: Lessons from Racially Restrictive Covenants." *Northwestern University Law Review* 117(1): 225–49.

Ross, Stephen, and John Yinger. 2002. *The Color of Credit*. Cambridge: MIT Press.

Rothstein, Richard. 2017. *The Color of Law: A Forgotten History of How Our Government Segregated America*. New York: Liveright.

Rothwell, Jonathan, and Douglas Massey, 2009. "The Effect of Density Zoning on Racial Segregation in U.S. Urban Areas." *Urban Affairs Review* 44(6): 779–806.

Rovner, Melissa. 2021. "The 'Social Science' of Segregation: Between the 'Charitable' Surveys of the Progressive Era and the 'Appraisal' Surveys of the New Deal Era." *Journal of Planning History* 20(4): 326–37.

Rubenstein, William. 1997. "Divided We Litigate: Addressing Disputes among Group Members and Lawyers in Civil Rights Campaigns." *Yale Law Journal* 106(6): 1623–81.

Ruggles, Steven, Sarah Flood, Ronald Goeken, Megan Schouweiler, and Matthew Sobek. 2022. IPUMS USA: Version 12.0 [dataset]. Minneapolis, Minn.: IPUMS.

Rugh, Jacob, and Douglas S. Massey. 2010. "Racial Segregation and the American Foreclosure Crisis." *American Sociological Review* 75(5): 629–51.

Rusk, David. 2001. "The 'Segregation Tax': The Cost of Racial Segregation to Black Homeowners." Washington, D.C.: Brookings Institution, Survey Series.

Saatcioglu, Argun, and Thomas M. Skrtic. 2019. "Categorization by Organizations: Manipulation of Disability Categories in a Racially Desegregated School District." *American Journal of Sociology* 125(1): 184–260.

Sahn, Alexander. 2022. "Racial Diversity and Exclusionary Zoning: Evidence from the Great Migration." University of California, Santa Barbara. Unpublished manuscript.

Sampson, Robert J. 2009. "Racial Stratification and the Durable Tangle of Neighborhood Inequality." *Annals of the American Academy of Political and Social Science* 621(1): 260–80.

———. 2012. *Great American City: Chicago and the Enduring Neighborhood Effect*. Chicago: University of Chicago Press.

Santucci, Larry. 2020. "Documenting Racially Restrictive Covenants in 20th Century Philadelphia." *Cityscape* 22(3): 241–68.

Sauter, Michael. 2017. "Black and White Inequality in All 50 States." *24/7 Wall Street*. Last modified January 12, 2020. https://247wallst.com/special-report/2017/08/18/black-and-white-inequality-in-all-50-states-2/10/.

Schelling, Thomas. 1963. *The Strategy of Conflict*. Cambridge, Mass.: Harvard University Press.

Schindler, Sarah. 2015. "Architectural Exclusion: Discrimination and Segregation through Physical Design of the Built Environment." *Yale Law Journal* 124(6): 1934–2024.

Schneider, Anne, and Helen Ingram. 1993. "Social Construction of Target Populations: Implications for Politics and Policy." *American Political Science Review* 87(2): 334–47.

Seiple, Emily, Ashley Zitzner, Jerry Anthony, Ryan Dusil, Kirk Lehman, Gabriel Martin. 2017. *Racial Segregation in Iowa's Metro Areas, 1990–2010*. Iowa City: University of Iowa Public Policy Center.

Sexauer, Cornelia Frances. 2003. "Catholic Capitalism: Charles Vatterott, Civil Rights, and Suburbanization in St. Louis and the Nation, 1919–1971." Ph.D. diss., University of Cincinnati.

Shapiro, Thomas. 2017. *Toxic Inequality: How America's Wealth Gap Destroys Mobility, Deepens the Racial Divide, and Threatens Our Future.* New York: Basic Books.

Sharfstein, Daniel J. 2003. "The Secret History of Race in the United States." *Yale Law Journal* 112(6): 1473–509.

Sharkey, Patrick. 2013. *Stuck in Place: Urban Neighborhoods and the End of Progress toward Racial Equality.* Chicago: University of Chicago Press.

———. 2020. "To Avoid Integration, Americans Built Barricades in Urban Space." *Atlantic*, June 20. https://www.theatlantic.com/ideas/archive/2020/06/barricades-let -urban-inequality-fester/613312/.

Sharkey, Patrick, and Jacob Faber. 2014. "Where, When, Why, and for Whom Do Residential Contexts Matter? Moving Away from the Dichotomous Understanding of Neighborhood Effects." *Annual Review of Sociology* 40: 559–79.

Shertzer, Allison, Tate Twinam, and Randall P. Walsh. 2016. "Race, Ethnicity, and Discriminatory Zoning." *American Economic Journal: Applied Economics* 8(3): 217–46.

———. 2022. "Zoning and Segregation in Urban Economic History." *Regional Science and Urban Economics* 94 (2022): 103652.

Shertzer, Allison, and Randall P. Walsh. 2019. "Racial Sorting and the Emergence of Segregation in American Cities." *Review of Economics and Statistics* 101(3): 415–27.

Shertzer, Allison, Randall P. Walsh, and John R. Logan. 2016. "Segregation and Neighborhood Change in Northern Cities: New Historical GIS Data from 1900–1930." *Historical Methods* 49(4): 187–97.

Shoenfeld, Sarah Jane, and Mara Cherkasky. 2016. "'A Strictly White Residential Section': The Rise and Demise of Racially Restrictive Covenants in Bloomingdale." *Washington History* 29(1): 24–41.

Silver, Christopher. 1991. "The Racial Origins of Zoning: Southern Cities from 1910–40." *Planning Perspectives* 6(2): 189–205.

Slingsby, Jerry A. 1980. "Racial Covenants in Kansas City: An Historical View of Their Effect on Housing Choice." MA (Urban Planning), University of Kansas.

Smith, Greta. 2018. "'Congenial Neighbors': Restrictive Covenants and Residential Segregation in Portland, Oregon." *Oregon Historical Quarterly* 119(3): 358–64.

Snowden, Kenneth. 2006. Data tables in *Historical Statistics of the United States, Earliest Times to the Present: Millennial Edition*, edited by Susan B. Carter, Scott Sigmund Gartner, Michael R. Haines, Alan L. Olmstead, Richard Sutch, and Gavin Wright. New York: Cambridge University Press.

Somers, Margaret R. 2008. *Genealogies of Citizenship: Markets, Statelessness, and the Right to Have Rights.* New York: Cambridge University Press.

Sood, Aradhya, William Speagle, and Kevin Ehrman-Solberg. 2019. "Long Shadow of Racial Discrimination: Evidence from Housing Covenants of Minneapolis." Unpublished manuscript. https://papers.ssrn.com/sol3/papers.cfm?abstract_id=3468520.

Soss, Joe, and Vesla Weaver. 2017. "Police Are Our Government: Politics, Political Science, and the Policing of Race-Class Subjugated Communities." *Annual Review of Political Science* 20: 567–74.

Spear, Allan H. 1967. *Black Chicago: The Making of a Negro Ghetto, 1890–1920*. Chicago: University of Chicago Press.

Squires, Gregory D., 2003. "Racial Profiling, Insurance Style: Insurance Redlining and the Uneven Development of Metropolitan Areas." *Journal of Urban Affairs* 25(4): 391–410.

———. 2005. "Predatory Lending: Redlining in Reverse." Shelterforce, January 1, 2005. https://shelterforce.org/2005/01/01/predatory-lending-redlining-in-reverse/.

Stach, Patricia Burgess. 1988. "Deed Restrictions and Subdivision Development in Columbus Ohio, 1910–1970." *Journal of Urban History* 15(1): 42–68.

Stebbins, Samuel, and Evan Comen. 2018. "The Worst Cities for Black Americans." *24/7 Wall St.*, November 16. https://247wallst.com/special-report/2018/11/09/the-worst-cities-for-black-americans-4/.

Sterner, Richard. 1943. *The Negro's Share: A Study of Income, Consumption, Housing, and Public Assistance*. New York: Harper.

Stone, Deborah. 2005. "How Market Ideology Guarantees Racial Inequality." In *Healthy, Wealthy, and Fair: Health Care and the Good Society*, edited by James A. Morone and Lawrence R. Jacobs. New York: Oxford University Press.

Sugrue, Thomas. 1995. "Crabgrass-roots Politics: Race, Rights and the Reaction against Liberalism in the Urban North." *Journal of American History* 82(2): 551–78.

———. 1996. *Origins of the Urban Crisis: Race and Inequality in Postwar Detroit*. Princeton: Princeton University Press.

———. 2011. "A Dream Still Deferred." *New York Times*, March 26, 2011. https://www.nytimes.com/2011/03/27/opinion/27Sugrue.html.

Taeuber, Karl E., and Alma Taeuber. 1965. *Negroes in Cities: Residential Segregation and Neighborhood Change*. Chicago: Aldine.

———. 1976. "A Practitioner's Perspective on the Index of Dissimilarity." *American Sociological Review* 41(5): 884–89.

Taylor, Keeanga-Yamahtta. 2019. *Race for Profit: How Banks and the Real Estate Industry Undermined Black Homeownership*. Chapel Hill: University of North Carolina Press.

Teaford, Jon C. 2000. "Urban Renewal and Its Aftermath." *Housing Policy Debate* 11(2): 443–65.

Tilly, Charles. 1998. *Durable Inequality*. Berkeley: University of California Press.

Tolnay, Stewart E. 2003. "The African American 'Great Migration' and Beyond." *Annual Review of Sociology* 29: 209–32.

Tretter, Elliot. 2012. *Austin Restricted: Progressivism, Zoning, Private Racial Covenants, and the Making of a Segregated City*. Austin, Tex.: Institute for Urban Policy Research and Analysis.

Troesken, Werner, and Randall Walsh. 2019. "Collective Action, White Flight, and the Origins of Racial Zoning Laws." *Journal of Law, Economics, & Organization* 35(2): 289–318.

Trotter, Joe William. 1985. *Black Milwaukee: The Making of an Industrial Proletariat, 1915–45.* Urbana: University of Illinois Press.

Trounstine, Jessica. 2018. *Segregation by Design: Local Politics and Inequality in American Cities.* New York: Cambridge University Press.

Tuttle, William M. 1970. "Contested Neighborhoods and Racial Violence: Prelude to the Chicago Riot of 1919." *Journal of Negro History* 55(4): 266–88.

University of Chicago Law Review. 1940. "Negro Restrictions and the 'Changed Conditions' Doctrine." *University of Chicago Law Review* 7(4): 710–16.

U.S. Census Bureau. 1920. *Fourteenth Census of the United States.* Manuscript census accessed via Ancestry.com.

———. 1930. *Fifteenth Census of the United States.* Manuscript census accessed via Ancestry.com.

———. 1940. *Sixteenth Census of the United States.* Manuscript census accessed via Ancestry.com.

———. 1950. *Seventeenth Census of the United States.* Manuscript census accessed via Ancestry.com.

———. 1952. *Census of Population: 1950.* Washington: U.S. Department of Commerce.

———. 1953. *Census of Housing: 1950.* Washington: U.S. Department of Commerce.

———. 1994. *Geographic Areas Reference Manual.* Washington: U.S. Department of Commerce. https://www2.census.gov/geo/pdfs/reference/GARM/GARMcont.pdf.

U.S. Commission on Civil Rights. 1977. *School Desegregation in Waterloo, Iowa: A Staff Report of the U.S. Commission on Civil Rights.* Washington: Government Printing Office.

U.S. Department of Commerce. 1966. *Housing Construction Statistics, 1899–1964.* Washington: Government Printing Office.

U.S. Department of the Interior. 1983. *A History of the Rectangular Survey System.* Washington: Government Printing Office.

U.S. News and World Report. 2022. "Best Places to Live in the U.S. in 2022–2023." Accessed April 16, 2023. https://realestate.usnews.com/places/rankings/best-places-to-live.

Valentino, Lauren, and Stephen Vaisey. 2022. "Culture and Durable Inequality." *Annual Review of Sociology* 48: 14.1–14.21.

Van Hecke. M.T. 1928. "Zoning Ordinances and Restrictions in Deeds." *Yale Law Journal* 37(4): 407–25.

Vargo, Scott. 2013. "Disinvestment Trifecta: Parking, Highways, & Urban Renewal in Minneapolis an Historical Analysis of the Gateway District." *Macalester Review* 3(1). https://digitalcommons.macalester.edu/macreview/vol3/iss1/4/.

Vock, Daniel, Brian Charles, and Mike Maciag. 2019. "Houses Divided: How States and Cities Reinforce Segregation in America." *Governing* (January). https://www.governing.com/archive/gov-segregation-main-feature.html.

Vose, Clement. 1959. *Caucasians Only: The Supreme Court, the NAACP, and the Restrictive Covenant Cases.* Berkeley: University of California Press.

Wacquant, Loïc. 1997. "Three Pernicious Premises in the Study of the American Ghetto." *International Journal of Urban and Regional Research* 21(2): 341–53.

———. 2002. "Resolving the Trouble with 'Race.'" *New Left Review* 133/134. https://newleftreview.org/issues/ii133/articles/loic-wacquant-resolving-the-trouble-with-race.

Walker, Rebecca H., Hannah Ramer, Kate D. Derickson, and Bonnie L. Keeler. 2023. "Making the City of Lakes: Whiteness, Nature, and Urban Development in Minneapolis." *Annals of the American Association of Geographers*, DOI: https://doi.org/10.1080/24694452.2022.2155606.

Walker, Renee E., Christopher R. Keane, and Jessica G. Burke. 2010. "Disparities and Access to Healthy Food in the United States: A Review of Food Deserts Literature." *Health & Place* 16(5): 876–84.

Ware, David. 2020. "The Black and White of Greenway: Racially Restrictive Covenants in Manchester Connecticut." LLM, Human Rights and Social Justice, University of Connecticut School of Law.

Weaver, Robert C. 1944. "Race Restrictive Housing Covenants." *Journal of Land and Public Utility Economics* 20(3): 183–93.

———. 1948. *The Negro Ghetto*. New York: Macmillan.

———. 1960. "Class, Race and Urban Renewal." *Land Economics* 36(3): 235–51.

Weisbord, Reid K. and Stewart E. Sterk. 2021. "The Commodification of Public Land Records." *Notre Dame Law Review* 97(2): 507–62.

Weiss, Debra Cassens. 2022. "Law That Keeps Racist Covenants in Separate Public Record Helps Preserve History, Top State Court Says." *ABA Journal*, April 4, 2022. https://www.abajournal.com/web/article/top-state-court-says-law-that-keeps-racist-covenants-in-separate-public-record-strikes-a-balance.

Weiss, Marc A. 1987. *The Rise of Community Builders: The American Real Estate Industry and Urban Land Planning*. New York: Columbia University Press.

Whittemore, Andrew H. 2018. "The Role of Racial Bias in Exclusionary Zoning: The Case of Durham, North Carolina, 1945–2014." *Environment and Planning* 50(4): 826–47.

———. 2020. "The Roots of Racial Disparities in Residential Zoning Practice: The Case of Henrico County, Virginia, 1978–2015." *Housing Policy Debate* 30(2): 191–204.

———. 2021. "Exclusionary Zoning." *Journal of the American Planning Association* 87(2): 167–80.

Widestrom, Amy. 2015. *Displacing Democracy: Economic Segregation in America*. Philadelphia: Penn Press.

Williams, Gil. 2013. "Specificity, Blight and Two Tiers of TIF: A Proposal for Reform of Tax Increment Financing Law." *Saint Louis University Public Law Review* 33(1): 255–80.

Wilson, William Julius. 1987. *The Truly Disadvantaged: The Inner City, the Underclass, and Public Policy*. Chicago: The University of Chicago Press.

———. 2011. *When Work Disappears: The World of the New Urban Poor*. New York: Vintage.

Wimmer, Andreas. 2013. *Ethnic Boundary Making: Institutions, Power, Networks*. New York: Oxford University Press.

Winling, LaDale. 2011. "Students and the Second Ghetto: Federal Legislation, Urban Politics, and Campus Planning at the University of Chicago." *Journal of Planning History* 10(1): 59–86.

Witgen, Michael. 2019. "A Nation of Settlers: The Early American Republic and the Colonization of the Northwest Territory." *William and Mary Quarterly* 76(3): 391–98.

Woods, Louis Lee. 2018. "'The Inevitable Products of Racial Segregation': Multigenerational Consequences of Exclusionary Housing Policies on African Americans, 1910–1960." *American Journal of Economics and Sociology* 77(3–4): 967–1012.

Wright, John A. 2001. *The Ville: St. Louis.* Chicago: Aldine.

Xu, Wenfei. 2022. "Legacies of Institutionalized Redlining: A Comparison between Speculative and Implemented Mortgage Risk Maps in Chicago, Illinois." *Housing Policy Debate* 32(2): 249–74.

Yinger, John. 1995. *Closed Doors, Opportunities Lost: The Continuing Costs of Housing Discrimination.* New York: Russell Sage Foundation.

Young, Iris Marion. 1990. "Residential Segregation and Differentiated Citizenship." *Citizenship Studies* 3(2): 237–52.

Zile, Zigurds L. 1959. "Private Zoning on Milwaukee's Metropolitan Fringe—Part II." *Wisconsin Law Review* 1959(3): 451–88.

INDEX

Tables and figures are listed in **boldface**.